Agents of European overseas empires

Manchester University Press

Seventeenth- and Eighteenth-Century Studies

Seventeenth- and Eighteenth-Century Studies promotes interdisciplinary work on the period c.1603–1815, covering all aspects of the literature, culture and history of the British Isles, colonial North America and the early United States, other British colonies and their global connections. The series welcomes academic monographs, as well as collective volumes of essays that combine theoretical and methodological approaches from more than one discipline to further our understanding of the period. It is supported by the Société d'Études Anglo-Américaines des XVIIe et XVIIIe siècles.

General editors
Ladan Niayesh, Université de Paris and Will Slauter, Sorbonne Université

Founding editor
Anne Dunan-Page

Advisory board
Bernadette Andrea, Daniel Carey, Rachel Herrman, Hannah Spahn, Claire Preston and Evan Haefeli

To buy or to find out more about the books currently available in this series, please go to:

https://manchesteruniversitypress.co.uk/series/seventeenth-eighteenth-century-studies/

http://1718.fr/

Agents of European overseas empires

Private colonisers, 1450–1800

Edited by

Agnès Delahaye, Elodie Peyrol-Kleiber,
L.H. Roper and Bertrand Van Ruymbeke

MANCHESTER UNIVERSITY PRESS

Copyright © Manchester University Press 2024

While copyright in the volume as a whole is vested in Manchester University Press, copyright in individual chapters belongs to their respective authors, and no chapter may be reproduced wholly or in part without the express permission in writing of both author and publisher.

Published by Manchester University Press
Oxford Road, Manchester M13 9PL

www.manchesteruniversitypress.co.uk

British Library Cataloguing-in-Publication Data
A catalogue record for this book is available from the British Library

ISBN 978 1 5261 6733 0 hardback
ISBN 978 1 5261 9579 1 paperback

First published 2024
Paperback published 2026

The publisher has no responsibility for the persistence or accuracy of URLs for any external or third-party internet websites referred to in this book, and does not guarantee that any content on such websites is, or will remain, accurate or appropriate.

EU authorised representative for GPSR:
Easy Access System Europe – Mustamäe tee 50,
10621 Tallinn, Estonia
gpsr.requests@easproject.com

Typeset by Newgen Publishing UK

Contents

Contributors	vii
Acknowledgements	xii
Abbreviations	xiii
Introduction – Agnès Delahaye, Elodie Peyrol-Kleiber, L.H. Roper and Bertrand Van Ruymbeke	1

Part I: Tensions within imperial projects

1 Global trade and its benefits for 'the nation': The examples of early modern France and Britain – Susanne Lachenicht	23
2 Comparing and criticising early modern imperial policies in the Age of Revolution: Abbé Raynal's *Histoire philosophique et politique des deux Indes* – François Brizay	45
3 Global pursuits: English overseas initiatives of the long seventeenth century in perspective – L.H. Roper	66

Part II: The limits of imperial control

4 The limits of royal control over migration to Spanish America in the sixteenth century – Eric Roulet	91
5 Imperial struggles, colonisation and the Dutch slave trade in seventeenth-century New Netherland – Anne-Claire Faucquez	108
6 The control of unfree labour across the Dutch Empire in the eighteenth century – Elisabeth Heijmans and Rafaël Thiebaut	129

Part III: Local adaptations and developments

7 Settler colonialism and early American history
 – Trevor Burnard and Agnès Delahaye   153

8 Colonising the Cape of Good Hope: Company policy and settlers' interests in a contested space of European occupation in Southern Africa
 – Marilyn Garcia-Chapleau   179

9 Shipping mules in the eighteenth century: New England's equine exports to the West Indies
 – Charlotte Carrington-Farmer   200

Epilogue: Perspectives on the mechanisms and impacts of overseas colonisation in the early modern era – then and now – Bertrand Van Ruymbeke   223

Select bibliography   233
Index   254

Contributors

François Brizay is Professor of Modern History at the University of Poitiers, France. He works on the history of travels and on international relations. He studies, more specifically, travel literature and the action of consuls. His more recent publications include *Identité religieuse et minorités. De l'Antiquité au XVIIIe siècle* (Presses Universitaires de Rennes, 2018) and (as editor with Thierry Sauzeau) *Les étrangers sur les littoraux européens et méditerranéens. À l'époque moderne (fin xve début xixe siècle)* (Presses Universitaires de Rennes, 2021).

Trevor Burnard is the Wilberforce Professor of Slavery and Emancipation at the University of Hull. He is a member of the Modern Slavery Policy and Evidence Centre Senior Management Board. In addition to many articles, book chapters and edited books on the Caribbean and the Chesapeake, he has authored *Planters, Merchants, and Slaves: Plantation Societies in British America, 1650–1820* (University of Chicago Press, 2015); *The Plantation Machine: Atlantic Capitalism in French Saint-Domingue and British Jamaica* (University of Pennsylvania Press, 2016); *The Atlantic in World History, 1492–1830* (Bloomsbury, 2020); *Britain in the Wider World* (Routledge, 2020); *Jamaica in the Age of Revolution* (Pennsylvania, 2020); *Writing Early America: From Empire to Revolution* (University of Virginia Press, 2023); and *Writing the History of Global Slavery* (Cambridge University Press, 2023). He has been the editor-in-chief of the *Oxford Bibliography Online in Atlantic History* since 2009.

Charlotte Carrington-Farmer (Ph.D., University of Cambridge) is an Associate Professor of History at Roger Williams University, Rhode Island, USA. She has a keen interest in equine history and has published an article on 'The rise and fall of the Narragansett Pacer' (*Rhode Island History*, 2018) and a chapter on 'Trading horses in the eighteenth century: Rhode Island and the Atlantic world', in *Equine Cultures* (University of Chicago Press, 2019). She is also interested in dissent and identity in seventeenth-century New England, and has published two biographies in edited collections, one on Thomas Morton in *Atlantic Lives: Biographies that Cross the Ocean* (Brill, 2014) and another on Roger Williams in *Law and Religion and the Liberal State* (Hart, 2020.)

Agnès Delahaye is Professor of American History and Civilisation at the University of Lyon (Lumière Lyon 2) and a specialist of early American settler historiography. She is the author of *Settling the Good Land: Governance and Promotion in John Winthrop's New England* (Brill, 2020), a study of early colonial formation and the importance of land appropriation and promotional writing in shaping the political archive of New England.

Anne-Claire Faucquez is Associate Professor of American Civilisation and History at Université Paris 8. She has published *From New Netherland to New York: The Birth of a Slavery Society 1624–1712* (Les Indes Savantes, 2021). She works on New York's colonial past and, more specifically, on the issues of race in colonial America. Her next project deals with history writing and the erasure of the history of slavery in nineteenth-century history books and textbooks. She is also interested in the commemoration and representations of slavery in public spaces (museums, monuments and contemporary art).

Marilyn Garcia-Chapleau teaches at the Institut catholique de Rennes (ICR) and at the Institut catholique d'études supérieures de la Roche-sur-Yon (ICES) in France. She is the author of *Le Refuge huguenot du cap de Bonne-Espérance – Genèse, assimilation héritage* (Honoré Champion, 2016), the first detailed monograph examining the French refugees of South Africa, and co-author of *L'Afrique du Sud de A à Z* (Versailles, 2011). She also continues her research on aspects of Dutch and British colonial history in South Africa and the Huguenot heritage.

Elisabeth Heijmans is a postdoctoral researcher in Early Modern History at the Centre for Urban History at the University of Antwerp. She obtained her Ph.D. at Leiden University in 2018 on the Early Modern French Empire and published *The Agency of Empire Connections and Strategies in French Overseas Expansion, 1686–1746* (Brill, 2020). Her first postdoctoral research focused on the governance of diversity in the Dutch Empire and she co-edited with Sophie Rose the volume *Diversity and Empires: Negotiating Plurality in European Imperial Projects from Early Modernity* (Routledge, 2023). Her current research explores future expectations of French merchants active in long-distance trade.

Susanne Lachenicht is Professor of Early Modern History at the University of Bayreuth, Germany. She works on Europe and the Atlantic World with a special focus on diasporas and nationhood, religious migrations, knowledge transfer and transformation, as well as temporalities in the early modern world. Her more recent publications include (as editor with Charlotte Lerg and Michael Kimmage) *The TransAtlantic Reconsidered* (Manchester University Press, 2018); (as editor with Mathilde Monge) 'Nations et empires' (*Diasporas: Circulations, Migrations, Histoire*, 2019); (as editor with Marianne Amar, Isabelle Lacoue-Labarthe, Mathilde Monge and Annelise Rodrigo) 'Négocier l'accueil / Negotiating asylum and accommodation' (*Diasporas: Circulations, Migrations, Histoire*, 2020); and (as editor with Guido Braun) *Spies, Espionage and Secret Diplomacy in the Early Modern Period* (Kohlhammer, 2021).

Elodie Peyrol-Kleiber is Associate Professor of American Civilisation and History at the University of Poitiers. Her book *Les premiers Irlandais du Nouveau Monde, une migration atlantique, 1618–1705* was published by Presses Universitaires de Rennes in 2016. Her research interests include the different systems of unfree labour as developed by the English and French Empires in the colonies of North America and the West Indies. She is also co-general editor of the *Journal of Early American History*, published by Brill.

L.H. Roper is SUNY Distinguished Professor of History at the State University of New York–New Paltz, USA, and a Fellow of the Royal Historical Society and the New York Academy of History. A recipient of a SUNY Chancellor's Award for Excellence in Scholarship, he is the author or editor of seven books, including, most recently, *Advancing Empire: English Interests and Overseas Expansion, 1613–1688* (Cambridge University Press, 2017) and *The Torrid Zone: Caribbean Colonization and Cultural Interaction in the Long Seventeenth Century* (University of South Carolina Press, 2018).

Eric Roulet is Professor of Modern History at the University Littoral-Côte d'Opale, France. He works on the genesis of colonial societies in Mexico (sixteenth century). He questions the development of European templates both socially and culturally (evangelisation, interbreeding, acculturation), the modalities of exchanges and the resistance organised by dominated populations in a colonial context. He is the author of *L'évangélisation des Indiens du Mexique. Impact et réalité de la conquête spirituelle (XVIe siècle)* (Presses universitaires de Rennes, 2008), *Écritures indigènes de la conquête du Mexique* (Shaker Verlag, 2015) and *Conquistadores, négriers et inquisiteurs. Trois figures majeures du monde colonial américain XVIe–XVIIIe siècle* (Harmattan, 2018).

Rafaël Thiebaut defended his Ph.D. dissertation 'Traite des esclaves et commerce néerlandais et français à Madagascar (XVIIe–XVIIIe siècles)' at the Université Paris 1 under joint supervision with the Vrije Universiteit Amsterdam in 2017. This research received the Thesis Prize of the Fondation pour la Mémoire de l'Esclavage. Subsequently hired as a postdoctoral researcher by the International Institute of Social History in Amsterdam, he worked on the project 'Resilient Diversity: The Governance of Racial and Religious Plurality in the Dutch Empire, 1600–1800'. He is now a postdoctoral researcher at the Musée du Quai Branly, where he studies the link between museum objects and slavery. He also contributes to a better knowledge of the Indian Ocean slave trade by participating in the newly created Indian Ocean Slave Trade Database and through the publications of two articles: 'French slave trade on Madagascar: A quantitative approach' (*Journal of Social History*, 2020) and 'Construire une base de données sur la traite des esclaves dans l'océan Indien. L'exemple du cas français à Madagascar au XVIIIe siècle' (*Esclavages & Post-Esclavages*, 2020).

Bertrand Van Ruymbeke is Professor of American History at Université Paris 8, France. Specialising in Early and Revolutionary America, he is the author of *From New Babylon to Eden: The Huguenots and their Migration to Colonial South Carolina* (University of South Carolina Press, 2006), *L'Amérique avant les Etats-Unis. Une histoire de l'Amérique anglaise 1497–1776* (Flammarion, 2013) and *Histoire des Etats-Unis. De 1492 à nos jours* (Tallandier, 2021). He is also co-editor of 'The American Revolution and Europe: Transnational perspectives', in *Revue Française des Etudes Américaines* (2022), *L'indépendance des Etats-Unis. Héritage et interprétations. Arts, lettres, politique* (Les Perséides, 2021), *Les fondations de villes sur les littoraux américains. Brésil et Etats-Unis, XVIe–XIXe siècles* (Les Perséides, 2021), *A Companion to the Huguenots* (Brill, 2016) and *The Atlantic World of Anthony Benezet (1713–1784): From French Reformation to North American Quaker Antislavery Activism* (Brill, 2016). He is currently working on two books (in French) on the American Revolution and is the principal investigator of a European and transatlantic consortium, America 2026, on the study of the American Revolution with scholars and institutions from France, the United Kingdom, the Netherlands, Germany, Italy, Spain, Hungary and the USA.

Acknowledgements

This edited volume results from a lively and enriching collaboration between international scholars who were drawn together around the study of agency in the complex structures and processes at the heart of the early governance of distant overseas imperial territories. We would like to thank the participants of the *Terres Lointaines* conference held in Poitiers in 2018, which was the starting and meeting point of the authors and editors of this volume. Our project was supported by the Société des Études Anglo-Américaines des XVIIe et XVIIIe siècles, the Mémoires, Identités, Marginalités dans le Monde Occidental Contemporain (MIMMOC) research unit and a multitude of colleagues who provided useful insights. As volume editors, we wish to thank the authors who have been enthusiastic from the beginning and whose contributions offer food for thought to our numerous readers. On behalf of the contributors, we are extremely grateful for the assistance provided by archivists and librarians of the British Library in London; the National Archives of Great Britain in Kew, London; the Archives Nationales in Paris; the London Metropolitan Archives in London; the Cape Town Archives Repository in South Africa; the Mystic Seaport Archives in Connecticut, USA; the Archives de l'Académie des Sciences, Belles-Lettres et Arts de Lyon in France; the Archives Nationales d'Outre-Mer in Aix-en-Provence, France; and the New York Public Library in the USA.

Abbreviations

CCMEIC	*A Calendar of Court Minutes etc. of the East India Company, 1635–1639 to 1677–1679*, 11 vols., edited with introductions by Sir William Foster
CIO	*La Compagnie des Iles Orientales* (French East India Company)
CO	Colonial Office series papers, National Archives of Great Britain, Kew
CP	*Ceylonees Plakkaatboek: Plakkaten en Andere Wetten, Uitgevaardigd door het Nederlandse Bestuur op Ceylon, 1638–1796*, L. Hovy (ed.) (Verloren, 1991)
CuP	*West Indisch Plakaatboek: Publikaties, en Andere Wetten Alsmede de Oudste Resoluties Betrekking Hebbende op Curacao, Aruba, Bonaire*, Jacob. A. Schiltkamp and J. Th. de Smidt (eds.) (Amsterdam: S. Emmering, 1978)
DIHST	*Documents Illustrative of the History of the Slave Trade to America*, 4 vols., Elizabeth Donnan (ed.) (Washington: Carnegie Institution, 1930–35)
DRCHNY	*Documents Relative to the Colonial History of the State of New York*, E.B. O'Callaghan (ed.) (Albany, 1855–83)
EIC	English East India Company
HCA	High Court of Admiralty series records, National Archives of Great Britain, Kew
KP	*Kaapse Plakkaatboek* 4 vols., M.K. Jeffreys and S.D. Naudé (eds.) (Cape Town: Cape Times, 1944–49)

NIP	*Nederlandsch-Indisch Plakaatboek, 1602–1811*, 17 vols., J.A. van der Chijs (ed.) (Batavia, 1885–1900)
NL-HaNa	Nationaal Archief, Amsterdam
PG	*Plakaatboek Guyana, 1670–1816*, J. Th. de Smidt, T. van der Lee and H.J.M. van Dapperen (eds.) (The Hague: Huygens Institute for the History of the Netherlands, 2014)
RLI	*Recopilación de Leyes de los Reynos de las Indias* [1681], reprint of the 1791 edition (Madrid: Centro de estudios políticos y constitucionales/Boletín oficial del estado, 1998)
SP	*West Indisch Plakaatboek. Plakaten, Ordonnantiën en Andere Wetten Uitgevaardigd in Suriname, 1667–1816*, J.A. Schiltkamp and J. Th. de Smidt (eds.) (Amsterdam: Emmering, 1973)
TWIC	Tweede West Indische Compagnie (Second Dutch West India Company)
VOC	Vereenigde Oostindische Compagnie (Dutch East India Company)
WIC	West Indische Compagnie (Dutch West India Company)
WMQ	*The William and Mary Quarterly*, third series

Introduction

*Agnès Delahaye, Elodie Peyrol-Kleiber, L.H. Roper
and Bertrand Van Ruymbeke*

Agents of European overseas empires is a collection of essays written in collaboration by a group of international scholars, whose work engages with the complexities of colonial enterprise. Combining their approaches and methods, the French, American, German, English and Dutch authors of this volume agreed to consider colonial agency in the overseas lands that they study in relation to the imperial thinking and decision-making that shaped imperial policies in the English, French, Spanish and Dutch metropolitan centres to which these spaces were connected. The objects of these essays are the private agents located in the metropolitan centres of Europe or in their respective colonial dominions, who promulgated and pursued the global expansion of European overseas interests during the fifteenth, sixteenth, seventeenth and eighteenth centuries. By interrogating their sources and objects under the prism of the nature and evolution of the imperial relation, our contributors provide an overview of the breadth and variety of the commercial structures, constitutional traditions and institutional innovations that advanced early modern overseas trade and colonisation, on the ground and in the texts where knowledge about these processes was shared and debated. They highlight the role of these colonisers in shaping both the processes behind early modern colonisation and commerce and global conceptions of the legitimacy, feasibility and profitability of colonial enterprise.

This volume takes a new and closer look at the collective 'engine room' of overseas endeavour: the people who effectively initiated, promoted and invested in these ventures, as well as those who managed commercial and colonising operations on the seas and on the ground. We have expanded the scope of colonisers beyond the corporation to include all the vehicles that were employed in the conduct of early modern European overseas colonisation and trade, as well as the array of actors who employed these vehicles. While the emergence of the corporate form in our period constitutes an important development in the histories of political economy and empire – and a vein of recent scholarship is devoted to companies and the conduct of empire in and of themselves – by no means did it constitute the only structure by which overseas colonisers and traders pursued their activities. Our book illustrates the phenomenon Jane Burbank and Frederick Cooper call 'repertoires of powers', as in the diversity of imperial experiences and the means by which imperial authority was validated and put into practice.[1] Research on such complex phenomena is necessarily collaborative, as shown in recent publications in Atlantic and global history, which cover the breadth of imperial experiences and compare, for instance, the varied labour regimes and racial and social hierarchies that developed in colonial scenarios across large swaths of overseas territories.[2]

Our volume builds upon the concept of Atlantic history, which over the last thirty years has shattered the old methodological and theoretical barriers that confined the history of empire within the study of each imperial nation-state. Circulation, mobility and interconnectedness have replaced more traditional approaches contained within the fluctuating borders of each imperial dominion, enabling scholars to follow their particular object around and across colonised spaces and to account for the dynamic diversity of colonial experiences and colonial lives.[3] The creative and innovative methods employed by Atlanticists have accordingly reconfigured and advanced our understanding of the directions, networks and progress of imperial commerce, starting with the centrality of slavery and the slave trade, in connecting the distant spaces with the competing ports and metropoles of Europe. In-depth studies of companies and maritime networks have enabled comparisons between institutions and between the imperial zones where they operated. Carrying Atlantic interconnectedness beyond national imperial frameworks enables us to understand the intra-imperial nature of the circulation of goods and ideas that transcends the 'Atlantic national framework'.[4] The aim of this collaborative volume is to further challenge the nation-centred paradigm that understands imperial development within national structures, institutions and cultures, to uncover the commonalities of aims and practices of the agents of trade and colonisation in the overseas spaces they sought to invest in and exploit.

We take a different tack from recent scholarship on early modern European empires, which still privileges 'the state' as a central player in imperial developments prior to circa 1800: one survey, while helpfully encouraging the jettisoning of the old, anachronistic concepts of 'mercantilism' and 'laissez-faire' when discussing early modern empires, nevertheless proclaims that 'scholars should characterize early modern economic culture' – the context from which these overseas empires arose – 'as a series of degrees of economic development between private and public spheres'.[5] The contributions to *Agents of European overseas empires* make clear that such 'spheres' – or even 'the state' as a protagonist in overseas endeavours or 'state interests' in the modern sense – did not exist as such in Western European 'economic culture', at least prior to the end of the eighteenth century.

The enduring – and also anachronistic – tendency to separate 'public' and 'private' is understandable, though, since the nature of the record can lead the unwary to focus on the metropolitan authorities upon whom agents of empire had to depend for legal approval and often protection for their activities. Promoters of overseas trade and colonisation naturally described *their* initiatives as public services to the Crown and the nation, in conformity with shared European understandings of the significance of westward expansion as the vehicle of providence, conversion and progress, with the Crown/nation/state generally occupying the van, correspondingly.[6] Yet, the pattern by which overseas ventures proceeded legally did not differ from domestic projects such as road-building or lighthouse construction. A focus on the multiplicity of agents who made imperial promotional plans into concrete commercial colonial enterprises requires a change of scale, to reveal the diversity and often conflicting interests that pitted investors, patrons and promoters in the cities of Europe against the experiences of the men, for they were overwhelmingly men, who sailed the ships or occupied the overseas territories these ships connected with one another and with the metropole.

The record of early modern European overseas interests is truncated by the dynamics of colonial promotion, which published and extolled colonial success while silencing the many exploratory and business failures that were also part of the process through which knowledge about distant places was accumulated. The authors in this collection, however, use the extant records of colonising companies, admiralties and governments, as well as the private papers of merchants, investors and colonisers involved, to explore and interrogate the motivations, abilities and practices of merchants, captains and colonial managers, who had to constantly adapt their actions and decisions to local conditions. These records reflect both the accumulation of knowledge and experience over time about the feasibility and profitability of colonial enterprise, and the reliance on accountability and publicity to stabilise ventures and protect reputations, without which there could be no imperial connections to speak of. From the first expeditions of the early modern era to the end of the nineteenth century, with the signing of the *Lei Áurea* (Golden Law) that marked the end of slavery in Brazil, the expansion of European interests overseas profoundly transformed non-European landscapes and societies, but it also led to the transformation of habits of sociability, taste, consumption and investment at home, where empires were widely discussed.[7] The multiple agents of empire of this volume shared the same private interests in furthering European presence overseas and understood their actions in the very public sphere of European imperial competition.

Companies and other private proprietary ventures took the lead, through the multiplicity of networks they established. These entities also assumed particular roles in imperial development, starting with their immediate concerns for the sustainability and efficiency of their operations on the ground, which often pitted their actions and interests against the expectations or exigencies of the metropolitan authorities under which they functioned. The tendency to refer to them through acronyms (WIC, VOC, EIC) points to their institutional endurance and legacy. They were established as long-term agents of empire through legitimising charters, whether or not pursuant to state initiative, as opposed to the unincorporated merchant associations and 'interlopers' who had no legal identity and were often devised or implemented for one specific mission through private funding.[8] These companies had different financial structures and different relationships with their sponsors, but they were fully institutional actors in overseas trade and colonisation.

Governments delegated privileges and some of their military and governmental power to these 'private' operators, which reveals the fiscal and bureaucratic frailty of those polities.[9] It is clear, however, that, in exchange for the powers, including monopolies, the recipients of charters undertook the responsibility for managing overseas affairs for their governments in accordance with the terms of their agreements. Thus, the institutional, financial and governing structures of the sort of ventures examined here existed as an extension of the central government, in order to carry out the public purpose that they agreed to provide. The contextual analyses of their commercial activities investigated in this volume widen the scope of these activities to include the social and political implications of such devolution in the spaces they entered and competed over, often in the name of the sovereignty of their sponsors.

It should be stressed, though, that these endeavours – while duly empowered to conduct operations on behalf of early modern polities – did not constitute 'company-states', a historiographical misconception that has amassed substantial recent currency. Rather, as with the various councils, aristocrats and viceregents who held wide discretion to govern as state representatives on the ground, the operators of early modern vehicles of overseas trade and colonisation received special powers to conduct their activities, both as matters of necessity – as their governments generally lacked either the resources or the capacity to initiate empire – and as an element in the incessant pursuit of political and economic advantage by patronage networks in these societies.[10]

As our volume also shows, these ventures had different structures and different relations with the polities that sponsored them, at least officially; while they might – and did – exercise state functions both by design and in the breach, in the first instance, their legal status could be changed, and their charters modified or even revoked. Moreover, the nature, scope and aims of overseas operators drastically evolved from the sixteenth and seventeenth centuries to the eighteenth century. The Virginia Company of London saw its charter modified twice before its dissolution by the Crown in 1624 after its management descended into a fierce, irreparable breach, while the Dutch East India Company first obtained a twenty-one-year monopoly on the spice trade with South Asian countries, which evolved into a larger array of trading activities, including slavery, until its end in 1800. The French East India Company and the English East India Company took on trade in those distant lands with different strategies. Both started as monopolistic trading bodies but, as opposed to the CIO, which remained a trading company, the EIC became involved in politics and acted as a major agent of British imperialism during the greater part of the eighteenth century, acquiring powers in diplomacy and military actions. The WIC was granted a monopoly on trade, navigation and conquest in the Western Hemisphere, but setbacks administered by the Portuguese and the English caused its liquidation and reorganisation in 1674 and it ended up administering the remaining faraway territories in Africa and America rather than a vehicle for furthering commerce and colonisation.[11]

Although their organisational structures and aims evolved differently under the pressure of international competition, these companies were the sites of the formation of networks of individual investors and stakeholders who, by contributing to various degrees in furthering or ending these ventures, increased the transformative impact of imperial expansion on metropolitan centres. Even though aristocrats enrolled in such ventures and in the overall process of colonisation, the proliferation of these entities led to the formation of merchant courtiers in European metropoles, remodelling societies and politics in the process. Whether in the United Provinces, France or England, merchants became indispensable political actors in search of increasing social distinction and favours from the Crown. Throughout Europe, patriciates of merchants dominated landownership. In France, Louis XIV's wars after 1661 helped develop a pool of wealthy merchants as they involved the sons of successful bankers and merchants in the state's affairs – the career of Louis' finance minister Jean-Baptiste Colbert providing a good example of this pattern. Every merchant wanted an official position by royal appointment to participate in the administration of this powerful nation. As long as states remained solvent enough to pay the interests on their loans, the merchant class would be staunch supporters of the throne.[12] In England, the same remodelling of society can be observed. Gentry families married into wealthy London, Bristol or Liverpool merchant circles to come closer to occupying seats in the House of Commons. As Daniel Defoe wrote in 1726, 'our merchants are princes, greater and richer, and more powerful than some sovereign Princes'.¹³ European colonial companies, merchant associations and other individual stakeholders were agents of empire, who competed nationally and internationally for overseas wealth, political access and social prestige, with different degrees of support from their sovereign.¹⁴

Commercial interests, however, represent only one end of the relationships this volume seeks to investigate. In the wake of Jack Greene's seminal 'periphery and centre' model, inspired by Edward Shils' sociological characterisation of imperial relations in oppositional – and ahistorical – 'colonial vs metropolitan' terms, constitutional historians of the British Empire have uncovered the dynamic nature of constitutional organisation in the spaces where settlement generated the formation of colonial proto-states.¹⁵ In the Spanish, Dutch and French Empires, power, authority and commercial terms were also perpetually negotiated between metropolitan stakeholders and creole agents, merchants and writers representing their own interests. The essays in this collection are in line with a spatial and political understanding of imperial development as the concurrent and, at times, overlapping formation of dynamic imperial constitutions, within the fluctuating claims and correspondingly fluid relations that existed between each empire and their respective colonial constituencies. Ideas of authority, property and governance circulated, were negotiated and evolved, making the study of creole actions, innovations, interests and politics increasingly relevant to a global understanding of the history of European overseas empires.¹⁶

Accordingly, *Agents of European overseas empires* considers overseas commercial and colonial enterprise as a global phenomenon, to reveal the diversity among the spaces of European occupation, which were fragmented, distant and contested, but also profoundly interconnected, through trade, migration and the exchange of letters and ideas. In doing so, these essays investigate the manners and the degrees to which metropolitan dominion and authority were either delegated to, or appropriated by, these individuals and institutions for 'the defence of remote American boundaries' and for remoter East Indian territorial claims, 'the cultivation of local government' as well as 'the need to recruit migrants'.¹⁷ They also question the extent to which individuals or companies were required or inclined to implement imperial orders and directives, they demonstrate the degree of autonomy and innovation these agents exerted to fulfil their commissions or enforce their own sustainable commercial, colonial plans and they address their contributions to early modern European polities.[18]

The sources on which these articles are based include the records, papers and narratives in which merchant adventurers and colonial sponsors devised and promoted their colonising projects, companies established their proceedings and company agents and recruits recorded the fulfilment or failure of their commissions. They analyse colonisation as a series of assumptions and innovations in trading practices and modes of imperial administration by which European interests extended globally during the early modern period. They also challenge the traditional view in which issues of authority and dependency in the history of empire are centred principally on the interests and power of the metropole. Instead, the essays highlight the common experiences of those who left Europe, temporarily or permanently, to labour and trade in overseas territories as part of imperial projects, but for their own benefit and for the benefit of the individuals and companies under whom they worked.[19]

Colonising agency is not a new concept. It initially referred to the official or identified captains and merchants who flew their country's colours and bore the seal of their sovereign or company to distant lands. On paper, these agents were in charge of claiming lands, and later, as trade routes became stable, of enforcing, or rather negotiating, measures and policies elaborated and adopted by corporate assemblies or dictated by royal commissions devoted to colonial matters. By the eighteenth century, British publicist Malachy Postlethwayt could confidently identify colonial agents as 'people entrusted, or appointed, with the conduct, management, and negotiation of the affairs of other peoples, or of a corporation', a particular type of professionals at the centre of imperial commerce.[20]

Early on, however, these agents included governors and captains who not only managed part of the capital of metropolitan investors but also the ships, cargoes, and crews they hired, and the soldiers, labourers, craftsmen and surveyors whom they transported abroad in order to sustain colonial locations, not to mention make them profitable. Taking stock of the diversity of colonial stakeholders within each empire, this collection highlights the processes of adaptation and innovation put in place and enforced by the men who travelled or settled in the spaces of colonial appropriation to make colonial expansion and profit a reality.[21]

This collection, in turn, sheds light on the shared experiences, practices and knowledge of some of the economic agents of colonisation – courtiers, merchants, captains, soldiers, privateers, missionaries and settlers – who sojourned or remained in the lands on the peripheries of the Spanish, French, Dutch and British Empires, beyond the classical typologies of expansion that define each one according to their respective practices of occupation and exploitation, within distinct geographical borders often defined in cultural terms. It offers a series of themes, structures and vantage points that consider expansion as a constant process of economic development leading to international competition over land and sea, from the perspective of its many actors in the merchant associations of the metropole, on the ships that connected the latter to its overseas dominions and in the colonial spaces that were created in their wake.[22]

European expansion led to European competition. Competition led to wars and negotiations over power and authority among Europeans and with African, Asian and Native American polities. Competition between empires was visible as almost permanent wars shook the centuries under scrutiny and overseas lands were taken or lost as the objects of greed and conflict between rival and competing imperial powers.[23] Less visible, though, were the conflicts that also emerged between the nations and corporations they had either created or agreed to create, as the example of the CIO shows, whose commercial policy led to petitions by French textiles workers in the 1670s who felt endangered by the importation of calico from India. A similar scenario occurred in England thirty years later. This volume therefore addresses the competition between the respective recipients of authority from the polities they represented, and the relations each of them entertained with their responsibilities as carriers of their nation's colonial projects. Corporations and other private agents were recipients of private and public funds and were carriers of metropolitan power and invested in public missions, such as spreading the nation's religion or increasing its wealth, but as commercial organisations, they tended to be guided by their own sustainability and interests. In addition, some owed their success to firm and enduring ties with their central governing body in the metropole, while others evolved through an immediate adaptation of corporate forms by local authorities, people and institutions, giving way to a form of corporate power shaped by the real needs of the territories and populations.

As competition often goes hand in hand with domination in the early modern period, this volume also seeks to address aspects of European overseas expansion in the colonised territories themselves. The wars mentioned earlier also took the form of civil wars within the conquered territories, sometimes displacing the inter-European tensions to the colonies, the latter becoming mirrors of their 'mother countries'. Agents of empires also faced the task of controlling, imposing rules and creating legislation to the detriment of local populations and unfree labourers, forcing us, as historians, to think more structurally in terms of evolving dominant/dominated relationships, framed, for instance, within the concept of settler colonialism or the study of violence, competition and conflict as constitutive of colonial regimes.[24]

This book began as a collaborative project around the theme of distant lands and the agents that operated links between Europe and those faraway territories. The authors came away from their initial discussions having agreed to revisit the object of their initial personal research through the prism of the nature of imperial interests and imperial authority, and to consider the complexities of colonial agency collaboratively. The resulting chapters are organised along three different perspectives that reflect the multi-directional nature of imperial connections. The first three chapters consider imperial expansion from the vantage points of European stakeholders who questioned the significance of colonisation in relation to the power and sovereignty of each imperial nation. In Chapter 1, Susanne Lachenicht introduces the reader to the complexity of the multiple agencies at work in the development of imperial plans and imperial thinking. She illustrates the negotiations and contestations surrounding the development of overseas operators in the first era of globalisation, through a comparison between French and British imperial policies and the resistance they triggered within each nation. She stresses the notion of imperial process in the formation of a political and economic definition of what a nation was, what it should be and how the nation's sovereignty should be transferred on to distant colonial territories.

François Brizay's chapter develops the issue of the criticism levelled in Europe at imperial expansion and its agents, through a close examination of the political economic thought of Abbé Raynal, one of the first critics of imperialism and globalisation, in the *Histoire philosophique et politique des établissements et du commerce des Européens dans les deux Indes*. Raynal compared the transfer of sovereignty from the Crown to the multiple agents of the British and French Empires, reflected on the modalities of this transfer and the most profitable economic strategies that resulted, and questioned the Europeans' motivations for settling in overseas territories. The political, economic and military depiction of the colonies that he provided reveals the extent to which knowledge about colonial spaces was shared across Europe. Using Raynal's argumentation, the chapter questions three aspects of this comparative study: the role and the economic activities companies practised in the distant colonies, an analysis of how the French and English Empires had managed, or failed, to spread across Asia, the West Indies and North America and, finally, the imperial strategies developed by both Empires in the process of colonising distant lands – Raynal positioning himself in favour of the English strategies.

In Chapter 3, L.H. Roper demonstrates that imperial endeavours were not only a question of negotiation between the nation and the agents of empire. He argues that private enterprise directed imperial state policy, and not the other way around, to further challenge and complexify the periphery-centre model of previous imperial thinking that assumed commonality of interests between the state and its agents overseas. This chapter therefore engages the latest literature on the part played by the English state in early modern empire-building, along with recent characterisations of the functions and roles of private agents in English imperial history. It argues that joint-stock companies and other private agents held activities that benefited 'public' prosperity and, thus, warranted the chartering of extraordinary 'public' powers to those who were willing to endorse them.

The second set of chapters carries the analysis into the distant spaces of colonial occupation and development in the Atlantic and the Indian Ocean worlds, for an even closer look at the institutional and commercial evolution of company policy, as well as the negotiations local agents engaged in on the ground to compensate for the difficult circumstances created by distant, inconsistent, or ill-adapted metropolitan strategies. In Chapter 4, Eric Roulet focuses on the Spanish migratory policy of the sixteenth century to demonstrate the limits of imperial control over the nature and evolution of the population invited to transform eras of Spanish occupation into spaces of Spanish sovereignty. His detailed study of the records of early modern Spanish migration shows both the scope and ambition of metropolitan control over the numbers and composition of colonial migration, and the limits imposed on these regulatory impulses by the realities of colonial occupation on the ground in Spanish America.

Engaging in colonisation meant potentially failing to control distant lands and the agents recruited to transform or exploit them. This failure often translated into the development of smuggling, illegal trade, autonomy or the ultimate rejection of imperial sovereignty. When negotiation was impossible with authorities in the metropole, agents of empires resorted to illegality. Because much was at stake in colonial agency, illegal trade or piracy developed at a fast pace, barely hurt by the desperate imperial attempts at curtailing them. In Chapter 5, Anne-Claire Faucquez turns the lens to agents of the Dutch Empire in the Atlantic, to underline the role of strategy in colonisation and stress the fact that intercolonial competition mattered at least as much as relations with the metropole. The Dutch Empire engaged in the slave trade to limit the expansion of the Spanish Empire, resorting to privateering to negotiate profits. In this case, privateering and piracy held blurred boundaries which were instrumentalised by the various national or colonial agents of empire, for the sake of commerce. Hence, looking at the correspondence between governors and the Dutch state, colonial legislation and ship registries, the chapter analyses how the introduction of slavery resulted from the colonists' personal motives and ambition as much as it did from the imperialist policies of the States-General and the implementation of the Dutch West India Company.

Lastly, in Chapter 6, Elisabeth Heijmans and Rafaël Thiebaut provide a wide-ranging analysis of labour legislation across the separate and distinct areas of the Dutch Empire, both in the Atlantic and the Indian Ocean worlds, as proof of the adaptability of company rule to the demands and interests of enslavers in these regions. Through an unprecedented and forensic analysis of labour by-laws in Suriname, Batavia and the Cape, they argue for the generalisation of unfree labour and slavery in all areas of this vast empire, and demonstrate the increasing racialisation of the social orders under company rule but designed and adapted to the advantage and for the profit of local elites, whose brutality and exploitative tendencies compare with the enslaved societies of the Caribbean and limited the scope of imperial authority and Dutch aspirations for more humanitarian labour management in the nation's overseas dominions.

Over the period covered in this volume, a great variety of New World societies were created, in which land and trade jointly defined the imperial projects these societies were part of. The forms and degrees of sovereignty the agents of colonisation held over these distant lands depended on the topography and the resources of the spaces they reached, and on their ability to compete with rival traders and occupiers overseas for the actual appropriation and exploitation of these lands. The last section of this volume focuses specifically on settler locales and settler interests on the margins of imperial policies and authorities, to highlight the importance of settler adaptation and settler action in shaping not only the social and political orders in which they evolved but also in challenging metropolitan perceptions and practices that were becoming increasingly critical of the violence and exploitation inherent in expansion and colonisation. Chapter 7 by Trevor Burnard and Agnès Delahaye explores the relevance of the concept of settler colonialism as an interpretative framework of the history of early America, to argue that settlers were indeed full-on actors of imperial expansion, in this case, the British Empire, but that they were not the all-powerful perpetrators of genocide upon Indigenous populations that much recent scholarship in the field likes to portray. A study of creole historiography in early America demonstrates that British settlers were both aware of the precariousness and frailty of their imperial ambitions, challenged at every step by Indigenous resistance and international competition, and determined to see their efforts integrated in the wider history of the imperial project to which they belonged. Settlers deserve to be studied in their own terms, as the experienced agents of expansion and conquest whose knowledge was an essential part of the development of imperial orders and whose voices help illuminate the complexity and failures of imperial plans from the metropole.

Chapter 8 by Marilyn Garcia-Chapleau illustrates the conflicts that power negotiations in the imperial context could lead to, through an analysis of the stages of colonial occupation in the Cape of Good Hope. Even though some agents of Dutch expansion would have settled this land permanently, their ambitions were limited by the decision-making of the leadership of the VOC, who considered the area as unprofitable and too costly to develop. Successive waves of Dutch and other settler migration contributed to the slow development of the area, highlighting the conflicting interests of settlers and companies when the latter refused to recognise and access to the demands of the former, who developed their activities in spite of the neglect of the company to whom they owed their sovereignty. The Cape instead became a prosperous colony under the British at the beginning of the nineteenth century, but its history is much longer and much more localised than previous historiography has cared to consider.

Considerable labour force was required to stabilise the presence of European earliest industries, so as to enable transatlantic shipping to become a profitable enterprise. Sustainability was hard to reach; profit could take time and various degrees of investment to materialise, providing ample stories of deadly seasoning, disease and starvation overseas, and financial loss in the metropole. Colonial failure was blamed on the cupidity, laziness and insubordination of hired soldiers, sailors and servants working and dying in distant lands, and colonial societies were slow to attract both sufficient labourers to work these lands and the interest and protection of the metropole. This tension between conducting commerce in the interest of the nation and generating private profit is illustrated by Charlotte Carrington-Farmer in Chapter 9, through the trade in mules bred in New England. Settlers struggled between attractive West Indian (non-British) markets and the national interests, often leading to reprimands and sometimes conflicts. These distant creole lands and societies entertained privileged connections with their respective metropolitan centres through networks of colonial investors, merchants and agents, yet they adapted the legal, constitutional, and financial structures and precedents at their disposal to the particular needs of their own ventures. In doing so, they competed with each other within and across imperial projects and dominions, adding their own experiences and models to existing colonial precedents, and contributing to European understandings of what empire entailed.

Finally, in the epilogue, Bertrand Van Ruymbeke presents an analysis of the reflection and debates on colonisation since the late fourteenth century that occurred in France – and in Europe – in the late eighteenth century through prize-winning essay contests offered by *Académies*. The contribution focuses particularly on the contest held in Lyon through the 1780s on the effects – disastrous or beneficial, as then perceived – of the colonisation of the Americas, in the shadow of the publication of Raynal's immensely popular *Histoire philosophique et politique des établissements et du commerce des Européens dans les deux Indes*. The epilogue thereby offers a contemporaneous vision on colonisation that covers many issues addressed in the volume.

Together, these essays provide a wide-ranging examination of colonial agency and the conflicting interests between stakeholders and actors of expansion within the Spanish, French, Dutch and British Empires, while highlighting the commonalities of interests between these agents and the similarities in the way they negotiated and appropriated the spaces they sought to exploit. By bringing together explorations of colonial processes and imperial negotiations in different spaces and at different periods of European expansion overseas, they offer a better understanding of the complexities of the imperial machinery, through the actions of the multiple agents of European empires, be they trading companies, courtiers, corporations, traders, merchants, privateers or colonisers. They also bring to view the many possibilities that localised and comparative analysis of colonising methods and processes brings to the study of European imperial expansion.

Notes

1 Jane Burbank and Frederick Cooper, *Empires in World History: Power and the Politics of Difference* (Princeton: Princeton University Press, 2010). Recent scholarship on corporations and empire includes Ron Harris, *Going the Distance: Eurasian Trade and the Rise of the Business Corporation, 1400–1700* (Princeton: Princeton University Press, 2020); William A. Pettigrew and David Veevers (eds.), *The Corporation as a Protagonist in Global History, 1550–1700* (Leiden: Brill, 2019); Andrew Philips and J.C. Sharman, *Outsourcing*

Empire: How Company-States Made the Modern World (Princeton: Princeton University Press, 2020).
2 Jeffrey A. Fortin and Mark Meuwese (eds.), *Atlantic Biographies: Individuals and Peoples in the Atlantic World* (Leiden: Brill, 2014); Gregory D. Smithers and Brooke N. Newman (eds.), *Native Diasporas, Indigenous Identities and Settler Colonialism in the Americas* (Lincoln: University of Nebraska Press, 2014); John Smolenski and Thomas J. Humfrey (eds.), *New World Orders: Violence, Sanction and Authority in the Colonial Americas* (Philadelphia: University of Pennsylvania Press, 2005); Lawrence Aje, Anne-Claire Faucquez and Elodie Peyrol-Kleiber, 'Servitudes et libertés dans les Amériques avant l'abolition de l'esclavage', *Les cahiers du MIMMOC* [online], 19 (2018), http://journals.openedition.org/mimmoc/3077; Esther Sahle, *Quakers in the British Atlantic, c. 1660–1800* (Martlesham: Boydell & Brewer, 2021); Jorge Cañizares-Esguerra and Benjamin Breen comment on a number of innovative studies on cross-imperial topics in Jorge Cañizares-Esguerra and Benjamin Breen, 'Hybrid Atlantic: Future directions for the history of the Atlantic World', *History Compass* 11, no. 8 (2013), 597–609.
3 David Armitage, 'Three concepts of Atlantic history', in D. Armitage and M. Braddick (eds.), *The British Atlantic World, 1500–1800* (New York: Palgrave Macmillan, 2002), 11–27. Examples include Ben Marsh, *Unravelled Dreams: Silk and the Atlantic World 1500–1840* (Cambridge: Cambridge University Press, 2020); Pierre Gervais, Yannick Lemarchand and Dominique Margairaz (eds.), *Merchants and Profit in the Age of Commerce, 1680–1830* (London: Pickering & Chatto, 2014); Maxine Berg, Felicia Gottmann, Hanna Hodacs and Chris Nierstrasz (eds.), *Goods from the East, 1600–1800: Trading Eurasia* (London: Palgrave Macmillan, 2015); Anne Gerritsen and Giorgio Riello (eds.), *The Global Lives of Things: The Material Culture of Connections in the Early Modern World* (Abingdon: Routledge, 2016).
4 Cañizares-Esguerra and Breen, 'Hybrid Atlantic', 600. See also Manuel Barcia, 'Into the future: A historiographical overview of Atlantic history in the twenty-first century', *Atlantic Studies* 19, no. 2 (2021), 181–99, doi/full/10.1080/14788810.2021.1948284; Philip J. Stern, 'British Asia and British Atlantic: Comparisons and connections', *WMQ* 63, no. 4 (2006), 693–712; Pierre Gervais, 'Neither imperial, nor Atlantic: A merchant perspective on international trade in the eighteenth century', *History of European Ideas* 34, no. 4 (2008), 465–73.
5 Jacob Soll, 'For a new economic history of early modern empire: Anglo-French imperial co-development beyond mercantilism and

laissez-faire', *WMQ* 77, no. 4 (2020), 525–50 at 530; see also Cátia Antunes and Amélia Polónia (eds.), *Beyond Empires: Global, Self-Organizing, Cross-Imperial Networks, 1500–1800* (Leiden: Brill, 2016), 1–11, 1–2, 8–10. For early modern European political culture, Robert von Friedeburg and John Morrill (eds.), *Monarchy Transformed: Princes and their Elites in Early Modern Western Europe* (Cambridge: Cambridge University Press, 2017).

6   Karen Kupperman (ed.), *America in European Consciousness, 1493–1750* (Chapel Hill: University of North Carolina Press, 1995); David Armitage, 'Greater Britain, 1516–1776', in *Essays in Atlantic History* (Aldershot: Ashgate Publishing, 2004), 1–19. For 'projecting' in early modern England, Koji Yamamoto, *Taming Capitalism before Its Triumph: Public Service, Distrust, and 'Projecting' in Early Modern England* (New York: Oxford University Press, 2018).

7   Emma Rothschild, 'Late Atlantic history', in Nicholas Canny and Philip D. Morgan (eds.), *The Oxford Handbook of Atlantic History* (Oxford: Oxford University Press, 2011), 634–48. For sociability and empire, Catherine Hall and Sonya Rose (eds.), *At Home with the Empire: Metropolitan Culture and the Imperial World* (Cambridge: Cambridge University Press, 2006); Lauren Working, 'Tobacco and the social life of conquest in London, 1580–1625', *Historical Journal* 65, no. 1 (2022), 30–48; Misha Ewen, *The Virginia Venture: American Colonization and English Society, 1580–1660* (Philadelphia: University of Pennsylvania Press, 2022).

8   Eric Roulet (ed.), *Les Premières Compagnies dans l'Atlantique, 1600–1650: Structures et modes de fonctionnement* (Aachen: Shaker Verlag, 2017), 5; Niels Steensgaard, 'Companies as a specific institution', in Leonard Blussé and Femme Gaastra (eds.), *Companies and Trade: On Companies during the Ancien Régime* (The Hague: Nijhoff, 1981), 245–64 at 246–7; Mark Freeman, Robin Pearson and James Taylor, *Shareholder Democracies? Corporate Governance in Britain and Ireland before 1850* (Chicago: University of Chicago Press, 2012), 2.

9   Stephen R. Brown, *Merchant Kings: When Companies Ruled the World, 1600–1900* (New York: Thomas Dunne Books, 2009), 1.

10 The pattern whereby 'private' entities initiated colonisation continued well into the nineteenth century: Matthew Birchall, 'History, sovereignty, and capital: Company colonization in Australia and New Zealand', *Journal of Global History* 16, no. 1 (2021), 141–57, doi:10.1017/S1740022820000133. For the 'company-state', Philip J. Stern, *The Company-State: Corporate Sovereignty & the Early Modern Foundations of the British Empire in India* (Oxford: Oxford University Press, 2012); Andrew Phillips and J.C. Sharman,

Outsourcing Empire: How Company-States Made the Modern World (Princeton: Princeton University Press, 2020); Edmond Smith, *Merchants: The Community That Shaped England's Trade and Empire* (London: Yale University Press, 2021); Roulet (ed.), *Les premières compagnies dans l'Atlantique, 1600–1650*.
11 Adam Clulow and Tristan Mostert (eds.), *The Dutch and English East India Companies: Diplomacy, Trade and Violence in Early Modern Asia* (Amsterdam: Amsterdam University Press, 2018), 15.
12 George F. Rudé, *Europe in the Eighteenth Century: Aristocracy and the Bourgeois Challenge* (Cambridge, MA: Harvard University Press, 1972), 78–9.
13 Daniel Defoe, *The Complete English Tradesman* (London, 1726), 240.
14 Elizabeth Mancke and Carole Shammas (eds.), *The Creation of the British Atlantic World* (Baltimore: Johns Hopkins University Press, 2005); Elizabeth Mancke, 'Empire and state', in Armitage and Braddick (eds.), *The British Atlantic World*, 193–213.
15 Jack P. Greene, 'Transatlantic colonization and the redefinition of empire in the early modern era: The British–American experience', in Christine Daniels and Michael V. Kennedy (eds.), *Negotiated Empires: Centers and Peripheries in the Americas, 1500–1820* (New York: Routledge, 2002), 267–82.
16 Stern, 'British Asia and British Atlantic'.
17 L.H. Roper and Bertrand Van Ruymbeke, 'Introduction', in *Constructing Early Modern Empires: Proprietary Ventures in the Atlantic World, 1500–1750* (Leiden: Brill, 2007), 1–19 at 7.
18 William A. Pettigrew, 'Political economy', in William A. Pettigrew and David Veevers (eds.), *The Corporation as a Protagonist in Global History, c. 1550–1750* (Leiden: Brill, 2018), 43–67. Vincent Grégoire alludes to the instrumentalisation of the agents by the states and the instrumentalisation of the states by the agents, where the agents are merchant companies, but it could be any other private agent, in *Théories de l'État et problèmes coloniaux (XVIe–XVIIIe siècles)* (Paris: Honoré Champion, 2017), 15.
19 L.H. Roper, *Advancing Empire: English Interests and Overseas Expansion, 1613–1688* (New York: Cambridge University Press, 2017), 9–11.
20 Cited in Michael Kammen, *A Rope of Sand: The Colonial Agents, British Politics, and the American Revolution* (Ithaca: Cornell University Press, 1968), 3.
21 William A. Pettigrew and Edmond Smith, 'Corporate management, labour relations, and community building at the East India Company's Blackwall Dockyard, 1600–57', *Journal of Social History* 53, no. 1

(2018), 133–56. See also Stern, *The Company-State*, for a reinterpretation of the role the East India Company played in shaping India. Both develop the idea of corporate management and corporate sovereignty in different parts of the English and (after 1707) British Empire.

22 Trevor Burnard, 'Empire matters? The historiography of imperialism in early America, 1491–1830', *History of European Ideas* 33, no. 1 (2007), 87–107; William A. Pettigrew, David Armitage, Paul Halliday, Vicki Hsueh, Thomas Leng and Philip Stern, 'Corporate constitutionalism and the dialogue between the global and the local in seventeenth-century English history', *Itinerario* 39, no. 3 (2015), 487–525.

23 Steve Pincus and James Robinson, 'Wars and state-making reconsidered: The rise of the developmental state', *Annales: Histoire, Sciences Sociales* 71, no. 1 (2016), 5–36.

24 David Chaunu and Séverin Duc (eds.), *La domination comme expérience européenne et américaine à l'époque moderne* (Brussels: Peter Lang, 2019), 13; John G. Reid and Thomas Peace, 'Colonies of settlement and settler colonialism in northeastern North America, 1450–1850', in Edward Cavanagh and Lorenzo Veracini (eds.), *The Routledge Handbook of the History of Settler Colonialism* (London: Routledge, 2016), 79–94.

Part I

Tensions within imperial projects

1

Global trade and its benefits for 'the nation': The examples of early modern France and Britain

Susanne Lachenicht

Politicians, the media, economists, political scientists and historians claim today that so-called new nationalisms – Brexit, former US president Donald Trump's 'Make America great again' and many others – are a response to increasing globalisation or hyper-globalisation.[1] Hence, nationalism is often understood as an ideology and as practices meant to limit globalisation and its negative effects and vice versa.[2] There are some indications, though, that the links between globalisation and nationalism are complex, more ambivalent and less purely antagonistic, especially when examined in a *longue durée*,[3] spatially diverse perspective and on different scales.[4]

This chapter considers the relationship between globalisation and nationalism *avant la lettre*[5] for the early modern Atlantic world. To this end, it assesses how European expansion, state- and empire-building, commerce and trade, and concepts of and identifications with the nation, which is not congruent with state, have developed since the late fifteenth century. It then zooms in on one aspect of the relationship between early modern globalisation and nationalism, namely, how between the seventeenth and the mid-eighteenth centuries, historical actors in France and Britain looked at global commerce and trade and discussed its benefits, or lack thereof, for the nation.

From the later seventeenth century, commerce and trade in the Atlantic and Indian Ocean worlds increased significantly, not least through proto-industrial plantation and slaveholding societies in the Caribbean that were a response to growing demand for specific consumer goods in Europe and the colonies, as much as to the need of European imperial powers to generate revenue and build powerful states.[6] Related to these processes, the same period saw major competition and conflict between imperial states, if not permanent war,[7] and between a variety of corporate institutions forming and transforming states and empires: the Crown, the Estates, the Catholic Church and its orders, Protestant churches and their missionary arms, cities, foreign nations or diasporas, trade companies and others.[8] The absolutist state as described by Jean Bodin (1529–96) or Thomas Hobbes (1588–1679) was by no means in place; it was 'more prescription than description'.[9] Sovereignty was far from being indivisible. We could consider the period between the later seventeenth and the mid-eighteenth centuries as a crucial phase when state- and empire-building, global commerce and trade were subject to significant changes. Questions about the sovereignty of states, nations (diasporas inclusive), trading companies and other corporations were being discussed and fought out for solutions to be found. The Seven Years' War, the new repartition of the world, including the loss of France's North American empire to Britain, British territorial gains in India and the repercussions these developments had in Europe and her colonies are often understood as other watersheds in these processes.[10]

This chapter sets out with a brief discussion of what globalisation and 'the nation' mean for the early modern period. It then looks into agents in the process of European expansion and colonisation and the role trading companies and other corporations played in this as much as in early attempts to regulate the effects of permanent war and global trade. Against this backdrop, the third and fourth parts will take examples from late seventeenth- to mid-eighteenth-century France and Britain to enquire into discussions about trade companies, manufacturing and protectionism, sovereignty rights and the benefits for the nation. These discussions not only included political economists, politicians, the directors of trading companies and their investors but also a wide range of other actors: manufacturers, artisans, consumers of all kinds, ship crews, trade company clerks in offices around the world and many others. These parts will highlight a specific spectrum of actors participating in a multivocal discourse (including practices) on state, the nation, trade, and commerce, and will end with a preliminary discussion of what this could mean for the relationship between globalisation, state-building and nationalism in the early modern Atlantic world.

Globalisation and nations in the early modern period

For the early modern period, there have been substantial discussions about whether processes of increased imperial expansion and the ensuing interconnectedness of world and peoples should be framed in terms of globalisation. Together with other scholars, historians Christopher Bayly and Jürgen Osterhammel have described the early modern period as a time of accelerated globalisation, as the first 'global age'.[11] The expansion of European and non-European empires triggered a degree of interconnectedness not known before the 1500s – especially not in the Atlantic realm. It produced a non-linear process of intensifying interconnections of spaces, finances, people, knowledge, institutions, production, distribution and consumption. Among the voluntary and involuntary actors of increasing interconnectedness, we find imperial states and their institutions, conquistadores and private venturers, trading companies, the Catholic Church and its religious orders, Protestant churches and their missionary arms, migrants – which included voluntary migrants, religious refugees, enslaved people and indentured servants – seamen, soldiers, maroons, privateers and pirates, smugglers, scientists, Indigenous nations, producers and consumers of goods, and authors, producers and readers of encyclopaedias, maps, dictionaries, and natural histories, in metropolitan and colonial spaces and in the so-called hinterlands or backcountry.[12] While these actors enhanced interconnectedness and what we might today dub globalisation, their intentions were more complex or even contradictory to their effects. Some of these actors had clear imperial, religious and 'national' agendas in their intentions and actions; at the same time, they produced increasing interconnections, transnational or supranational spheres, all of which we could describe as globalisation.

For the early modern period, there has not only been much debate about the term 'globalisation' but also about concepts of the nation and nationalism *avant la lettre*. Today, literatures coming out of early modern history and literary studies hold that the fifteenth and sixteenth centuries not only saw attempts at creating sovereign states[13] but also shifting paradigms in what was considered to be a nation. For late sixteenth-century England, Richard Helgerson and others have shown how in the context of British expansion and empire-building at home and abroad, contemporaries such as William Shakespeare, Edmund Spenser, Richard Hakluyt, Walter Raleigh and Christopher Marlowe imagined the English nation as a cultural community conceived in a common origin and sharing a history, a language and cultural artefacts imagined through chivalric romance, historical narrative, topographical description, travel narratives, theatre and others.[14] However, these writers were at odds with questions about the body of the English nation, its sovereignty and who represented it: some thought that 'the people', so those having inhabited England since times immemorial and sharing a common history, language and traditions, formed the nation. Others held that the monarch and Parliament embodied the nation, and others still that the nation was a combination of both. Discussions and conflicts also arose around the question of the relationship between nation and state: should the monarch, Parliament, the people, the law or the economy establish and control state institutions that were to benefit the nation? Different and interrelated foundations of the nation rivalled with each other for hegemony within England, and at the same time thickened the lines that separated one nation from another.[15] For the British Empire or state system, this meant both competition within – between the English, Irish, Scottish and Welsh nations[16] – and between dynasties, states, empires and nations. In later instances, as a consequence of the Civil Wars, during the Commonwealth period, the nation was identified with the republican state which recognised its subjects as citizens and governed their daily lives through various forms of law and administration. At the same time, so still in pre-Restoration England, we find notions of the nation as an imagined community much along the lines of what Helgerson described for the late sixteenth century.[17]

Not only early modern England but also the Holy Roman Empire saw the development of concepts of the nation from the late Middle Ages onwards, with which Germans identified, next to religion, dynasties or economic interests. Through a blend of discourses on *patria*[18] and nation, the nation became a universal category which defined people as equal and identifiable nations competing for territory, other economic resources, honour and might. The nation also came to be associated with freedom, sovereignty, social and economic progress, and with security and the equality of all members within it. The nation thus turned into a parallel and entangled concept of late medieval and early modern estate-based societies, of imaginations of a God-given social hierarchy of people and a universal religious community (Catholicism).[19] Again, one of the crucial questions was, however, who was to defend and protect the nation and its sovereignty rights. Debates centred around the role of the Emperor, the Estates (*Reichstag*), the German Princes, the people, the law, commerce and trade, and non-state actors such as the church(es) or an international political and economic system. For all these early modern nations, commerce and trade were to generate revenues that were supposed to build competitive states. One of the major questions raised was the extent to which early modern imperial states needed transnational or even global trade to turn into mighty powers.

Agents of colonisation and governance in early modern conflicts

New institutional historians have shown that diverse actors organised as corporations at home and abroad were involved not only in processes of colonisation and state-building but also in regulating international relations along with commerce and trade.[20]

There clearly was a complex, mutually enabling but nonetheless competitive relationship between a variety of corporations, which made state-building, European expansion and colonisation possible. Conquistadores, private venturers, trading companies, trade diasporas, churches and missionary orders played an important role in the process of European expansion.[21] Between the fifteenth and eighteenth centuries, the Crown and/or the Estates were often too weak and their fiscal basis too poor to finance colonisation, its institutions and its necessary structures, and to take the permanent risk of financial investments in long-distance trade. It has often been held that Portugal and the composite Spanish monarchy were only able to start the *conquista* into North Africa and to the eastern Atlantic islands, the Canaries, Madeira and the Cape Verde Islands off the Atlantic coast of Africa, thanks to increased centralisation of fiscal and state power.[22] At the same time, though, the *conquista* largely depended on high-risk private ventures, sometimes by foreign conquistadores and groups of private investors funding their travels. Imperial states and their economies therefore hinged on specific corporations willing to take major financial and personal risks: colonial proprietors, trade companies, religious orders and trade diasporas, who competed against each other within one and the same imperial enterprise. In later phases of colonisation, these actors were in some instances replaced by state administration and centralisation, but with great difficulty, as Eric Roulet demonstrates in his contribution to this volume. When private ventures, trading companies or religious orders managed to make greater profits from the colonies or failed to fulfil the state government's expectations in terms of profits and domination, European imperial states often cut back on these actors' original privileges, as the cases of French Canada from 1660 onwards, of South Carolina in 1729 or of French Louisiana in 1731 illustrate.[23] Some of these measures came as a punishment for resisting colonial orders. In other instances, commercial or religious corporations preserved their rights and autonomy for quite some time.

With the process of European expansion taking off, state and imperial conflicts and wars increased, requiring new, substantial state finances which often came out of colonial ventures and profits made by trading companies, of which a specific percentage had to be conceded to the Crown. Private ventures, trading companies and other corporations were granted substantial rights and powers, as most of the royal charters of the late fifteenth to the mid-eighteenth centuries indicate, including the right to exploit natural resources and human beings in the colonies, to install and administer law, to perform regular governance, to have their own currencies and organise their own militia, and often also to enjoy monopolies for certain goods or over certain shipping routes. This meant conferring, delegating and thus limiting the Crown's sovereignty rights, which was, nevertheless, normal procedure in that period. Early modern imperial states were made up of powerful corporations, the Crown, Estates, church(es), guilds, universities, foreign nations and trade companies, bound together in a complex legal framework that 'administer(ed) over and on behalf of the collectivity', or the nation.[24] Competition and conflicts between these corporations was the order of the day and included discussions on whether and how this multitude of corporative actors benefited and protected the nation.

The period of European expansion, thus, was not only a process of increased interconnections and globalisation. It was inextricably linked to, or rather driven by, imperial, national and religious competition, by conflicts and almost permanent wars, in the Atlantic as much as in the Indian Ocean and Southeast Asian realms, from a Eurocentric perspective between the Portuguese, the Spanish, the French, the English and the Dutch, as the most powerful and prominent European empires. Globalisation in that period could thus be understood as the connections enabling states and empires and the corporations within them to develop and compete with each other and vice versa. All of this happened more often than not in the name of the nations over which sovereignty state and imperial governments had stewardship.

Contemporaries held that the relationships and competition between nations and states needed to be regulated as much as commerce and trade. Hugo Grotius' (1583–1645) *Mare Librum* (1609), commissioned by the directors of the VOC, has often been understood as one of the key writings helping to legitimise the seizure of Spanish and Portuguese ships by the Dutch Republic and, later, France and England, as well as the latter's early seventeenth-century efforts to build their own colonial, that is, commercial and territorial, empires. Ever since Portugal and Spain had benefited from the papal bulls of the late fifteenth century, wars between the forming European states not only raged in Europe but increasingly so in non-European seas and territories.[25] Wars were fought about souls, territories, natural resources, products, and consumption, for the benefit of each nation.

Political thinkers such as Thomas Hobbes and Samuel von Pufendorf (1632–94) held that nations were sovereign, had natural equality and an imperative duty to defend their right to self-preservation, which legitimised all possible measures, including war. In Hobbes' understanding, the state, his Leviathan, had to be all-powerful, an absolutist power suppressing all rivalling corporations within (whom Hobbes judged to be parasites), to be able to defend the nation's rights against other nations. For both Pufendorf and Hobbes, states that represented and protected nations could acquire rights over other states and thus restrict their freedom of action by concluding treaties – in the political sphere as much as in the realms of commerce and trade. Natural law required these treaties to be respected (*pacta sunt servanda*).[26] For Hobbes, wealth was necessary for self-defence and should be primarily acquired by domestic industry, less so by expansion and grand commercial ventures. He considered merchants making large profits to be unpatriotic, as their businesses could ruin the safety of the state. Private or partial economic interests had to be suppressed for the benefit of the state and thus the security of the nation.[27]

However, Grotius' *Mare Librum* also opened up ideas for a code of international law, which was to regulate trade and commerce, between but also beyond states and empires, which could attribute a rather important role to private venturers, trading companies and corporative actors other than the Crown.[28] The sovereign autonomy held by state or empire and its monarch or estates, as critiques of Britain's commercial empire and hegemony put it, could hinder peace and the wealth of nations. Pufendorf, Hobbes and, later, David Hume (1711–76) were struggling with *the* conundrum of their time, the relationship between global trade, state and nation: 'they wanted to explain how the conflation of the logics of war and trade arose in the seventeenth century and why it was so difficult to exorcise them afterward'. They also struggled for how the nation could be best protected.[29]

At the latest with the Treaty of Utrecht (1713), new political and economic thinking developed along with treaty practices in interstate relations as well as commerce and trade, which were supposed to end the permanent state of war between Europe's imperial states.[30] Contemporaries hoped that regulating, and establishing a legal international order for trade and commerce in particular, was to produce a civil society of states and peaceful competition between nations.[31] Based on principles of sovereignty, reciprocity, the equality of nations and international security, the Treaty of Utrecht was supposed to bring about lasting peace and relative tranquillity up to the 1740s.[32] Those regulating interstate treaties and treaties of commerce and trade were by no means simply state governments and their officials but other corporations, which could be at odds or conflicting with each other even when acting officially in the name of nation and state.[33] This was the case for private ventures, proprietary or trade company governors, religious orders and their global networks or trade diasporas.[34] Many of them claimed to act for the benefit of the nation when using the latter's sovereignty rights.

France and global trade

France had two major competitors in its efforts towards imperial expansion and dominance in global trade: the Dutch Republic and Britain. The following paragraphs lay out a few features of the manner in which France was to compete internationally, and how this resonated with 'the French nation'.

As much as other European imperial states, France highly depended for her early colonial ventures on domestic and foreign investors, seafarers or adventurers, commissioned and entitled by the French Crown to explore, 'discover', appropriate and exploit 'unknown' territories and resources. This was the case during the so-called contact phase with the Florentine Giovanni da Verrazzano in 1524, the Breton Jacques Cartier in 1534 or with the official founding of Quebec in 1608, under the auspices of Pierre Gua de Monts and Samuel de Champlain respectively. After 1610, other non-state actors were active in colonising and setting up missions in French Canada, namely Jesuits, Récollets and Ursulines. In France's colonial enterprises, trade companies became more important from the later 1620s onwards, with the founding of Richelieu's *Compagnie des Cents Associés* (or *Compagnie de la Nouvelle France*). Endowed with monopolies and the powers of a *seigneur*, a number of small trade companies had to find settlers for New France, to defend France's overseas territories against the British and Indigenous Americans and to convert the latter to Catholicism. Many trade companies in New France and the Antilles failed to accomplish these aims, not least because of inter-imperial competition with Britain and because they were too small in comparison to their Dutch and British rivals. Neither the *Compagnie des Cents Associés* nor the *Compagnie des Habitants* (founded in 1645) managed to fulfil their promises, which meant that, officially, in New France, the Crown took over to centralise colonial government from 1661 onwards.

However, in other parts of France's empire, the importance of trade companies as actors for the imperial state's colonial endeavours prevailed, and they became even more important, especially from the later seventeenth century onwards. As François Charpentier, a member of the *Académie française*, claimed in 1665: 'A great realm is never fully prosperous when trade fails to flourish there as in other dominions; ... among all the trades done in all parts of the world, there is none as rich ... as that of the East Indies'.[35] Thus, he urged the entire French nation to invest in the French *Compagnie des Indes*, founded in 1664, in order to render the people prosperous and happy and to make the state a mighty one.

The *Compagnie des Indes* was thus founded much later than the VOC or the English East India Company. As a latecomer, it was supposed to make France rise up to the rank of successful player in global colonial commerce and trade, to rival, equal and outdo the Dutch, Portuguese, English, Danes and Swedes.[36] It was to contribute to the development of a mighty navy and to spread French civilisation and Catholicism across the world, becoming a powerful arm of the French nation, of state and empire. It was a question of national honour and pride to turn France into an important economic player in commerce and trade.[37] Merged together in 1719 with the *Compagnie du Sénégal*, the *Compagnie de Chine*, the *Compagnie du Mississippi* and the *Compagnie de la Louisiane* into the *Compagnie perpétuelle des Indes*, it held together much of the French Empire, from the Upper Mississippi Valley to the West African coast to the Bay of Bengal in South Asia, and it became responsible for the collection and management of taxes in France. More than a century later than England and the Dutch Republic, France had finally created one powerful company acting on a global level. In 1720, the *Compagnie perpétuelle des Indes* merged with the royal bank of France. It was dissolved in 1769 after the crisis and losses incurred during the Seven Years' War, and a third trade company was founded in 1770, which in turn came to an end during the era of the French Revolution.

In the later seventeenth century, rivalling the Dutch and English East India Companies was problematic. At the onset of the personal reign of Louis XIV, Charpentier and other authors of his time alluded to France as an inferior nation when it came to trade and commerce.[38] As a weaker player in global trade, France sought to introduce a legal framework for foreign exchanges for the purpose of furthering its economic and political interests. Colbert was very much aware that international trade had to be free to a certain degree and competition permitted, but he equally insisted on the condition that France was allowed in return to sell her agricultural and pre-industrial products abroad. From the 1660s onwards, Colbert made attempts at regulating international trade towards a middle ground between open market rivalry and state protectionism. However, France failed to persuade the Dutch Republic and Britain, its two major competitors, to abide by the legal principles France wanted to impose upon them: that trade had to be reciprocal and mutually beneficial while simultaneously guaranteeing each state's sovereignty in matters of custom duties.[39] In consequence, France turned into a war-waging machine and the absolutist regime of Louis XIV 'welded war and trade into a single new policy'.[40]

The idea of more peaceful solutions to a workable form of commercial competition between the imperial states was not dead, though. A stable European state system was envisaged that would guarantee the security of all nations by creating a European free trade area.[41] As mentioned above, during the War of the Spanish Succession and with the Treaty of Utrecht, ideas developed towards what we would call today multilateral and reciprocal trade treaties, for the purpose of avoiding, on the one hand, perpetual war between Europe's imperial states and their respective trading companies, and, on the other, the damage done by specific forms of trade to manufacturing at home. These developments, for which the British were held responsible, would not even benefit the English nation itself, as David Hume held.[42] Some French authors, such as the Abbé de Saint Pierre, became famous for proposing a confederation of European states. Saint Pierre dreamed of a 'permanent society' to 'secure the advantages of commerce', which would have resulted in downscaling the existing system of tariffs in Europe. It would have affected the degree of sovereign power of the European states and could have included other, non-European powers.[43] Most French authors considered Britain as the most unwilling probable partner in any such scheme because of its aggressive imperial politics, and thus had little hope to see their ideas evolve into concrete measures.[44]

Obviously, granting trade companies major privileges to found new colonies or to have monopolies over specific goods of trade was but one option in making imperial states wealthier, more powerful, more rational and modern. Manufacturing and selling goods at home and abroad could also enrich the early modern nation. While Britain and France took profit from their respective East India Companies in their trade with Asian textiles, at the same time, Indian cotton posed a threat to European domestic textile production.[45] In the 1670s, textile workers in France grew anxious to avoid global competition with regard to their manufactured textiles. Again and again, they petitioned the Government to introduce a complete ban on calico imports to protect French domestic products, which was eventually conceded and put in place in 1686. From then onwards, France's East India Company was, in theory, only allowed to bring Indian calico and silk into France for re-exportation to African and Caribbean markets, where they became an important factor in the slave trade triangle and clothed larger and larger parts of the world. The ban was thus supposed to serve French commercial state interests while simultaneously protecting its textile workers from direct competition from the East India Company's trade. It was impossible, though, to enforce the ban on Indian textiles. The free port of Marseille and the calico printing industry there had a keen interest in the import of these products, as did an increasing number of French people, for reasons of price and fashion. Cotton had become a 'populuxe good'. In terms of function and aesthetics, cotton was fashionable and cheap and had already replaced European textiles to some extent. It had become indispensable for many consumers but also producers of textiles in Europe and it had also changed the structures in European commerce and trade.[46] The 'calico craze' of the early eighteenth century meant that protectionism in France ran counter not only to the interests of its international rivals but also to the interests of larger parts of the French nation, such as producers, shopkeepers, peddlers and consumers.[47]

Britain and global trade

While England (and from 1707 Britain) had some powerful corporations such as the Levant and New England companies or the City of London, one specific corporation preoccupied contemporaries and historians most prominently: the English East India Company (EIC). It was founded in 1600, in clear opposition to

Dutch economic and imperial competition. On the one hand, it was to stimulate free trade and globalisation, and, on the other, it was an important player in the making of the British Empire and, also, of English nationalism. As some contemporaries put it, English EIC merchants were the vanguard of the English nation abroad.[48] At the latest in 1670, the EIC acquired rights to territorial acquisitions, to mint money, to command fortresses and troops and form alliances, to make war and peace and to exercise both civil and criminal jurisdiction over the areas it acquired. During the eighteenth and much of the nineteenth centuries, it became a rather autonomous and powerful arm of the British empire, promoting not only commerce and trade but also English civilisation and Protestantism. In the eighteenth century, it turned into an important money lender for Britain's imperial wars against France. Dissolved in 1873/74, as a late effect of the crisis of 1857, it was no longer looked upon as guaranteeing English/British national/imperial interests.

This section will take the EIC as one example to enquire into discussions about trade companies, manufacturing and protectionism, sovereignty rights and the benefits for the nation. How did England consider the EIC between the late seventeenth and mid-eighteenth centuries, before the Company acquired substantial territories in India during the Seven Years' War and before it came to rule over one fifth of the world's population, generating revenues far beyond the domestic British economy?[49] Prior to these developments, how did the English look on to the EIC, its sovereignty rights and its role in benefiting the nation?

Before the Glorious Revolution, the major legal challenge to the EIC's corporative rights and monopolies came from a specific group of members of the English nation, independent merchants, whom the EIC considered as interlopers, who sought to get shares in the lucrative East India trade. The most prominent case was *East India v. Sandys*, also known as the Great Case of Monopolies, heard in the Court of King's Bench in the mid-1680s. Advocates of the EIC argued that the latter had no monopolies as such, yet, as a sovereign corporation, it was the only possible institution capable of handling the East India trade for the benefit of the English nation, provided it efficiently governed this trade by royal privilege and by a set of specific rules and laws.[50] Quoting Hugo Grotius, Thomas Sandys' lawyers in return argued that trade was free to all men and should not be controlled by any one corporation. Furthermore, they held that the EIC, due to its limited stock, was unable to fully develop the potentials of trade with East India. From the free merchants' or 'interlopers'' perspective, there was more trade and benefits out there than the EIC could manage. Therefore, other members of the English nation would have to do it in their place. Ironically, in the early seventeenth century, the EIC had used some of these arguments to justify its royal charters and its infringing on the Portuguese and Spanish trades. Now, these arguments turned against the Company itself. In the end, however, the King's Bench took over, representing the Crown, and ruled that regulating trade in foreign parts of the world fell to the King's prerogatives. The Crown had delegated some of these prerogatives to the EIC, so that the latter could govern and rule the East India trade at the pleasure of the King.[51] Prior to 1688–89, two corporations, the EIC and the Crown, and Sandys as a representative of the free English nation of merchants, struggled for sovereignty and the freedom to trade, and all argued that their perspective was the one which was best for the entire English nation.

Further attacks on the EIC's privileges and sovereignty rights came with the Glorious Revolution. While the ascendance of the Dutch *stadtholder* William of Orange to the throne of England, Scotland and Ireland could have ended the competition between the VOC and the EIC, conflicts in fact grew between the two trade companies. The two nations' most prominent trading companies, the VOC and the EIC, still were competing with each other, as the two nations, the Dutch and the English, had not been united with the Glorious Revolution.

However, after 1688, greater challenges came from within, with another corporation, the English Parliament, gaining in importance and sovereignty. It gave a voice to some members of the English nation, such as artisans, ship crews, textile workers and manufacturers, who had not necessarily been heard before, and all complained about the EIC's practices in East India and its effects at home. From the complainants' perspective, the EIC trade in Indian textiles had ruined domestic textile production in England, the shipbuilding industry and many other trades at the basis of the nation's livelihoods.[52]

One of the EIC's most eloquent advocates was Charles Davenant (1656–1714), an English economist and member of Parliament, who published his *Essay on the East India Trade* in 1697. Discussing whether the 'East India trade is hurtful or beneficial to this [the

English] nation', Davenant held that England's might and its potential to wage wars against other imperial powers depended on its 'plantation trade' and the 'East India traffic'. He went on:

> The plantation trade gives employment to many thousand artificers here at home and takes off a great quantity of our inferior manufactures. The returns of all which are made in tobacco, cotton, ginger, sugars, indico, etc. by which we were not only supplied for our own consumption, but we had formerly wherewithal to send to France, Flanders, Hamburg, the East Country and Holland, for 500,000. Per annum, besides what we shipped for Spain and the Streights, etc.

Furthermore, he argued that since Europeans had discovered East India and the textiles trade in particular, England as a nation could not afford to abstain from it, not even to protect its own textile industries. International competition, in trade, war, colonies and power, forced England as a nation to continue the East India trade and to refrain from banning Indian textiles from the Isles.[53]

Members of Parliament and a number of complainants of the English nation were not convinced by these arguments. Many of Davenant's contemporaries would not agree with his stance on the EIC and the importance of global trade. Manufacturers went on to petition the English Government to ban imports of calico; Londoners took to chasing women wearing Indian calicos in the streets and stripping them of this undesired fabric, because it was seen to threaten the nation's interests. While the ban on calico finally came into force in 1721, consumers in England continued to buy calicos imported through the VOC.[54] As was the case in France, the demand for Indian cotton had already changed production, distribution and consumption chains in England, and could not be terminated.

The critique of the EIC's practices continued. Considering the 'abuses' of the privileged group of EIC governors and stockholders, in 1693, under the pressure of non-EIC merchants and other lobby groups, Parliament and the Privy Council revoked the EIC's original charter to replace it with another that transferred some of the Company's sovereignty rights to Crown and Parliament. The Company was impelled to increase its stock and had to export a large amount of English manufactured goods to the East Indies, with the intent to satisfy English non-EIC merchants, manufacturers and textile workers. However, these efforts did not succeed in calming the wrath of those who objected to the EIC's privileges and the effects of global trade. In 1697, weavers and workers in the linen and dying industries besieged the East India House in London to end the tyranny of this corporation and its sovereignty rights over the English nation. In the long run, especially with the United English East India Company that emerged in 1707, Parliament and the Crown gained more control over the EIC. The latter was incorporated into the state and became part of it, while the dominating institutions or corporations now clearly were the Crown and Parliament, or so it seemed.[55] These conflicts between EIC, King, Parliament and other members of the English nation illustrate how one corporation, Parliament, tried to bring another, the EIC, under control, and how state formation in late seventeenth-century Britain meant that Parliament turned into the most powerful state institution capable of controlling global trade.

Conclusions

From zooming in on these late seventeenth- to mid-eighteenth-century French and British examples, it seems that global trade, which, among other factors, enhanced globalisation, was considered to be an important tool to make nations prosperous and to develop mighty imperial states protecting nations. Early modern imperial states seem to have depended on their trading companies and on global trade to finance inter-imperial wars, to modernise and finance their institutions and grow more stable and more powerful. At the same time, the examples provided show that contemporaries struggled with the effects of global and globalising trade, in particular with the effects of permanent war between imperial states and threats posed by imperial trade to domestic manufacturing. Furthermore, it was not clear which corporations within early modern imperial states – whether it was Crown, Parliament or other Estates, trading companies, cities, church(es), guilds or other corporations – were best suited to protect the nation's interests in global commerce and trade. Some political thinkers, such as the Abbé de Saint Pierre, even opted for what we might want to dub early liberal designs, that is, for less powerful states and a European system of reciprocal, free trade.

The questions of the time seem to have pertained to the relevance of global trade in making early modern nations powerful among other nations and empires, to the necessity of building a mighty imperial state to cope with global competition and to the imperatives of making the state aggressive to deal with the latter to its best advantage. Contemporaries also discussed the instruments by which global trade was to be regulated among equal nations. Equally important was the conundrum of how much a nation needed to protect its own national manufactures from global trade and competition, and for the benefit of which producing, distributing or consuming segment of the population. Finally, the question remained whose claims for protection within the nation were legitimate, or more legitimate than others.

Approaching the relationship between globalisation, state-building and nationalism from an early modern perspective can thus shed light on how entangled these processes were at the time. Globalisation, state-building and nationalism also stand for a crucial discussion, if not a major modern conundrum: which institutions, state or international, and of what nature, are best fitted to regulate trade and commerce while protecting the interests of all nations? Furthermore, globalisation and nationalism interrogate the nature and contours of the nation and demonstrate the tensions between the different interests that compose it, who equally require and demand the protections of state institutions. The notion of the nation has, ever since the sixteenth century, promised freedom, social and economic progress and integrated identities for all, but this was, as we have seen, an impossible promise to fulfil, that produced conflicting and competing forms of nationalistic claims within the nation, dividing it into multiple, antagonistic groups all invoking the interests of the whole to protect and further their own.

Notes

1 For example, John B. Judis, 'What the left misses about nationalism', *New York Times*, www.nytimes.com/2018/10/15/opinion/nationalism-trum-globalization-immigrationhtml (accessed 21 March 2021). On the resurgence of nationalism in the 1990s, see I. Clark, *Globalization and Fragmentation* (Oxford: Oxford University Press, 1997), 4; Stuart Hall, 'The question of cultural identity', in T. McGrew, S. Hall and

D. Held (eds.), *Modernity and Its Futures* (Cambridge: Polity Press, 1992), 273–325 at 314.
2 Michael Ignatieff, *Blood and Belonging* (London: Vintage, 1994), 2.
3 A *longue durée* perspective (English: long term) is an approach to history, developed by the French *Annales* school, which studies long-term historical structures instead of *histoire événementielle* ('event history'), that is, the short-term timescale. The foundational work is Fernand Braudel, *La Méditerranée et le Monde Méditeranéen à l'Epoque de Philippe II* (Paris, 1949).
4 See, for example, Anna Lowenhaupt Tsing, *Friction: An Ethnography of Global Connection* (Princeton: Princeton University Press, 2005); Natalie Sabanadze, *Globalization and Nationalism: The Cases of Georgia and the Basque Country* (Budapest: Central European University Press, 2010), 1; Volker Depkat and Susanne Lachenicht, 'Rückkehr des Nationalismus?', https://geschichtedergegenwart.de (accessed 9 September 2019); Volker Depkat and Susanne Lachenicht, 'Nations, nationalism, and transnationalism revisited', *Yearbook of Transnational History* 5 (2022), 1–39.
5 Before the specified concept existed.
6 The 'plantation machine', as Trevor Burnard and John Garrigus have dubbed this, fully developed from the 1740s onwards, see T. Burnard and J. Garrigus, *The Plantation Machine: Atlantic Capitalism in French Saint-Domingue and British Jamaica* (Philadelphia: University of Pennsylvania Press, 2018).
7 Charles Tilly, *Coercion, Capital, and European States, AD 990–1992* (Cambridge: Cambridge University Press, 1990).
8 Philip J. Stern, *The Company-State: Corporate Sovereignty and the Early Modern Foundations of the British Empire in India* (Oxford: Oxford University Press, 2012), 8; Istvan Hont, *Jealousy of Trade: International Competition and the Nation-State in Historical Perspective* (Cambridge, MA: Harvard University Press, 2010), 15–17. On this topic, see also Lou Roper's chapter in this volume.
9 Stern, *The Company-State*, 9.
10 *Ibid.*, 3.
11 Christopher A. Bayly, *The Birth of the Modern World, 1780–1914* (Oxford: Oxford University Press, 2005); Jürgen Osterhammel and Niels P. Petersson, *Geschichte der Globalisierung. Dimensionen, Prozesse, Epochen* (Munich: Beck, 2003); André Gunder Frank, *ReOrient: Global Economy in the Asian Age* (Berkeley: University of California Press, 1998); J.R. McNeill and William H. McNeill, *The Human Web: A Bird's-Eye View of World History* (New York: Norton and Company, 2003). See also Pim de Zwart, *Globalization and the*

Colonial Origins of the Great Divergence (Leiden: Brill, 2016), who, contrary to many other scholars, finds significant evidence for the integration of global commodity markets already for the seventeenth and eighteenth centuries.

12 For example, Susanne Lachenicht, *Europeans Engaging the Atlantic: Knowledge and Trade* (Frankfurt/Main, New York, Chicago: Campus and University of Chicago Press, 2014).

13 Geoffrey R. Elton, *The Tudor Revolution in Government: Administrative Changes in the Reign of Henry VIII* (Cambridge: Cambridge University Press, 1953), 3.

14 Richard Helgerson, *Forms of Nationhood: The Elizabethan Writing of England* (Chicago: University of Chicago Press, 1992), 2, 152.

15 Ibid., 8–10, 14, 299–300.

16 Brendan Bradshaw and Peter Roberts, 'Introduction', in Brendan Bradshaw and Peter Roberts (eds.), *British Consciousness and Identity: The Making of Britain, 1533–1707* (Cambridge: Cambridge University Press, 2000), 1–7.

17 David Loewenstein and Paul Stevens, 'Introduction: Milton's nationalism: Challenges and questions', in David Loewenstein and Paul Stevens (eds.), *Early Modern Nationalism and Milton's England* (Toronto: University of Toronto Press, 2008), 3–21, 5.

18 Latin for 'fatherland'.

19 Caspar Hirschi, *Wettkampf der Nationen. Konstruktionen einer deutschen Ehrgemeinschaft an der Wende vom Mittelalter zur Neuzeit* (Göttingen: Wallstein, 2005).

20 Antonella Alimento and Koen Stapelbroek, 'Trade and treaties: Balancing the interstate system', in Antonella Alimento and Koen Stapelbroek (eds.), *The Politics of Commercial Treaties in the Eighteenth Century: Balance of Power, Balance of Trade* (New York: Palgrave Macmillan, 2017), 1–75 at 10–11. See also Jean-Pierre Jessenne, Renaud Morieux and Pascal Dupuy (eds.), *Le Négoce de la Paix. Les Nations et les Traités franco-britanniques, 1713–1802* (Paris: Société des études robespierristes, 2011).

21 On proprietary ventures, see L.H. Roper and Bertrand van Ruymbeke, 'Introduction', in L.H. Roper and Bertrand Van Ruymbeke (eds.), *Constructing Early Modern Empires: Proprietary Ventures in the Atlantic World, 1500–1750* (Leiden: Brill, 2007), 1–19; on trade diasporas, see Daviken Studnicki-Gizbert, *A Nation upon the Ocean Sea* (Oxford: Oxford University Press, 2007) and Dagmar Freist and Susanne Lachenicht (eds.), *Connecting Worlds and People: Early Modern Diasporas* (London: Routledge, 2016); on missionary orders, see Susanne Lachenicht, Lauric Henneton and Yann Lignereux (eds.),

'The spiritual geopolitics in the early modern world', special issue, *Itinerario* 40, no. 2 (2016), 182–353.
22 See Bartolomé Yun Casalilla and Patrick K. O'Brien, *The Rise of Fiscal States: A Global History, 1500–1914* (Cambridge: Cambridge University Press, 2017) and B. Yun Casalilla, *Iberian World Empires and the Globalization of Europe 1415–1668* (New York: Palgrave Macmillan, 2018), especially Chapters 1–2.
23 Roper and Van Ruymbeke, 'Introduction', 3–5, 7–8, 10.
24 Stern, *The Company-State*, 6, 7, 24–5. For this argument, see also Lou Roper's chapter in this volume.
25 See Martine J. van Ittersum, *Profit and Principle: Hugo Grotius, Natural Rights, Theories and the Rise of Dutch Power in the East Indies, 1595–1615* (Leiden: Brill, 2006). For the 'total war mentality', see Alimento and Stapelbroek, 'Trade and treaties', 6–7.
26 Moritz Isenmann, 'Égalité, réciprocité, souveraineté: The role of commercial treaties in Colbert's economic policy', in Alimento and Stapelbroek, Politics of Commercial Treaties, 77–103 at 79; Stern, *The Company-State*, 213.
27 Hont, *Jealousy of Trade*, 18–19.
28 Grégoire Holtz, 'The model of the VOC in early seventeenth-century France', in Siegfried Huigen, Jan L. de Jong and Elmer Kolfin (eds.), *The Dutch Trading Companies as Knowledge Networks* (Leiden: Brill, 2010), 319–35 at 328–9. See also the chapters by Elizabeth Heijmans and Rafaël Thiebaut and Lou Roper in this volume.
29 Hont, *Jealousy of Trade*, 6–7.
30 Alimento and Stapelbroek, 'Trade and treaties', 10–11. See also Jessenne, Morieux and Dupuy, *Le Négoce de la Paix*.
31 Eric Schnakenbourg, 'The conditions of trade in wartime: Treaties of commerce and maritime law in the eighteenth century', in Alimento and Stapelbroek, Politics of Commercial Treaties, 217–42; Alimento and Stapelbroek, 'Trade and treaties', 3–4.
32 John G.A. Pocock, *Barbarism and Religion: Vol. I: The Enlightenment of Edward Gibbon, 1734–1764* (Cambridge: Cambridge University Press, 1990), 110; Andreas Osiander, 'Sovereignty, international relations, and the Westphalian Myth', *International Organization* 55, no. 2 (2001), 251–87; Marc Belissa, *Repenser l'Ordre Européen (1795–1802): De la Société des Rois aux Droits de Nations* (Paris: Kimé, 2006); Heinhard Steiger, 'Was haben die Untertaten vom Frieden?', in H. Duchhardt and M. Espenhorst (eds.), *Utrecht-Rastatt-Baden 1712–1714. Ein Europäisches Friedenswerk am Ende des Zeitalters Ludwig XIV* (Göttingen: Vandenhoeck & Ruprecht, 2013), 141–66.
33 Alimento and Stapelbroek, 'Trade and treaties', 10–11. See also Jessenne, Morieux and Dupuy, *Le Négoce de la Paix*.

34 See Donald C. Coleman, 'Politics and economics in the age of Anne: The case of the Anglo-French trade treaty of 1713', in D.C. Coleman and A.H. John (eds.), *Trade, Government and Economy in Pre-Industrial England* (London: Weidenfeld and Nicolson, 1976), 187–213.

35 '*Il manque quelque chose à la prospérité d'un grand royaume, quand le commerce n'y fleurit pas à l'égal des autres possessions; ... entre tous les commerces qui se font dans toutes les parties du monde, il n'y en a point de plus riches ... que celui des Indes orientales*', F. Charpentier, *Discours d'un Fidèle Sujet du Roi touchant l'Établissement d'une Compagnie Française pour le Commerce des Indes Orientales* (Paris, 1665), 3–4, 6, 60.

36 Erin M. Greenwald, *Marc-Antoine Caillot and the Company of the Indies in Louisiana: Trade in the French Atlantic World* (Baton Rouge: Louisiana State University Press, 2016), 13–14. See also Charpentier, *Discours d'un Fidèle Sujet*, 7–8, 16, 18.

37 Charpentier, *Discours d'un Fidèle Sujet*, 18, 29–30.

38 Marie Ménard-Jacob, *La Première Compagnie des Indes, 1664–1704: Apprentissages, Échecs et Héritage* (Rennes: Presses Universitaires de Rennes, 2016), 219–25.

39 Isenmann, 'Égalité, réciprocité, souveraineté', 79, 102.

40 Hont, *Jealousy of Trade*, 23.

41 *Ibid.*, 27.

42 Alimento and Stapelbroek, 'Trade and treaties', 28; David Hume, 'Of the balance of power', in E. Miller (ed.), *Essays Moral, Political, and Literary* (Indianapolis: Liberty Fund, 1975), 332–41, 315.

43 Alimento and Stapelbroek, 'Trade and treaties', 28–9.

44 *Ibid.*, 31–2.

45 Felicia Gottmann, *Global Trade, Smuggling, and the Making of Economic Liberalism: Asian Textiles in France 1680–1760* (New York: Palgrave Macmillan, 2016).

46 Cissie Fairchilds, 'The production and marketing of populuxe goods in eighteenth-century Paris', in J. Brewer and R. Porter (eds.), *Consumption and the World of Goods* (London: Routledge, 1993), 228–48.

47 J.C. Nierstrasz, *Rivalry for Trade in Tea and Textiles: The English and Dutch East India Companies (1700–1800)* (New York: Palgrave Macmillan, 2015), 11. For the eighteenth-century 'calico craze', see also the following contemporary texts: Jacob-Nicolas Moreau, *Examen des Effets que doivent produire dans le Commerce de France, l'Usage & la Fabrication des Toiles Peintes: ou Réponse à l'Ouvrage intitulé* (Geneva, 1759); André Morellet, *Réflexions sur les Avantages de la Libre Fabrication et de l'Usage des Toiles Peintes en France;*

pour servir de Réponse aux divers Mémoires des (Geneva, 1758). See also Giorgio Riello, *Cotton: The Fabric That Made the Modern World* (Cambridge: Cambridge University Press, 2013).
48 Stern, *The Company-State*, 42.
49 John McAleer, 'Introduction', in H.V. Bowen, J. McAleer and R.J. Blyth (eds.), *Monsoon Traders: The Maritime World of the East India Company* (London: Scala, 2011), 1–21 at 1.
50 Stern, *The Company-State*, 44–58.
51 *Ibid.*, 53–4.
52 Stern, *The Company-State*, 15, 143–4.
53 Charles Davenant, *Essay on the East India Trade* (London, 1697).
54 Natalie Rothstein, 'The calico campaign of 1719–1721', *East London Papers* 7 (1964), 3–21; Beverly Lemire, 'Fashioning cottons: Asian trade, domestic industry and consumer demand, 1660–1780', in D. Jenkins (ed.), *The Cambridge History of Western Textiles*, Vol. 1 (Cambridge: Cambridge University Press, 2003), 493–521.
55 Stern, *The Company-State*, 148–63.

2

Comparing and criticising early modern imperial policies in the Age of Revolution: Abbé Raynal's *Histoire philosophique et politique des deux Indes*

François Brizay

The *Histoire philosophique et politique des établissements et du commerce des Européens dans les deux Indes* (*A Philosophical and Political History of the Settlements and Trade of the Europeans in the East and West Indies*) was originally published in three editions and quickly earned a great reputation, giving rise to many counterfeits. Conceived as an encyclopaedia of European expansion in modern times, this book provided information and commentaries on the discourses of the 1770s about the way the Portuguese, the Spanish, the French, the English, the Dutch and the Scandinavians had conquered and developed territories overseas. It was presented as a sum of the historical, geographical and economic knowledge that Europeans had accumulated on this subject at the end of the *ancien régime*.

Commonly attributed to Abbé Guillaume-Thomas Raynal (1713–96), an anti-slavery priest and writer, the *Histoire des deux Indes* was a joint publishing enterprise of vulgarisation, accompanied by a critical dissertation.[1] Its second edition was blacklisted and the third one burnt in public in Paris on 29 May 1781, after it had been condemned by the Parliament of Paris and the Church. Consequently, Raynal used the services of several collaborators, whose anonymity he preserved. Among the main authors, scholars have recognised Diderot and the Baron d'Holbach, but Raynal also asked others to contribute, such as the man of letters Alexandre Deleyre (1726–96), the encyclopaedist Valadier, the Marquis de Saint-Lambert and the astronomer and mathematician Joseph-Louis Lagrange.[2] He also mobilised others' works to feed his own, such as the memoirs of farmer-general Paulze (Lavoisier's father-in-law) and those of the Comte d'Aranda.[3] He copied passages from the *Histoire Générale des Voyages* by Abbé Prévost and from other famous books by some of his contemporaries, such as the *Recherches Philosophiques sur les Américains* by Cornelius de Pauw and *Common Sense* by Thomas Paine. Several of these sources appear throughout the work, such as the *Histoire générale* by the Abbé Prévost and the contributions of Diderot and Jussieu; others, such as the travel accounts of Jean de Léry about Brazil or Lafitau's account of Native American life, were confined to a segment of the work describing the economy, the society, the flora and the fauna of a particular area.[4]

Several developments of this text were updated from one edition to the next, which makes it often confusing because it contains digressions and uses many registers of writing combining historical narrative, descriptions and philosophical and political essays.[5] The diversity of the information provided and the success of the book since its publication explain its complete or partial reissues and the varied studies scholars have devoted to it. Indeed, Raynal, who was particularly interested in slavery and trade, relayed much information about trading companies, trade routes, commercial factories and overseas commodities. Context is also relevant, since Raynal wrote in the aftermath of the Treaty of Paris (1763), which marked the defeat of the French by the British in America and Asia. This chapter examines the explicit and implicit criticism Raynal levelled at the British and French Empires and their respective founding agents in successive editions of the *Histoire des deux Indes*. It focuses on three recurrent themes that highlight the impact of colonial rivalry between the French and the British and the negotiations they undertook to further their respective advantage: first, their trading companies and early economic activity in the colonies, then the politics of the factories led by France and Great Britain in Asia, and, finally, colonisation undertaken by the two monarchies in the West Indies and in North America.[6]

Trading companies and early colonial trade

As a supporter of the ideas of the Physiocrats, Raynal defended a liberal conception of the economy, in which the state was not to impede trade through taxes and regulations that would hinder commercial exchanges. He trusted private enterprise to promote trade, the effects of which were supposed to be beneficial to consumers and producers. Nevertheless, in his view, the role of commercial companies was not always favourable to the interests of settlers and consumers, and he underlined the fact that to gain new markets, European trading companies had not hesitated to use force against their rivals. He noted that the East India Company, the commercial company founded by London merchants in 1600, had not immediately embarked on conquests, but had first devoted itself instead only to a form of trade which he considered useful to nations, and which was practised, he wrote, by 'humane and just merchants'. Unfortunately for the company, the 'love' it aroused among the native populations allowed it to acquire only a small number of factories that did not have fortified places and good ports, as opposed to those of the Dutch and the Portuguese who knew, besides, how to inculcate fear. This observation nourished Raynal's reflection on the violence perpetrated by the Europeans against their European rivals and the Indigenous populations whose lands they took. He believed the English, in the seventeenth century, 'felt that it was difficult to obtain great wealth without perpetrating great injustices' (Amsterdam, 1770, 1: 245–6).

Raynal offered a laudatory characterisation of the East India Company, especially its post-1709 incarnation when the company recovered from its Jacobite associations:

> Since that time, the affairs of the company have been conducted with more light, wisdom, and dignity. The principles of trade which developed more and more in England influenced its administration as much as the interests of its monopoly permitted. It improved its old settlements. It formed new ones. The happiness it had of never failing in its engagements gave it more credit than it needed. It sought to get by larger sales the profits it was deprived of by greater competition. Its privilege was attacked with less violence since it had received the sanction of the laws and got the protection of the parliament.[7]

Raynal admired the East India Company because it had expanded and achieved institutional, reputational and financial success, without compromising too much of its commercial autonomy. One of the secrets of its success was its ability to let private traders take advantage of its freightage.

In the *Histoire des deux Indes*, the effectiveness of British private traders contrasted with the economic performance of the CIO, which was too tightly controlled by the Crown. Raynal immediately presented it in an unfavourable light because he believed that at the time of its creation, trade with Asia had disadvantages. The French would import expensive luxury items that competed with their own production, a point of contention discussed by Susanne Lachenicht in Chapter 1 of this volume, and cost more than what their export sale of manufactured goods could pay for. In addition, from the outset, the CIO was an exclusive monopoly company, which the state financially and militarily supported by providing it with soldiers and escorting its squadrons (Geneva, 1780, 1: 407–8).

The development titled 'Decadence of the company of France. Causes of its withering'[8] is a good illustration of Raynal's manner of proceeding. He pointed out the mistakes the French company made from the 1640s until the end of the reign of Louis XIV. In Madagascar, which was the company's initial target, settlers had only experienced famine and discord, and many had died, in part because shareholders at home had not got involved enough, and the company had not gathered the resources necessary to maintain the factories where it first implanted. Consequently, it had been forced to abandon those at Siam, Bantam, Rajapour, Tilseri, Masulipatam and Bandar Abbas (Geneva, 1780, 1: 450–1). To compensate for the company's lack of financial means, Colbert had authorised French and foreign private traders to load goods on the company's ships on payment of a 5 per cent duty on the proceeds of their sale. However, the CIO continued to be underfunded and its administrators and agents not properly directed. Lastly, Raynal accused financials of having hampered the development of the CIO during the War of the League of Augsburg (1688–97), because they wanted to support French manufactures at the expense of trade with India. At the close of his analysis, he concluded that the ultimate failure of the company had been due to 'the conduct of an ignorant and corrupt administration, the levity, the impatience of the shareholders, the interested jealousy of finance, and the oppressive spirit of the Treasury'[9] in the context of a series of international conflicts, including the War of the Spanish Succession, that had precipitated its ruin.

According to Raynal, the situation did not improve much under the reign of Louis XV (1715–74). On the one hand, the Government's control over the Company was too tight. From 1723 onwards, the Court chose its directors, and the commissioner of the King, appointed in 1730 in the administration of the company, prevented its members from deliberating freely. The appointment of two directors between 1731 and 1746 also led to the division of the company into two factions, whose intrigues had consequences as far as India. On the other hand, the company was penalised by a debt which, according to Raynal, who shared the opinion of Dupont de Nemours, was contracted through to the negligence and incapacity of CIO agents and the very high material and financial cost of the operations carried out in India during the Seven Years' War, which were wrongly evaluated (Geneva, 1780, 1: 510–12).[10] On 13 August 1769, Louis XV suspended the monopoly privilege of the CIO and granted all his subjects the right to sail and trade beyond the Cape of Good Hope. Raynal regretted, however, that this trade was still controlled by the Government, echoing thereby the 1769–70 controversy in which he and Diderot participated, along with political leaders like Necker and the economists Gournay and Dupont de Nemours, about the CIO deficit and the high cost of maintaining its factories, despite the large profits ensured by the monopoly of the importation into France of certain colonial products. Raynal, however, did not mention the other reasons that explained the relative failure of the French to build an efficient trading company, such as their inability to raise substantial capital, because the kingdom had different tax regimes and provinces separated by internal customs, and the weakness of Paris, which, unlike London and Amsterdam, had no direct access to the sea and suffered from lower financial and economic weight than its rivals.[11]

Consistent in his criticism of the economy of the colonies, Raynal severely condemned the monopoly of trade (*Exclusif* in French). This colonial system, established in the seventeenth century, re-enacted in 1727 and maintained until 1769, prohibited commercial relations between colonies and between colonies and foreign countries. It obliged the Europeans settled overseas to consume only the products supplied by the mother country and to sell their products only to the latter. Raynal illustrated with examples the absurdity of this policy, which was much criticised elsewhere by political economists such as Adam Smith, Josiah Tucker, François Quesnay and Anne Robert Turgot.[12] He detailed the manner in which the French colonies in the West Indies needed cattle, salt fish and wood in quantities that the metropole failed to provide, so they imported them from New England by resorting to smuggling, a practice also discussed by Charlotte Carrington-Farmer in Chapter 9 of this volume, and which Raynal viewed from a metropolitan point of view as 'too expensive, dishonest and insufficient'.[13] Burdened by unnecessary taxes, colonies were unable to enrich themselves, that is, to produce enough and sell freely at the best price. The monopoly meant that products imported from the colonies were sold in the mother country at non-competitive and artificially high prices, while metropolitan goods exported to the colonies were sold at artificially low prices. In the West Indies, however, the inhabitants still found these prices excessive, so they turned to smuggling to get supplies at a lower cost.[14]

Raynal argued that the monopolistic system in force from the 1660s harmed the economic interests of France. The islands could only trade with France, where only a small number of ports were allowed to receive their goods, and French ships had to return directly to the ports from which they had departed. These constraints caused costs which themselves triggered an increase in prices for many American products. In addition, the French West Indies only managed to sell three quarters of their sugar production in France. They therefore produced the basic necessary quantities of poor quality, leading to lower raw sugar 'cent' prices, which fell from fourteen or fifteen francs in 1682 to five or six francs in 1713. Metropolitan taxes on American products such as tobacco, cocoa, cotton, ginger and sugar further impeded trade (Geneva, 1780, 3: 339–41).[15]

Raynal showed that the settlers of the British colonies of North America also suffered from mercantilist policies. Foreign ships were not allowed to enter British colonial ports unless they were shipwrecked or carrying gold or silver, and British ships could only enter these ports if they came from an English port. As for the ships of the North American colonies that went to Europe, they could only bring English goods to American ports and the only foreign products they could import were salt for their fisheries and the wines of Madeira, the Azores and the Canaries. Raynal's economic thought condemned commercialism and clung to the competition and the freedom of imperial commerce defended in the 1730s and 1740s by French economists like Vincent de Gournay and François Véron Duverger de Forbonnais, who recommended a mixture of liberalism and interventionism. Raynal also shared the ideas of the Physiocrats. He criticised the colonial monopolies, which he blamed for impoverishing colonies and consumers for the exclusive benefit of greedy traders.

French and British factory colonies in Asia

In the *Histoire des deux Indes*, the evocation of French and British colonial expansion is imbedded in narratives and ideas of conquest and violence. According to Raynal, the opening of factories and the implantation of settlers gave rise to a predatory economy he condemned, and to violent encounters between Europeans, who pursued overseas the rivalries that opposed them throughout the Old Continent. From the very end of the seventeenth century, wars between the French and the British were carried out both in Europe and in the colonies, and diplomats began integrating the defence of their colonial interests during negotiations with economic competitors and diplomatic enemies. In addition, from the middle of the eighteenth century, overseas territories were no longer secondary theatres of operations, as shown by the examples of the wars waged in India and North America. In India, neither the French nor the British were satisfied with coastal factories and they began interfering militarily and politically in the affairs of the states of inner territories. Trading companies were major players in these conflicts, which were no longer about a return to the *status quo antebellum* but about defining a new territorial order, and they took military and sometimes diplomatic initiatives.[16]

Raynal illustrated the violent role of trading companies in the colonies through the example of the conflict between the English East India Company and its Dutch equivalent in the early seventeenth century. In order to capture markets for spices, the East India Company built forts in Java, Ambon and the Banda Islands, causing an immediate reaction from the Dutch, who, in turn, drove the English from their trading posts 'by trickery and force' (Amsterdam, 1770, 1: 247), a series of early conflicts described by Marilyn Garcia-Chapleau in Chapter 8 of this volume. To illustrate his point, Raynal mentioned the Amboyna massacre of February 1623, which provoked a long controversy between the two nations. In 1619, the English and the Dutch had signed a treaty providing that the Maluku, Ambon and Banda would belong to both trade companies, who shared their productions, two thirds going to the Dutch and one third to the English. Despite this agreement, the Dutch executed twenty men at Ambon, whom they accused of preparing a plot to deliver the fortress to the English. Raynal remained vague about these events, neither dating them nor indicating the number of victims – ten Englishmen, nine Japanese and one Portuguese. His main point was to denounce the brutality of the Dutch presented as conquerors hungry for colonial products and colonial dominion.[17]

The English, however, were not always the victims of these conflicts. They were as greedy as other Europeans in Asia. According to Raynal, they arrived and settled in Sumatra in 1688 and 'soon would the agents of the company indulge in that spirit of rapine and tyranny so typical of Europeans in Asia'.[18] Tensions erupted between the English and the islanders, who took up arms when they saw a fortress was being built – Fort York, rebuilt as Fort Marlborough in the 1710s – which they perceived as an instrument of oppression. They expelled the English, before allowing them to return in 1724 (Geneva, 1780, 1: 348).

Despite his criticism of English greed in Indonesia, Raynal described more than a series of thefts and pointed to the skill they had shown to achieve their ends. In his presentation of English expansion in India, he showed how they had artfully combined the purchase of cities, such as Gondelour (modern Cuddalore), in 1686, with trade, military operations and alliances with Indian princes. They pursued conquest in many forms and on a grand scale, often motivated by economic and financial reasons.[19] More generally, Raynal admired the English for their understanding of the advantages of practising trade from one Asian country to another, and for their consequent willingness to establish themselves in the Indian subcontinent. Raynal emphasised the pragmatism of the East India Company, which, unlike the Dutch VOC, founded in 1602, allowed English individuals to gain access to Asian countries and to take shares in the commissioning of its own ships. He judged that this policy had widely contributed to developing and strengthening English establishment on the continent (Amsterdam, 1770, 1: 362).[20] Raynal also offered an analysis of the policy implemented by the British to establish their domination in India by reminding his readers that they had begun to expand their presence in the wealthy provinces of Burdivan, Midvapour, and Chatigam in Bengal in 1757, only after having driven the French out of the region. He proposed that their endless conquests revealed both their skilful strategic thinking and their disproportionate ambition (Amsterdam, 1770, 1: 375).[21]

The British conducted the same policy as Jean-François Dupleix, Governor General of all French establishments in Asia between 1742 and 1754, which consisted of engaging in a flurry of alliances that allowed them to become involved in Indian affairs. After the East India Company in October 1764 defeated a coalition hostile to its ally, the Nawab of Bengal, Mir Jafar, it obtained from the Mughal emperor the Government of Bengal and the right to raise taxes and to exercise civil and criminal justice. Bengal thus passed under British dominion and the East India Company was able to enjoy the public revenues of this state henceforth at its disposal (Amsterdam, 1770, 1: 376).[22] Raynal argued that the economic exploitation of India was a profitable business for the British, and therefore justified their military expenditure. Around 1770, they sold three million pounds' worth of merchandise and bought half of this amount, financing half of their imports from their export sales. Raynal estimated the net income generated by the East India Company in Bengal to be around £1,250,000, a number in line with that of Mr Dow who, in April 1766, had estimated the income of Bengal at 10,575,968 rupees, or £1,321,994 (Amsterdam, 1770, 1: 376-7).[23] The East India Company owed £400,000 to the Government for its protection, which left it with the considerable sum of £921,994 of profit.

If we are to believe Raynal, the economic adroitness of the British included not making the same mistakes as their European predecessors, who had demanded considerable advances on rents from their Indian tenants, forcing these farmers to take loans at monthly interest rates of 12 per cent, or even 15 per cent, prices so exorbitant that they were in time pushed off their land and out of their *aldeas*, as boroughs and villages colonised by Europeans were called since the Portuguese conquest and until the nineteenth century. Informed by knowledge of these practices that carried little benefit for the economy, and aware that most of the *aldeas* were inhabited by a few families closely related to each other, the British proceeded differently: fields were rented yearly and the heads of families served as sureties for their families and allies, family solidarity contributing to the regularity of payments (Amsterdam, 1770, 1: 381). This adaptation to local social conditions would be one of the keys to the success of the British in India. By 1780, however, Raynal was no longer taken in by British methods, because of the way they exploited their benefits in India, to the disadvantage of their European competitors. They controlled textile production and trade, especially in Bengal, preventing the French from exploiting Chandernagor, and leading Raynal to castigate 'this domineering people' who 'so much abused their unjust right of victory' (Geneva, 1780, 1: 526).[24]

The French, indeed, gradually failed in India, principally because the agents of the French trading companies depended on the state. The King, for example, was represented on the board of directors of the CIO. Their room for manoeuvre was therefore more limited than that of its English counterpart. The British company had been created by merchants who wanted to make a profit and were able to develop a fruitful trade between the countries of Asia by installing factories in ports and not hesitating to use force against their European rivals. The East India Company was therefore no longer just a trading company; it was becoming a military and administrative organisation, whose initiatives at times were beyond the control of the British Government. In accordance with his liberal thinking, Raynal presented the settlement of the French in India not as a concerted state policy but as a series of epic episodes centred on the outstanding actions of exceptional figures distinct from the state they issued from: 'Everywhere great men did more than public bodies', he wrote. 'Peoples and societies are only the instruments of men of genius; they are the ones who founded states and colonies', and

France, 'more than most', was 'more indebted for its fame to some happy private persons than to its government' (Geneva, 1780, 1: 480).[25]

Particularly worthy of praise was Pierre-Benoît Dumas, CIO envoy to Pondicherry, who negotiated with Delhi for the right to mint money and the ownership of the territory of Karikal, allowing the CIO to trade in the Rajah state of Tanjore (or Thanjavur) (Geneva, 1780, 1: 477–8).[26] Another of Raynal's colonial heroes was Joseph François Dupleix, whose know-how and efficiency he contrasted with the incompetence of the directors of the CIO. Between 1731 and 1741, Dupleix developed Chandernagor into a very active post, trading with places subject to the Great Mughal and even Tibet. When he became governor of French India in 1742, Dupleix collided with the CIO directors who, during the months before the outbreak of the war between the French and the British in 1744, did not understand the motives of the English and remained persuaded that, in the event of a conflict between France and England, the India Companies of the two powers would observe neutrality. The 'Court of Versailles', on whose behalf the directors acted, failed to see that the British powers, 'whose cornerstone was trade', could not seriously give up fighting in the Indian Ocean, and that their show of neutrality was only a strategy to buy them time (Geneva, 1780, 1: 482). Entirely absorbed in his admiration for Dupleix, Raynal failed to mention the fortune amassed by the governor through smuggling and dwelled instead on the latter's activities between 1750 and 1754, when he exploited the discord and anarchy raging in India since the Persian Nadir Shah had entered Delhi in 1739, allowing the French to take control of several principalities, one of which was the Subaby of the Deccan.[27] Dupleix was then able to behave like an Eastern prince and received the title of nabob; Raynal presented this success as a sign of the possibility of sustainable trade benefits in India.

Raynal blamed the French defeat in the war they waged in India against the British between 1757 and 1761 on the failings of the French Government and the directors of the CIO, who did not understand that France should do whatever it took to keep the Carnatic, a region with abundant goods and food and sufficient revenue to pay for the troops, those of the fleet, that lacked the skills to defeat the British, and those of General Lally-Tollendal, whom Raynal made into a scapegoat for his poor performance as a political and military leader (Geneva, 1780, 1: 505). At the end of his analysis of the French presence in Asia, Raynal, who adhered to the theory of climates, proposed that the French had also been corrupted by 'the voluptuous climate of the Indies', which, curiously, did not seem to have hindered the British. He repeated that the corruption and the negligence of the many agents of the trade company were also to blame. The desire to get rich quickly pushed officers to divert the pay of their *sepoys* for their own profit by halving their numbers; the CIO clerks swindled the directors of the company by diverting for themselves profits from the sale of products imported from Europe and by selling Asian products to the CIO at a very high price; and those in charge of the land administration rented parcels for their own benefit. Lastly, Raynal described incompetent and corrupt directors of the CIO, who practised shameless nepotism by giving the most important posts to unfit parents, increased the number of factors to make themselves protectors at the Court of Versailles and undertook expensive and unproductive tasks. He thus called into question the complicity of the Government, which allowed and covered up these abuses (Geneva, 1780, 1: 507–8).

French and British settlements in the West Indies and North America

Raynal also discussed the societies that formed overseas after the French and the British undertook to develop the lands they occupied. As in other Europeans overseas territories, settlers faced land reclamation and labour-seeking problems that led them to resort to slavery. Once again, Raynal compared and contrasted French and British methods, to emphasise the economic superiority of the British model in the West Indies.

Despite the wealth and diversity of their crops, which included indigo, cochineal, cocoa, roucou, cotton, coffee and sugar, the West Indies were presented by Raynal as islands where the Europeans had met many difficulties. The French had come to the region solely to make a fortune. The place had failed to attract nobles, burghers or persons of independent means, and was peopled instead by commissioners, innkeepers and adventurers, all eager to get rich quickly and leave these islands, where one lived 'without distinctions, without honours, without enjoyments, and without any spur except that of interest'. Settlers and adventurers saved their income to return to France and, once ready to leave, sought to get rid of their plantations by selling them on credit (Geneva, 1780, 3: 448, 478). Other drawbacks that impeded economic development in the West Indies included insects, whose increase was favoured by heat; rats brought from Europe, that destroyed up to a third of the harvest; the lack of fertiliser, because manure was insufficient and drove farmers to resort to weeds that grew at the foot of the coffee trees but provided nests from which insects attacked the trees; and the degeneration of domestic animals imported by Europeans (Geneva, 1780, 3: 388).[28] Raynal attributed this degeneration, which spared pigs only, to 'the vice of the climate' (Geneva, 1780, 3: 208) and to the lack of care given to malnourished animals. The oxen were given small burdens, the mules carried loads half as small as in Europe and draft and pack animals remained weak, because settlers did not seek to make them stronger by crossing them with stallions from Europe, a topic addressed by Charlotte Carrington-Farmer in Chapter 9 of this volume. Even European trees planted in the West Indies degenerated, victims of the strong night dew and the abundant daytime heat, while African plants such as pigeon pea and cassava acclimatised there successfully (Geneva, 1780, 3: 206–11).

In stark contrast to the French situation, Raynal described British planters in the West Indies as enterprising and prosperous, because the British Government had let them get rich. He asserted that London never subjected them to taxation and that these islands, with the exception of Jamaica, had freely agreed in 1663 to pay each year to the mother country a tax of 4.5 per cent on the value of their exports. In addition, as the West Indies had to support their own financial needs, settlers had decided to pay new taxes when fortifications were needed, but in any case, in the 1770s, taxes were very low (Geneva, 1780, 3: 598–9). After generalities about the supposed appetite of the English for money, Raynal observed that English wealth was not confined to the mother country but had spread to the colonies and was particularly visible in the English settlements of the West Indies (Geneva, 1780, 3: 600). The reasons he gave to explain this phenomenon were precisely the reasons for the failure of settlement in the French West Indies: the tax system did not crush the taxpayers, the plantations belonged to rich men who had the financial means to properly develop them, the settlers could borrow money easily and cheaply because their estates were mortgaged to their creditors, wars did not prevent or delay their exports and English ports provided West Indian produce a more advantageous market than that of their rivals. These conditions explained why the value of West Indian land was also very high.

The counterpart to this economic success, however, was slavery. Raynal noted that here too, the English proceeded differently from the French, the Portuguese, the Dutch or the Danes. They sold entire cargoes of enslaved Africans to single merchants who then retailed them to planters, and they sent the people these wholesalers did not want to foreign colonies. French traffickers from Guinea, on the other hand, sold enslaved individuals to different buyers. The Crown first entrusted the transatlantic slave trade to monopoly companies, but in 1698, there were under twenty thousand people of African descent in the entire French West Indies, most of whom had been transported by unlicensed traffickers. Raynal's estimation was close to actual numbers: according to modern studies, there were perhaps 2,102 enslaved Africans living in Santo Domingo in 1680, 4,602 in Guadeloupe in 1687 and 8,777 and 14,566 in Martinique in 1682 and 1700 respectively (Geneva, 1780, 3: 341).[29]

Raynal was aware that West Indian planters owed their wealth to the labour of enslaved persons. He extolled the importance of the crops the latter raised in the production cycle, but he also described the appalling living and working conditions of enslaved labourers and the brutality of the methods used by their enslavers to claim ownership and exert control over their labour force (Geneva, 1780, 3: 187–204). Raynal's vigorous plea against slavery was accompanied by a remark on the different attitudes the British and the French would adopt regarding the status of people of African descent in America. The British considered the enslaved as a workforce that had to be kept physically fit, but they did not smile or talk to them, so enslaved people hated them. The French, on the contrary, spoke to them, but, impatient to make a fortune, they mistreated them by overwhelming them with work and by not giving them enough sustenance (Geneva, 1780, 3: 178). Physiocrats criticised slavery for economic reasons, arguing that it did not encourage innovation and was expensive. Raynal did not ignore these arguments, but he also condemned slavery in moral terms.

His critique of settler violence extended to British North America. He described the effectiveness of farmers, fishermen and traders on the northern continent, but he did not turn a blind eye to colonial violence they exerted against Native communities and individuals who they considered dangerous or suspicious. For instance, he explained that in the seventeenth century, the English settlers of Virginia had shown bad faith towards the Native population in refusing to take Indian women, which earned them the hatred of the Powhatans who killed 347 colonists in 1622, as related by John Smith in his *General History of Virginia*.[30] Raynal added that both Amerindians and English settlers subsequently engaged in innumerable atrocities, interspersed between periods of relative truce most often broken by the latter. In addition, he referred to two wars in the Carolinas, during which 'without interest and without motive, all wandering or fixed nations between the Ocean and the Appalachians were attacked and massacred' (Geneva, 1780, 4: 311).[31] Lastly, he reported that scalping was practised by the New England settlers, and that a bonus was given to those who killed Indians. He told the story of John Lovewell, who, in 1724, after this bonus had been raised to £2,250, had gone along with some of his friends, killed ten Native men while they slept and carried their scalps to Boston. This episode led the author to remind his readers that the Spaniards did not have the monopoly of violence in America, despite the criticism Anglo-Americans had levelled at them since the beginnings of colonisation (Geneva, 1780, 4: 240). Protestant colonists also pursued opponents with vindictiveness, as with the persecution of the witches of Salem in 1692, which Raynal related in detail, among other examples of violence committed in New England against religious minorities (Geneva, 1780, 4: 237–9).[32]

Conclusion

Between 1770 and 1796, *L'Histoire des deux Indes* went through around thirty editions and counterfeits, and many selected extracts were published in the reviews of the periodical press. In addition, the book was rapidly translated into English, German, Dutch and Italian between 1781 and 1783. Several themes, approached in a style that did not shy away from pathos, dear to the sensitivity of the time, explain this success: the denunciation of slavery and a precise description of the system of the African slave trade in the West Indies, but, above all, the criticisms formulated against fanaticism and ministerial despotism, the incitement to radical reforms of society and of the Government. The book is a compendium of political maxims that pleased supporters of the Enlightenment.

Raynal did not idealise the British East India Company. In the 1774 edition, which utilised a different source from the one he used in 1770, he completed the account of the conquest of Bengal and the incomes of that province, and he ended the third volume with a rather optimistic reflection about the future of that place, given the behaviour of the British which he considered exemplary. Six years later, however, the tone was more pessimistic, emphasising the 'methodical tyranny' of the British there. He also stressed the corruption of East India Company agents but still trusted Parliament to reasonably intervene in the affairs of the Company. Over a decade, Raynal's hostility to the British and the East India Company had grown steadily. By 1780, he painted a darker picture of British thirst for expansion and colonisation, emphasising the violence perpetrated by soldiers and the greed of administrators.[33] This point of view completed the harsh judgement levelled at the colonies by the Physiocrats, whose views Raynal shared: they were expensive for the state, which had to invest in 'primitive advances' such as vessels, forts and artillery, as well as in 'annual advances' like wages and goods; their economies remained archaic and unproductive; their operating mode, devoid of sustainable investments, was based more on the hoarding of wealth than on the creation of renewable wealth; and they also lacked freedom and economic efficiency.

In Raynal's eyes, then, colonisation had more drawbacks than advantages. Led by men who lived too far away from the metropole to be efficiently controlled, it seduced unscrupulous adventurers, encouraged the lure of easy gain at the expense of productive investment, encouraged the state to develop taxation that hampered the overseas economy and promoted corruption and, above all, it was built on slavery. Unafraid of paradox, Raynal proposed remedies for these evils, such as the development of the merchant marine and navy, freedom of commerce between the colonies and the mother country and a more humane attitude of enslavers towards those they enslaved, as if colonisation could become more bearable under the authority of men inspired by reason and concerned about the common good.

Notes

1 Raynal was the organiser of collective publications, as were Diderot and d'Alembert for the *Encyclopédie*, but unlike the latter, he often resorted to compiling the texts he received.
2 Gilles Bancarel and Gianluigi Goggi (eds.), *Raynal, de la Polémique à l'Histoire* (Oxford: Voltaire Foundation, 2000); Gilles Bancarel, *Raynal ou le Devoir de Vérité* (Paris: Honoré Champion, 2004); David Diop, 'Raynal, les colonies, la Révolution Française et l'esclavage', *Outre-Mers, revue d'Histoire* 103, no. 386–7 (2015), 218–21; Hans-Jürgen Lüsebrink and Anthony Strugnell (eds.), *Lectures de Raynal: L'Histoire des deux Indes: Réécriture et Polygraphie* (Oxford: Voltaire Foundation, 1995), 1–4; Michèle Duchet, *Diderot et l'Histoire des deux Indes ou l'Écriture Fragmentaire* (Paris: Nizet, 1978).
3 Jacques Paulze, *Mémoires sur le Commerce, Recueil d'Informations sur … les Relations Commerciales avec l'Inde, les Côtes d'Afrique, les Colonies d'Amérique et d'Asie*, Archives Nationales, Répertoire numérique, 129ap/; Pedro Pablo Abarca de Bolea (1719–98), tenth Count of Aranda, was the Spanish ambassador to France between 1773 and 1784. The use of his memoirs by Raynal about Spanish and Portuguese colonies in the Americas is reported in several nineteenth-century biographies and dictionaries. See, for instance, Antoine-Alexandre Barbier, *Dictionnaire des Ouvrages Anonymes et Pseudonymes*, 4 vols. (Paris, 1823), 2: 139, or L'abbé Glaire et le vicomte Walsh, *Encyclopédie Catholique*, 18 vols. (Paris, 1848), 16: 425.
4 Antoine François Prévost, *Histoire Générale des Voyages*, 20 vols. (Paris, 1746–50), 3: 188–466, 4: 1–336, 30 (about Dutch policy in the East Indies from 1600 to 1620): 1–443, and 31 (1750): 1–503; Corneille de Pauw, *Recherches Philosophiques sur les Américains, ou Mémoires Intéressants pour Servir à l'Histoire de l'Espèce Humaine*, 3 vols. (Berlin, 1768–70), 3: 10–16, 38–45, 119–32; Thomas Paine, *The Writings of Thomas Paine*, 4 vols. (New York: G.P. Putnam's Sons, 1894), 1: 84–111; Jean de Léry, *Histoire d'un Voyage fait en*

Terre du Brésil (Geneva, 1578); Joseph François Lafitau, *Mœurs des Sauvages Américains comparées aux Mœurs des Premiers Temps* (Paris, 1724).

5 For the sake of convenience, we will refer to successive editions of the *Histoire des deux Indes* by indicating the place and year of publication, volume and page reference within parenthesis after each quotation. By the same token, we are also attributing the work to Raynal, its master builder, who did not hesitate to send detailed sets of questions to correspondents living in the British colonies in North America. I wish to thank Bertrand Van Ruymbeke for this information.

6 Hans Wolpe, *Raynal et sa Machine de Guerre: L'Histoire des deux Indes et ses Perfectionnements* (Stanford: Stanford University Press, 1957); Hans-Jürgen Lüsebrink and Manfred Tietz (eds.), *Lectures de Raynal: L'Histoire des deux Indes en Europe et en Amérique au XVIIIe siècle*, Actes du colloque de Wolfenbuttel (Oxford: The Voltaire Foundation, 1991); Antonella Alimento and Gianluigi Goggi (eds.), *Autour de l'Abbé Raynal. Genèse et Enjeux Politiques de L'Histoire des deux Indes* (Ferney-Voltaire: Centre international d'étude du xviiie siècle, 2018).

7 '*Depuis cette époque, les affaires de la compagnie furent conduites avec plus de lumière, de sagesse et de dignité. Les principes du commerce qui se développoient de plus en plus en Angleterre influèrent sur son administration, autant que le permettoient les intérêts de son monopole. Elle améliora ses anciens établissemens. Elle en forma de nouveaux. Le bonheur qu'elle avoit de n'avoir jamais manqué à ses engagemens lui donnoit un crédit plus étendu que ses besoins. Ce qu'une plus grande concurrence lui ôtoit de bénéfices, elle cherchoit à se le procurer par des ventes plus considérables. Son privilège étoit attaqué avec moins de violence depuis qu'il avoit reçu la sanction des loix et obtenu la protection du parlement*' (Amsterdam, 1770, 1: 295).

8 '*Décadence de la compagnie de France. Causes de son dépérissement.*'

9 '*La conduite d'une administration ignorante et corrompue, la légèreté, l'impatience des actionnaires, la jalousie intéressée de la finance, l'esprit oppresseur du fisc*' (Geneva, 1780, 1: 453).

10 Pierre-Samuel Dupont de Nemours also criticised the CIO agents for having 'neither the knowledge necessary for all the different operations, nor a keen interest in success' ('*ni toutes les connaissances nécessaires à toutes les opérations différentes, ni un intérêt assez vif au succès*'), 'Du commerce et de la compagnie des Indes', in *Œuvres politiques et économiques*, 10 vols. (Nendeln: KTO Press, 1979), 2: 270.

11 Georges Dulac, 'Les Gens de Lettres, le Banquier et l'Opinion: Diderot et la Polémique sur la Compagnie des Indes', *Dix-huitième Siècle* 26 (1994), 177–99; Alain Clément, 'Du bon et du mauvais usage des colonies: politique coloniale et pensée économique française au XVIIIe siècle', *Cahiers d'Économie Politique* 56, no. 1 (2009), 101–27; Philippe Haudrère, *Les Compagnies des Indes orientales. Trois Siècles de Rencontre entre Orientaux et Occidentaux (1600–1858)* (Paris: Éditions Desjonquères, 2006), 71.

12 Alain Clément, 'Le Discours Économique Libéral à l'encontre des Pratiques Coloniales ou le Rejet de l'Empire Britannique (1750–1815)', in Jean-Pierre Potier, Jean-Louis Fournel and Jacques Guilhaumou (eds.), *Libertés et libéralismes* (Lyon: ENS Éditions, 2012), 87–115.

13 '*trop chère, malhonnête, et insuffisante*' (Geneva, 1780, 1: 486).

14 Jean Tarrade, *Le Commerce Colonial à la Fin de l'Ancien Régime. L'Évolution du Régime de 'l'Exclusif' de 1763 à 1789* (Paris: PUF, 1972).

15 In the eighteenth century, the '*cent*', or '*quintal*', was the usual French measure of sugar, which corresponded to a weight of one hundred pounds. It already existed in the seventeenth century and its rate was still five francs in 1682 according to J.-B. Patoulet, then intendant of Martinique, before its price increased suddenly through a change in taxation. I wish to thank Vincent Cousseau for this information: V. Cousseau, 'Population et Anthroponymie en Martinique du XVIIe s. à la Première Moitié du XIXe siècle: Étude d'une Société Coloniale à travers son Système de Dénomination Personnelle' (Ph.D. diss., Université des Antilles et de la Guyane, 2009).

16 Éric Schnakenbourg and François Ternat (eds.), *Une Diplomatie des Lointains. La France face à la Mondialisation des Rivalités Internationales, xviie–xviiie siècles* (Rennes: Presses Universitaires de Rennes, 2020).

17 Robert Markley, *The Far East and the English Imagination, 1600–1730* (Cambridge: Cambridge University Press, 2006); Benjamin Schmidt, *Innocence Abroad: The Dutch Imagination and the New World, 1570–1670* (Cambridge: Cambridge University Press, 2001); Karen Chancey, 'The Amboyna massacre in English politics, 1624–1632', *Albion* 30, no. 4 (1998), 583–98; Adam Clulow, *Fear and Conspiracy on the Edge of Empire* (New York: Columbia University Press, 2019); Alison Games, *Inventing the English Massacre: Amboyna in History and Memory* (New York: Oxford University Press, 2020).

18 'bientôt les agents de la compagnie se livrèrent à cet esprit de rapine et de tyrannie que les Européens portent si généralement en Asie.'
19 See, for instance, Peter James Marshall, *Trade and Conquest: Studies on the Rise of British Dominance in India* (Aldershot: Variorum, 1993); Antony Wild, *The East India Company: Trade and Conquest from 1600* (London: Harper Collins, 1999).
20 About the history of the VOC, see C.R. Boxer, *The Dutch Seaborne Empire, 1600–1800* (London: Hutchinson, 1965); Jonathan I. Israël, *Dutch Primacy in World Trade (1585–1740)* (Oxford: Clarendon Press, 1990); Om Prakash, *Precious Metals and Commerce: The Dutch East India Company in the Indian Ocean Trade* (Aldershot: Variorum, 1994).
21 Midvapour and Burdivan are today Midnapore and Bardhaman respectively, two Indian cities in West Bengal. Chaticam (or Chatigam) is Chittagong, Bangladesh.
22 Claude Markovits (ed.), *Histoire de l'Inde Moderne 1480–1950* (Paris: Fayard, 1994), 280–3; Jean-Louis Margolin and Claude Markovits, *Les Indes et l'Europe. Histoires Connectées XVe-XXIe siècles* (Paris: Gallimard, coll. folio, 2015), 187–8; Peter James Marshall, *East Indian Fortunes: The British in Bengal in the Eighteenth Century* (Oxford: Clarendon Press, 1976).
23 The pound was worth eight rupees.
24 'ce peuple dominateur ... a tellement abusé de l'injuste droit de la Victoire.'
25 'Partout les grands hommes ont fait plus que les grands corps. Les peuples et les sociétés ne sont que les instruments des hommes de génie: ce sont eux qui ont fondé des états, des colonies. ... La France, surtout, est plus redevable de sa gloire à quelques heureux particuliers, qu'à son gouvernement.'
26 The allies of France included Chanda Sahib, ruler of Trichinopoly (or Tiruchirapalli), and Dost Muhammad, Nabob of Arcot; France's opponents included the Rajah of Tanjore (or Thanjavur) and the Marathi chief Raghuji Bhonsle, who seized Trichinopoly.
27 This polity controlled a territory located in the Indian subcontinent from Pondicherry to the upper course of the Narmada River and southern Bengal.
28 Raynal mentioned an ant, hitherto unknown in America, which ravaged the plantations of Barbados and Martinique between 1764 and 1775.
29 Modern statistics are extracted from Bernard Gainot, *L'Empire Colonial Français de Richelieu à Napoléon (1630–1810)* (Paris: A. Colin, 2015), 61–2.

30 This is the massacre of more than three hundred Jamestown colonists, a quarter of the population of the colony, following the instructions of Opechancanough, the chief of the Powhatan Indians, Bertrand Van Ruymbeke, *L'Amérique avant les États-Unis. Une Histoire de l'Amérique Anglaise 1497–1776* (Paris: Flammarion, 2013), 111. This event is related by John Smith in his *General History of Virginia* (London, 1624), 145.

31 '*sans intérêt et sans motif, on attaqua, on massacra toutes les nations errantes ou fixées entre l'Océan et les Apalaches.*'

32 About the persecution of New England dissidents, see Van Ruymbeke, *L'Amérique avant les États-Unis*, 395–401.

33 Peter Jimack, 'Deux Modèles de Réécriture: la Compagnie des Indes (livre III) et les Jésuites du Paraguay (livre VIII)', in Lüsebrink and Strugnell, Lectures de Raynal, 158–62.

3

Global pursuits: English overseas initiatives of the long seventeenth century in perspective

L.H. Roper

The subject of seventeenth- and eighteenth-century English overseas trade and colonisation continually vexes the scholarly and popular imaginations. How could it be otherwise given the phenomena, the effects of which resonate deeply into the present, that these activities entailed: large-scale participation in the transatlantic and hemispheric slave trades, the establishment of beachheads from which control of the Indian subcontinent was launched and – last but not least – the creation of Anglo-American colonies in the course of the creation of an empire upon which the sun famously never set, administered from a relatively small, remote island off the northwest coast of Continental Europe?

The platform for an entity that coloured one quarter of the earth pink by 1914 was laid by what we would term 'private' interests today, although contemporaries did not distinguish between 'private' and 'public' interests as we do: an array of aristocrats and merchants – rather than government, which always lacked the fiscal and administrative resources, and often the interest, required to undertake and coordinate long-range commercial, privateering and colonising operations. They did so, as this chapter relates, in their pursuit of trade in exotic commodities ranging from cinnamon to Canary wines to chintzes, a schema in which the acquisition of labour, markets and locations for securing those commodities was essential; trafficking in labour constituted a vital element of the expansion of overseas interests – and the profits to be derived therefrom – in itself.[1]

These networks recruited migrants, mariners and other participants in the expansion of English interests on the ground, they chose the sites from which to conduct trade along with targets for territorial expansion and they solicited charters that legitimised their ventures, although they did not necessarily bother with legitimacy. In addition to metropolitan backers, these associations included 'colonial-imperialists' – promoters of territorial and commercial expansion who fully subscribed to the social, economic and political worldviews and ambitions held by their connections, with whom they consulted in the metropolis as occasion warranted – within their numbers, these connections constituted the points of contact between the imperial centre and its extensions. The nature of the expansion of overseas interests means, moreover, that it is difficult to find any set ideology – other than that the interests of commercial and colonising adventurers should hold sway – for the development of the seventeenth-century English Empire. Moreover, as the contributions of Agnès Delahaye and Trevor Burnard, as well as Charlotte Carrington-Farmer, Anne-Claire Faucquez, Susanne Lachenicht and Eric Roulet, to this volume suggest, early modern European overseas trading and colonising endeavours generally followed this pattern.[2]

The 'private' character of early modern English overseas operations requires emphasis because the historiographical perspectives on the 'British Empire' have remained fundamentally conventional: on the one hand, on the societies that were forged through the experiences of European colonists in their encounters with foreign environments – with at least half an eye on the United States to be; and, on the other, on the formation of the English state – with at least half an eye on the British Empire that came to colour over a quarter of the map of the world pink by the early twentieth century.[3]

Beyond even these epic results lurks the enduring conception that the movement of people, ideas and commodities over unprecedentedly long distances is a key aspect of the advent of modernity in the form of the international flow of ideas and commodities, aka 'globalisation'. Other prominent approaches to the history of the seventeenth-century English Empire have joined the quest for the origins of modernity in terms of the development of the English state, by focusing upon what has been identified as resistance – especially on the part of colonists – to the encroachment of an expanding state, and/or by privileging the importance of ideologies in fuelling the expansion of English overseas interests in conjunction with that encroachment.[4]

These quests for the origins of the modern world are certainly understandable, but they amount to a search for a scholarly El Dorado since they necessarily direct the investigator away from the context within which the history of English overseas interests took place. First, contemporaries not only did not think in terms of 'origins' but their comprehensions of society and government were quite different from those devised by subsequent generations. The pursuit of 'origins' consequently tends towards the anachronistic; moreover, it obscures, rather than clarifies, our understanding of the world that gave rise to increasingly intensive overseas trade and colonisation on the part of the English, the behaviour of the historical actors responsible for promoting those activities and, thus, the consequences of those activities, including the social formation of colonies and the processes through which colonies became independent.

Ex post facto approaches to the history of the English Empire, and its by-product, the history of 'early America', also ignore a fundamental political reality: while the English state did grow larger and did come to play a greater imperial role, it did so often reluctantly, as noted below, and customarily only when management proved beyond the capabilities of private enterprise.[5]

The Crown performed imperial functions through its sovereign power but in a reactive way: it did not set imperial policy; rather, in addition to issuing charters, it arbitrated disputes between rivals, both domestic and foreign, and, once ventures gained some running, sought its share of revenue from them. These circumstances were reinforced by the Government's habitually cash-strapped and skeletal state and arose from its corresponding practice, which dated from the Plantagenet monarchy, of delegating the oversight of 'public' purposes, such as the operation of markets, the employment of mariners and the promotion of the wool industry, as well as governmental powers over remote areas, to such entities as the Council of the North and the bishopric of Durham that administered those locations and connected, ideally, royal justice to those entitled to royal protection. The Crown issued charters under seal that formalised the powers and rights that it devolved to recipients as well as the responsibilities that those recipients assumed sometimes in corporate form, on some occasions as proprietorships. It is important to stress that this system was not 'feudalism' – a nineteenth-century characterisation of earlier societies – but the method by which the Crown rewarded loyal associates with lands and other means of cultivating their own patronage networks, while formally binding those associates and the places over which they had responsibility to the royal person.[6]

Private investors, as the other contributors to this volume make clear, possessed the fiscal and patronage resources that enabled them to bear the substantial risks and costs of long-distance ventures that the state could not absorb, and the system in place was seamlessly adopted to trade with the Continent as early as the thirteenth century.[7] It thus provided the constitutional basis for the conduct of overseas trading and colonising activities well into the nineteenth century despite its increasing unpopularity, usually generated by those who had been denied official favour. Grantees received monopolies for conducting commercial and/or colonising affairs in fixed areas to pursue their pecuniary interests along with such sub-governmental rights as recruiting migrants, building forts, conducting diplomacy and creating local institutions: seventeenth-century English people did not draw nearly as fine a distinction between 'public' and 'private' interests as we do, and overseas commercial and colonising projects fell squarely within a system that also included the delegation of more domestic concerns such as lighthouse construction, harbour repair and even the creation of grammar schools.[8] Notwithstanding appearances, however, this arrangement did not mean that the recipients of chartered powers exercised sovereignty: the Government always retained the right to investigate their behaviour and if the courts, usually at the instigation of concerned parties, found that grantees had exceeded their powers under the legal doctrine of ultra vires, they could revoke charters, as in the case of the Virginia Company in 1624, although the 'royalisation' of Virginia had not been intended to be permanent.[9]

By 1613, English privateering, smuggling and colonisation were beginning to be conducted on a more intensive basis. The chief undertakers of these activities included Robert Rich, Earl of Warwick, and the Anglo-Dutch merchant Sir William Courteen; Warwick's clients conducted raids on Spanish colonies and the Earl became involved in the Virginia Company partly to secure bases for his freebooters, while Courteen's agents founded colonies in

St Christopher's in 1624 and Barbados in 1627, which extended the plantation-style model of colonisation, grounded in tobacco cultivation initially, to Anglo-America. Sir William, drawing upon the tailoring firm he inherited from his father and his connections in Middleburg, Zeeland, became active in the colonisation of the Essequibo River after 1616, having been attracted to that area initially by the profits to be made through the Venezuelan salt pans. In 1623, his colonies, inhabited by African and Native enslaved individuals along with Dutch, English and Irish migrants, were producing a reported 800,000 pounds of tobacco annually, and, four years later, a Courteen ship established a colony in Barbados (at a cost of £8,000); its skipper, enamoured of that island's prospects, convinced Sir William to colonise it. Within a year, the colony had one hundred inhabitants, a figure that included forty enslaved persons, although the Courteen interests in the Caribbean ultimately fell victim to the habit of Charles I of demonstrating the limitations of the early seventeenth-century English state, in this case, creating competing patents for colonisation in the West Indies that convulsed colonial politics for the next forty years.[10]

The nature of the Portuguese sugar operations in Brazil, the Spanish plantations on Hispaniola and their Dutch counterparts in Guiana, with which Warwick, Courteen and their associates had familiarity, had made apparent the need for a regular supply of bound labour for plantation success. In line with this understanding, the Virginia Company implemented reforms in 1618 that converted that enterprise from a military-exploratory one to a plantation one, including the creation of a House of Burgesses that enabled Virginia's planters to govern local affairs as well as the device of indentured servitude. This system, which became the favoured means of transporting Europeans to Anglo-America through the independence of the United States and was employed in transporting Asian migrants to Africa, the Caribbean and Fiji after the abolition of enslavement in the British Empire in 1834, bound the servant to the eponymous indenture for a customary term of four or five years in exchange for his or her passage to a plantation location and their maintenance over the term of the contract. In its classic, American form, the servant who survived the indenture term could receive 'freedom dues' in the form of land, tobacco seed and tools.[11]

The supply of servants, though, remained entirely dependent on the success of recruitment efforts, the effectiveness of which remains entirely unclear notwithstanding the enduring conception of Europeans fleeing economic hardship and religious persecution and overcoming obstacles – including the ocean-crossing in the first instance – to pursue opportunities in the future United States: not only did migrants return to England in significant numbers but prospective members of the servant pool could vote with their feet when presented with the promise of life in Anglo-America. Convicts and prisoners of war who travelled across the Atlantic on indentures generally lacked, of course, the degree of choice available to other European migrants, but their numbers fell short of requirements.[12]

Slavery always presented an enticing labour option, but the problem of supply remained vexing; can it have been a coincidence that the English presence in Africa intensified as the English presence in America spread? In the event, private enterprise, both legitimate and otherwise, led English involvement in 'Guinea' just as it did in the Western Hemisphere, and the scale of these enterprises increased dramatically over the course of the seventeenth century; it is also apparent that English traders to Guinea had an understanding of how this commerce worked, including the commodities, such as Swedish iron and Indian fabrics, that Africans desired, and how to transport enslaved Africans to America without incident before 1640.[13]

These circumstances make it difficult to accept the textbook comprehension of 'early American history' that claims various English colonies underwent a 'transition to slavery' because of a purported change in planter preferences for labour from servants to enslaved people. Rather, planters always sought – or were encouraged to seek – enslaved persons: even as English access to the Guinea trade and, correspondingly, the enslaved population of Anglo-America increased, imports of the enslaved never matched colonial demands. This finding ranks among the most significant revelations we obtain from considering English overseas expansion from a wider geographical perspective, and from restoring private enterprise to its proper place in the engine room of that expansion.[14]

Indeed, the English had an awareness of the traffic in enslaved Africans before the invention of indentured servitude: Warwick's privateers had brought enslaved individuals to Bermuda by 1615.

Then, the first recorded English slave-trading voyage to an English colony (St Christopher's) occurred in 1626 under the direction of the Warwick client and London merchant Maurice Thompson. Thus, Africans could be brought to English colonies on a haphazard basis as in the case of the famous record of a shipment to Virginia at the end of 1619, but regular English access to the slave trade was not possible until the 1630s. Until then, the Portuguese had dominated the 'Guinea trade' through their trading citadels at Saõ Jorge da Mina on the Gold Coast and Luanda in Angola and their monopoly to supply Spanish America with enslaved persons; they took a dim view of competitors, especially 'heretics'. The war between the domains of Philip IV, including Portugal, and the Dutch Republic, though, spread to Africa, and the West India Company swept the Portuguese from the Gold Coast, capturing El Mina in 1637, thereby opening the region to other Europeans, and a revamped Guinea Company headed by Sir Nicholas Crispe and John Wood, as well as other operators, invigorated the English presence; by 1632, the merchant Samuel Vassall was sending slaving voyages to the Bight of Benin. Within a decade, Thompson – who became the pre-eminent English overseas adventurer by the middle of the seventeenth century – had become a leading Guinea trader, having already cornered the provision trade to Anglo-America.[15]

At the same time, the Providence Island Company devised the most fully fledged and ambitious of the English colonising schemes to date. This entity involved the most important and experienced operators, including Warwick and, inevitably, Thompson, in a plan that illustrates the ambiguity of ideology in the expansion of European overseas interests: while the establishment of a tobacco-growing plantation colony/privateering base in the western Caribbean provided a location for harassing Spanish interests while advancing the version of Calvinism to which the corporate leadership subscribed against 'popery', it also offered a site from which to conduct illicit trade with neighbouring Spaniards.[16]

Providence Island provides a splendid illustration of the nature of seventeenth-century English colonisation: a 'private' enterprise pursuing 'public' purposes without state involvement aside from the granting of a charter, to an entity the membership of which opposed the religious policies of Charles I, as it happens, the use of political and economic connections to advance the plan and a colonisation venture in which slavery and the slave trade comprised the vital component. It also amounted to another failure as the Spanish overwhelmed the colony in 1640. The effort made here was – and is – more important than this result, however: in addition to shining helpful light on the conduct of seventeenth-century overseas activities, Providence Island constituted a sort of laboratory in which various individuals – such as the ubiquitous Thompson but also Philip Bell, Daniel Elfrith and William Jessop – gained imperial experience that they employed subsequently in their involvement in initiatives ranging from the Indian Ocean to Barbados. The collective resilience of entrepreneurs and their agents in the face of the extensive list of expensive setbacks they incurred is another highly significant – and customarily overlooked – element of the expansion of seventeenth-century English overseas interests.[17]

Warwick, Vassall, Thompson and others connected to the Providence Island Company were also involved in the colonisation of New England, the most celebrated of the seventeenth-century English colonisation efforts and another first-rate example of the centrality of private enterprise to those efforts. Take the establishment of New Plymouth in 1620, for example, in which a group of Separatists living in Leiden in the Dutch Republic negotiated their removal to Virginia but, for reasons that remain suspiciously obscure, ended up off the coast of Cape Cod outside of the jurisdiction of any government. Almost a decade on, the 'Pilgrims' were followed by the 'Great Migration' sponsored by the Massachusetts Bay Company (chartered in 1628). Unlike their neighbours, this was, in the first instance, a legitimate operation conducted by a chartered company. Yet, that company, as with its Providence Island counterpart, governed as it was by men hostile to the religious policies of Charles I, easily defeated the attempts of its enemies to investigate its activities. Then, its success – unique in the annals of seventeenth-century Anglo-American colonisation – in dispatching some fifteen thousand people to New England in a little over a decade proved too great: the migrants spread south, west and north from Massachusetts, founding an array of communities from Long Island to Maine and three new colonies: Rhode Island, Connecticut and New Haven. This spread of settlement occurred without the knowledge, let alone the impetus, of the Crown.[18]

In actuality, notwithstanding the animosity that the likes of Warwick maintained towards Spain, the English had a new and much fiercer overseas competitor from the 1630s. The Dutch removal of the Portuguese presence along the Gold Coast enabled English involvement in West Africa, but it also aggravated the friction between these Protestant nations that had started in Asia in the first decade of the seventeenth century over access to spices and fabrics. As in other theatres, the advancement of English interests in Asia fell to private enterprise, in this case, the East India Company, arguably the best known of these ventures, which was chartered at the end of 1600 and retained primary responsibility for the English presence east of the Cape of Good Hope until it was wound up in 1858, as the chapter by Marilyn Garcia-Chapleau and the joint contribution of Elizabeth Heijmans and Rafaël Thiebaut in this volume discuss.

Over the first seventy-five years of its existence, this company's fortunes mostly waned in the face of the fierce hostility of its great rival, the Dutch East India Company, to its activities. The VOC's headquarters at Batavia (Jakarta), established by that company's vigorous agent, Jan Pietersz Coen, after he had routed the English and their Javanese allies there, provided a formidable base for Dutch operations in the Indian Ocean and so constituted a festering source of envy and deep concern for its English competitors. For instance, Coen expelled the English and their native allies from the Banda Islands.[19] The English fared somewhat better in India, securing a licence from the Mughal Emperor Jahangir to trade at Surat in 1613, while in 1639, Shah Jehan granted it the right to create a municipal government for Madras. Later, it recruited Indian weavers to produce the fabrics desired by African traders for resale in Guinea pursuant to arrangements grounded in local practice but not dissimilar to indentured servitude.[20]

Meanwhile, though, English interests in Asia nearly fell victim to the confusion that Charles I's involvement in overseas affairs generally brought. Sir William Courteen, probably the most ambitious of the early English imperial undertakers, both in terms of the capital at his disposal as well as his vision of overseas activity, secured a royal patent for a voyage that hoped to revive the flagging English presence in the East by visiting India, Indonesia, China and Japan, and to explore the Pacific Ocean as far as California to search for a

Northwest and Northeast Passage. Six Courteen Association ships left London in April 1636 backed by a capital fund of an astronomical £120,000 supplemented by an unprecedented agreement by the King to contribute an additional £10,000.[21] Sir William's venture in the Eastern Hemisphere, however, resulted in most spectacular failure – a reported loss of £151,612 altogether – in conjunction with the fatal problems his Caribbean interests suffered.[22]

The problems of the Courteen Association began practically as soon as its fleet departed: Sir William died, the East India Company ordered its agents to withhold cooperation in defiance of royal instructions and the Dutch and Portuguese harassed the expedition. Sir William's son (also named William) sent another fleet to the Indian Ocean in 1641 to investigate the colonisation of Madagascar as well as to support the trading factories that the 1636 undertaking had established in India. This second attempt envisioned integrating activities in Asia and Africa: acquiring gold in Guinea that would purchase fabrics, saltpetre and spices in India. Despite initial success, however, the effort again fell victim to the fierce opposition of the East India Company in defiance of royal instruction, the inhabitants of Madagascar, the Dutch, who seized two of its vessels, the Chinese and the Portuguese, along with mismanagement by its agents, and the Courteen presence was abandoned.[23]

In 1642, the wreckage of the Courteen Association came into the hands of Maurice Thompson and a group of like-minded merchants, including Samuel Moyer, William Pennoyer, Rowland Wilson, John Wood and Thomas Andrews, as William Courteen fled his creditors. Thompson's group sought to perfect the Courteen imperial vision, and they did so by enlisting the state – paradoxically, at a time when the English state had fractured – to support their plans: as these stretched geographically, they dragged national interests along. I have used the word 'national' here deliberately since Thompson and his associates wholeheartedly enlisted in the parliamentary regime that dispossessed Charles I in early 1642: Thompson and his associates assumed various offices that their patron Warwick and his aristocratic partners had created in the King's name (with that king in the field with an army trying to recover his realm).[24]

Having gained control of state power, thereby enabling them to bring that power to bear directly in their endeavours, the position of these operators became more vigorous as the royalists were defeated and then the King executed on 30 January 1649: they began work on a plan to integrate their interests by colonising the uninhabited island of Assada (Nosy Be) near Madagascar that they presented for parliamentary approval. The East India Company, which included a number of these 'Assada Adventurers' in its membership, opposed this perceived threat to its monopoly, as it did all colonisation schemes, which they regarded as pretences for conducting piracy, but the political strength of the Assada party and the argument for linking the Guinea and Asian trades compelled the EIC to accept an unwanted merger. In furtherance of this, the Adventurers prepared new slaving voyages for the Gold Coast. Thompson, Pennoyer, Wood and others had, meanwhile, acquired Barbados plantations, which they turned to the cultivation of sugar, the commodity that came to define the history of that place, by enslaved labourers. With the creation of the English Republic came the chance to bring their new state to bear against their rivals, both foreign and domestic.[25]

The foremost of these continued to be the Dutch, the list of whose 'insolencies' were dated back to Coen's success in the Bandas (which the Assada Adventurers sought to recover), including the 'unlawful' occupation of territory in North America, from 1614, and the 'massacre' of East India Company employees in Ambon (1623) in the Moluccas. More recent – and thus more directly connected to the Thompson group – complaints included repeated 'interference' with English operations on the Gold Coast and in the Spice Islands, the seizure of the Courteen ships, tobacco-smuggling in North America and, above all, a persistent refusal to redress these grievances, which itself became a grievance. The existence of support among the Orangist party in the Netherlands for Charles Stuart's claim to his father's throne, at a time when the English pretender had been crowned King of Scotland, added urgency within the new regime for resolving these issues – aggravated by a refusal to accept the Commonwealth in Barbados and Virginia. It hoped to do so by forming a union with its Dutch counterpart. Unfortunately for this plan's supporters, the designated allies regarded the decidedly subordinate place that it assigned to them askance.[26]

The 'carrot' having failed, the Assada Adventurers pressed the application of the 'stick' and the Commonwealth agreed, enacting the first Navigation Act on 9 October 1651, which sought to curb the colonial smuggling that deprived the new regime of customs revenue and encouraged resistance to its authority. The group then worked up an expedition led by Sir George Ayscue that, with the help of connections on the ground, subjugated Barbados and Virginia, and seized a reputed £100,000 worth of goods from a Dutch fleet it encountered at the former place.[27]

These measures were not enough, however: the East India Company presented the Council of State with a demand for the recovery of itemised damages amounting to £1,681,996 15s that it alleged it had suffered at Dutch hands dating from 1622, followed by a compilation of thirty-six petitions 'of divers, sea commanders, mariners, widows, and orphans' seeking letters of reprisal against the VOC to recover alleged damages for lost property and wages. This increasing pressure brought the first of three Anglo-Dutch wars fought within twenty-five years in July 1652 and demonstrates how 'mercantilism' worked in the seventeenth-century English Empire: private enterprise directed 'state' policy rather than the other way around.[28]

To the undoubted disappointment of its proponents, however, the war resolved none of their grievances as Oliver Cromwell, who had seized power in the middle of it, preferred to treat the Dutch with lenience in order to turn attentions to Spain. The new Lord Protector's renewal of antipathy against the old and fading foe included the arguably sole English instance of stereotypical imperialism during the seventeenth century, the 'Western Design', that targeted the Spanish Caribbean: at least, it is the view of recent studies of this endeavour that it reflected the vigour of the Cromwellian Protectorate and an eagerness to flex its new muscles that, in turn, furthered English imperial activities after the restoration of the monarchy in May 1660.[29]

Yet, even though the Protector's Government approved the expedition, it remains at best unclear whether the Design constituted 'Oliver Cromwell's Bid for Empire' or 'a single moment in the development of the English imperial vision'. Cromwell's enmity towards Spain presented an opportunity to the Thompson group: in addition to its alliance with the Dutch, English traders had long sought to open the Spanish Empire to their trafficking in enslaved individuals and other commodities; the Protector's determination to fight the Spaniards might have been manipulated to best advantage to include the Caribbean. Regardless, with a certain inevitability, Thompson and partners provided advice and logistical support while a veteran colonial-imperialist – the 'Pilgrim Father' Edward Winslow – was appointed as one of its leaders.[30]

Regardless of Cromwell's general imperial intentions or degree of involvement here, the Design, from his perspective, was a disaster, at least in the short term: beset by disease and bickering, it failed to take its designated target, Santo Domingo, obliging its leaders to improvise by attacking the smaller and more poorly defended Jamaica; the struggle to capture that island took five years. Its career, thus, demarcates, once again, the limitations of the seventeenth-century English state, even at its fiscal-military zenith. Yet, the acquisition of Jamaica also set a precedent for closer cooperation between private enterprise and the state in overseas affairs, and it restored an English presence in the western Caribbean, twenty years after the demise of the Providence Island establishment; this result entrenched the plantation pattern and formed – not coincidentally – what became the wealthiest and most important Anglo-American colony of the eighteenth century.[31]

English interests in the Eastern Hemisphere proceeded in an equally fitful manner. Cromwell negotiated the perfection of the merger between the East India Company and the Assada Adventurers at the behest of these parties, and Maurice Thompson assumed the leadership of the reinvigorated company in 1657. Having endured a torrid period in which additional Dutch 'insolencies' and the presence of 'interlopers' in the company's theatre had made the EIC's position perilous, this corporate reorganisation brought an influx of capital, morale and vision to the enterprise. Most particularly, it enabled a renewed implementation of the Courteen plan to link the Indian Ocean and Guinea trades: this involved the revitalised EIC's absorption of the Guinea Company, whose situation had also become precarious; the acquisition of the South Atlantic island of St Helena, which the EIC envisioned as a transit point for commerce from Guinea, Asia and America; and the reclamation of Pulau Run in the Banda Islands from the Dutch that would serve as the eastern terminus of its operations. The EIC also renewed its claims for damages that it and its predecessors had allegedly suffered from the Dutch.

The imperial reach here again fell rather short of the imperial grasp. The Dutch continued to frustrate efforts to negotiate while the attempt to recover Pulau Run was summarily rebuffed. Then, the EIC's efforts to recover the English position in the lucrative slave trade – already recognised as essential to the success of, as well as success in, Anglo-America – attracted the attention of James, Duke of York, and his clients after the Restoration.[32] The EIC could not resist York's group and their direct connections to the King; thus, the company was obliged to disgorge its African assets to a new Royal Company of Adventurers Trading into Africa that incorporated EIC membership with the Duke and his friends. The creation of this entity, which received the monopoly over the Guinea trade, also put paid to the Courteen–Thompson dream of a seamless English Empire as the Crown severed the connection of the East India Company with Guinea just as that connection had finally been perfected. The Crown did, though, award the EIC an unwanted Bombay, which it had acquired as part of the dowry of Charles' new Portuguese queen, Catherine of Braganza. So far, then, from centralising English overseas interests, the Crown divided these interests. These circumstances contradict the oft-repeated view that the 'Restoration empire' reflected the 'absolutist' tendencies of Charles II and James II who, building on the new fiscal-military capabilities commanded by the Cromwellian Protectorate, brought increasingly direct authority to bear over an increasingly mighty English Empire and provoked corresponding objections to that authority.[33]

This perception is erroneous: the familiar pattern by which English overseas matters were conducted remained evident with respect to the Western Hemisphere as it did with the Eastern after 1660, unsurprisingly, since most of those who assumed control of overseas affairs during the Interregnum continued in place, albeit in conjunction with new partners, as we have seen in the case of the Royal Company of Adventurers Trading into Africa. These partnerships also found new endeavours, as in the case of the Carolina proprietorship, which received its charter in 1663.

Meanwhile, colonial-imperialists, such as Lord Willoughby, intensified their involvement in – and, thus, their importance to – imperial development as they queued in London seeking royal favour after Charles II was enthroned. Willoughby, who had been primarily responsible for the founding of a colony in Suriname in 1650, not only solved the thorny political situation in Barbados but he also secured a regular customs revenue for the Crown (and thus royal gratitude, not coincidentally) when the colony's assembly acquiesced in the Staple Act (1663). At the same time, Willoughby's Connecticut counterpart, John Winthrop Jr, with thirty years of experience spearheading the territorial expansion of New England, petitioned the Crown for a charter for his colony, the terms of which were to include half of neighbouring Rhode Island and the entirety of the Dutch colony of New Netherland.

The Connecticut desire to eliminate the Dutch presence in North America added to the persistently deep loathing held by English overseas adventurers towards their bitter rivals; the King, who detested the Dutch governmental system and was concerned about the position of his nephew, the Prince of Orange, in the Dutch Republic, needed no encouragement towards an anti-Dutch policy. In the summer of 1664, the Crown provided the necessary support for the capture of New Netherland and sent a fleet to the Gold Coast against the West India Company's factories there as a prelude to the outbreak of formal war; York retained the seized Dutch province as his own proprietorship – although he immediately gave its territory west of the Hudson River to his friends, Sir John Berkeley and Sir George Carteret. The prospect of dealing a fatal blow to their bitter foe brought the political nation to a fever pitch: Parliament granted the King a massive £4,000,000 to achieve it.

This unprecedented scale of support yielded even poorer returns than even the Western Design did. First, a Dutch fleet under De Ruyter regained their African posts, expelling the English and destroying their factories as well as a trade worth a reported £100,000. The Royal Company never recovered from this blow and it was dissolved in favour of a new Royal African Company chartered in 1672.[34] Then, despite victory at Lowestoft at the outset of the conflict, Tangier (like Bombay, a 'money pit' offloaded by the Portuguese as part of the royal dowry and later abandoned embarrassingly to Morocco in 1684) came under intense pressure, the requirements of war caused a settlement on Cape Fear in Carolina to wither, while the Dutch seized Suriname and subjugated the Sultan of Macassar, an English ally in the Spice Islands, as the parliamentary grants were frittered away. The outbreak of plague in

1665, followed by the Great Fire that consumed most of London the following year, and De Ruyter's destruction of the English fleet at its Medway anchor where it had been mothballed due to lack of funds, underscored the dismal state of affairs; the peace did nothing to correct this.

In the aftermath of these fiascos, the Crown, at the behest of the New Englanders Thomas Breedon and Samuel Maverick, for the first time employed commissioners to report on colonial affairs directly to a new Commission on Trade and Plantations – the creation of which had been recommended by two of the most successful colonial-imperialists, Thomas Povey and Martin Noell, both of whom promptly accepted appointments to it.[35] The creation of this commission is customarily regarded as a typically centralising intervention by Charles II, which was resisted by the Government of Massachusetts. In actuality, many New Englanders, especially those residing north of the Merrimack River, regarded 'the Bay' as tyrannical while the commissioners were almost universally welcomed by the King's colonial subjects, who regarded their appearance as an opportunity for relief in resolving long-standing grievances, especially regarding their land titles with their southern neighbour. The delay and obfuscation of the Bay Colony enabled by virtue of its charter, though, succeeded in seeing off these complaints.[36]

The Third Anglo-Dutch War (1672–74), fought primarily because Charles II wanted revenge but that failed to attract the financial and popular support accorded to its predecessor, brought no change, although the Dutch briefly recaptured New York before burning the Virginia tobacco fleet and the fishing settlement in Newfoundland. This conflict, though, brought the ascendancy of France at the expense of the Dutch. In the first instance, the French invasion of the Dutch Republic in the *Rampjaar* of 1672 that reached Utrecht and caused the overthrow of the Government of Johan de Wit compelled the Dutch to adopt a more pacific overseas policy; Anglo-Dutch friction dramatically receded. In conjunction with Louis XIV's own hostility to republicanism, French antipathy to the Dutch arose from the Sun King's desire to pursue a greater commercial and territorial presence in accordance with his general attitude of aggrandisement, one that confirmed France as the English global bogey after 1675. Yet, even while enjoying a greater institutional and fiscal capacity than that possessed by his

English cousins, Louis still relied to some degree on private enterprise to carry out French ambitions worldwide: a comparison of the English and French cases could provide a fruitful assessment of the degree of power – 'absolutism' – that the respective monarchies both sought and were able to exercise, at least with respect to the initiation and implementation of overseas policies. This comparison, in turn, might bring a better appreciation of the nature of seventeenth- and eighteenth-century European states and of the history of states in general.[37]

The relatively febrile character of the English state was confirmed when the Prince of Orange, William III, and his adherents overthrew the Government of William's father-in-law/uncle, James II, in 1688–89. Recently heralded by one school of thought as the advent of 'modernity', in actuality, this 'Glorious Revolution', as the Civil Wars four decades before had also done, reflected how the conduct of overseas affairs remained essentially in place: the English Empire was still governed through the royal prerogative, and commercial and colonising rights continued to be issued under that prerogative, as in the case of the Georgia Trustees (1732), even as state involvement in these matters increased in order to combat increasing French threats.

Furthermore, this increasing state involvement still customarily occurred due to the activities of private enterprises and their networks, in which more numerous and more sophisticated colonial-imperialists participated, such as the membership of the Ohio Company of Virginia who received authorisation to colonise territory west of the Appalachian Mountains in 1747, the Indian slave-trading ring that operated illicitly, but notoriously, out of South Carolina, and the agents of the East India Company based at Bencoolen (Bengkulu) in western Sumatra whose activities also involved recruiting colonists (Chinese rather than German) and engaging in diplomacy with Indigenous nations to secure territorial and commercial concessions. In the end, variations on the 'frontier thesis', such as the fashionable concept of 'settler colonialism', provide as misleading a vantage point from which to consider Anglo-American territorial expansion and its effects as the privileging of 'state formation' does.[38]

After all, the political culture that the history of English overseas interests had generated remained firmly in place after William's coup d'état: colonial-imperialists and their patronage connections still took the lead in promoting overseas territorial and commercial interests, whether as smugglers, pirates or legitimate adventurers, such as Cecil Rhodes' South Africa Company chartered as late as 1889. After all, people have always sought wealth, power, connections, favours and similar advantages; seventeenth-century English private enterprise, having been bequeathed an ever-commercialising economy, certainly widened the scope and scale of these pursuits and generated profound global effects. *Mais plus ça change plus c'est la même chose?*[39]

Notes

1 L.H. Roper, 'Reorienting the "origins debate": Anglo-American trafficking in enslaved people, c. 1615–1660', *Atlantic Studies* (2022), doi: 10.1080/14788810.2022.2034570.

2 L.H. Roper, 'The fall of New Netherland and seventeenth-century Anglo-American imperial formation, 1654–1676', *New England Quarterly* 87, no. 4 (2014), 666–708, doi:10.1.1162/TNEQ_a_00417; David Veevers, '"Inhabitants of the universe": Global families, kinship networks, and the formation of the early modern colonial state in Asia', *Journal of Global History* 10, no. 1 (2015), 99–121; Edmond Smith, 'The social networks of investment in early modern England', *Historical Journal* 64, no. 4 (2021), 912–39, doi: 10.10107/S0018246X2000045X.

3 The classic formulation of 'early American origins' remains Edmund S. Morgan, *American Slavery, American Freedom: The Ordeal of Colonial Virginia* (New York: W.W. Norton, 1975).

4 For example, Steven Pincus, James Robinson and Élodie Grossi, 'Faire la Guerre et faire l'État: Nouvelles perspectives sur l'essor de l'État développementaliste', *Annales: Histoire, Sciences sociales* 71, no. 1 (2016), 5–36. For a comprehensive discussion of the issues raised in this essay and further citations, L.H. Roper, *Advancing Empire: English Interests and Overseas Expansion, 1613–1688* (New York: Cambridge University Press, 2017).

5 This imperial scenario remained pre-eminent well into the nineteenth century: Frank J.A. Broeze, 'Private enterprise and the peopling of Australasia, 1831–50', *Economic Historical Review* 35, no. 2 (1982), 235–53.

6 Elizabeth A.R. Brown, 'The tyranny of a construct: Feudalism and historians of medieval Europe', *American Historical Review* 79, no. 4

(1974), 1063–88. For proprietary ventures in English and other cases, L.H. Roper and B. Van Ruymbeke (eds.), *Constructing Early Modern Empires: Proprietary Ventures in the Atlantic World, 1500–1750* (Leiden: Brill, 2007).

7 Eneas Mackenzie, 'Incorporated companies: Merchant adventurers', in *Historical Account of Newcastle-upon-Tyne including the Borough of Gateshead* (Newcastle-upon-Tyne, 1827), 662–70; British History Online, www.british-history.ac.uk/no-series/newcastle-historical-account/pp662–670.

8 Paul Slack, *The Invention of Improvement: Information & Material Progress in Seventeenth-Century England* (Oxford: Oxford University Press, 2015), 66–76.

9 L.H. Roper, *The English Empire in America, 1602–1658* (London: Pickering & Chatto, 2009), 88–90; Cf. Philip J. Stern, *The Company-State: Corporate Sovereignty and the Early Modern Foundations of the British Empire in India* (Oxford: Oxford University Press, 2011); Felicia Gottmann and Philip Stern, 'Introduction: Crossing companies', *Journal of World History* 31, no. 3 (2020), 477–88.

10 Nicholas Darnell Davis (ed.), 'Papers relating to the early history of Barbados and St. Kitts', *Timehri* 6 (1892), 327–49, 328; Henry Winthrop to John Winthrop, 15 October 1627, and John Winthrop to Henry Winthrop, 30 January 1627/28, in N.D. Davis, *The Cavaliers and Roundheads of Barbados, 1650–1652* (Georgetown: Argosy Press, 1887), 33–6; Sarah Barber, 'Power in the English Caribbean: The proprietorship of Lord Willoughby of Parham', in Roper and Van Ruymbeke, *Constructing Early Modern Empires*, 189–212.

11 Aaron Spencer Fogleman, 'From slaves, convicts, and servants to free passengers: The transformation of immigration in the era of the American Revolution', *Journal of American History* 85, no. 1 (1998), 43–76; Rachel Sturman, 'Indian indentured labor and the history of international rights regimes', *American Historical Review* 119, no. 5 (2014), 1439–65.

12 Joseph West to Anthony Lord Ashley, 10 September 1669, in Langdon Cheves III (ed.), *The Shaftesbury Papers* (Charleston: South Carolina Historical Society, 2000), 153–4.

13 Cloberry v Lamberton, 4 May 1636, Deposition of Thomas Brooks, HCA 13/52, fos. 381r-384v.

14 Deposition of Walter Smith, 8 February 1648/9, HCA 13/61, fos. 268r-269r; The East India Company's Answers to the Assada Adventurers propositions, 19 November 1649, HCA 13/71, fos. 70–71; Examination of Samuel Meade, 14 September 1653, HCA 13/67, fo. 496r.

15 The humble answer of the Guinea Company unto the Remonstrance of Mr. Samuel Vassall, 25 May 1650, CO 1/11, fo. 29; Deposition of Maurice Thompson, London merchant [May-June 1638], HCA 13/54, fos. 137r-137v.
16 Deposition of Thomas Hewitt, 22 April 1652, and deposition of William Eales, 22 April 1652, London Metropolitan Archives, Depositions (unfoliated), Mayor's Court, City of London, 1652–53, CLA/024/06/004.
17 Karen Ordahl Kupperman, *Providence Island: The Other Puritan Colony* (New York: Cambridge University Press, 1993).
18 Virginia DeJohn Anderson, 'New England in the seventeenth century', in Nicholas P. Canny (ed.), *The Origins of Empire* (Oxford: Oxford University Press, 1998), 193–217.
19 Martine Julia van Ittersum, 'Debating natural law in the Banda Islands: A case study in Anglo-Dutch imperial competition in the East Indies, 1609–1621', *History of European Ideas* 42, no. 4 (2016), 459–501; Vincent C. Loth, 'Armed incidents and unpaid bills: Anglo-Dutch rivalry in the Banda Islands in the seventeenth century', *Modern Asian Studies* 29, no. 4 (1995), 13–35.
20 William Foster, *The Founding of Fort St. George, Madras* (London, 1902); East India Company to Fort St. George, 2 February 1661/62, British Library, IOR H/33, fo. 12.
21 The King's Undertaking to join in the Adventure to the Indies, 6 December 1635, in *CCMEIC*, 1: 123–4; Reasons to move the King to confirm under the Great Seal Captain Weddell's Commission, [May 1637], *CCMEIC* 1: 274–5.
22 Edward Graves, *A Brief Narrative and Deduction of the Several Remarkable Cases of Sir William Courten, and Sir Paul Pyndar* (London, 1679), 5.
23 Reparation of Courteen's Damages to be demanded of the States, 19 March 1646/7, *Lords Journal* 8: 220; Petition of William Courteen III to the King, 25 June 1663, British Library, Sloane Ms. 3515, fol. 4.
24 Graves, *A Brief Narrative*, 4.
25 A Meeting of Divers Committees and Others of the Assada Adventurers, 27 November 1649, *CCMEIC* 3: 379; Simon Groenveld, 'The English Civil Wars as a cause of the first Anglo-Dutch War', *Historical Journal* 30, no. 3 (1987), 541–66; The Agreement between the East India Company and the Assada Adventurers, 21 November 1649, *CCMEIC* 3: 377–8.
26 Gijs Rommelse, 'The role of mercantilism in Anglo-Dutch political relations', *Economic History Review* 63, no. 3 (2010), 591–611.

27 John Paige to Gowen Paynter and William Clerke, 16 February 1651/52, and same to same, 13 March 1651/52, 'Letters of 1642', G.F. Steckley (ed.), *The Letters of John Paige, London Merchant, 1648–58* (London: London Record Society, 1984), 57–82; J.E. Farnell, 'The Navigation Act of 1651, the first Dutch War, and the London merchant community', *Economic History Review* 16, no. 3 (1964), 439–54.
28 Abstract of damages, [January 1651/52], CO 77/7, fos. 83r–84r; William Cockayne, Governor, and Council of the East India Company to the Council of State, 29 January 1651/52, CO 77/7, fo. 93, with the humble petition of divers sea commanders, mariners, widows, and orphans to the Council of State [May 1652], CO 77/7, fos. 97–181.
29 Carla Gardina Pestana, 'English character and the fiasco of the Western Design', *Early American Studies* 3, no. 1 (2005), 1–31; Carla Gardina Pestana, *The English Conquest of Jamaica: Oliver Cromwell's Bid for Empire* (Cambridge, MA: Harvard University Press, 2017); David Armitage, 'The Cromwellian protectorate and the languages of empire', *Historical Journal* 35, no. 3 (1992), 531–55.
30 Mr Andrew Riccard, &c. to the Protector, 14 August 1654, in Thomas Birch (ed.), *A Collection of the State Papers of John Thurloe*, 7 vols. (London, 1742) (hereafter 'TSP'), 2: 542: Commissioners for the southern expedition to the protector, 7 March 1654/55, TSP, 3: 203–4; Jeremy Dupertuis Bangs, *Pilgrim Edward Winslow: New England's First International Diplomat* (Boston: New England Historic Genealogical Society, 2004), 384–401; Deposition of Thomas Hewitt, 22 April 1652, and deposition of William Eales of Lime-house, 22 April 1652, London Metropolitan Archive, Depositions (unfoliated), Mayor's Court, City of London, 1652–53, CLA/024/06/004.
31 Trevor Burnard, 'Prodigious riches: The wealth of Jamaica before the American Revolution', *Economic History Review* 54, no. 3 (2001), 506–24.
32 Letter from Suriname, 8 November 1663, CO 1/17, fos. 226–7.
33 See Note 2.
34 A Brief Narrative of the Trade and Present Condition of the Royal Company of England Trading into Africa [January 1664/65], CO 1/19, fos. 7–8.
35 [Draft] Overtures touching s Council to be Erected for Foreign Plantations, [1660], Egerton Ms. 2395, fos. 270r–271r, British Library.
36 For example, The petition of the inhabitants of Portsmouth and Strawberry Bank [July 1665], CO 1/19, fos. 163–4.

37 Helen Dewar, 'Government by trading company? The corporate legal status of the company of New France and colonial governance', *Nuevo Mundo Mundos Nuevos* (2018), http://journals.openedition.org/nuevomundo/72105, doi: 10.4000/nuevomundo.72105; Kenneth J. Banks, 'Financiers, factors, and French proprietary companies in West Africa, 1673–1713', Leslie Choquette, 'Proprietorships in French North America', Cécile Vidal, 'French Louisiana in the age of the companies' and Philip Boucher, 'French Proprietary colonies in the Greater Caribbean', in Roper and Van Ruymbeke, *Constructing Early Modern Empires*, 79–116, 117–32, 133–62, 163–88.

38 Warren Hofstra, '"The extention of His Majesties dominions": The Virginia backcountry and the reconfiguration of imperial frontiers', *Journal of American History* 84, no. 4 (1998), 1281–312; Anthony Farrington, 'Bengkulu: An Anglo-Chinese partnership', in H.V. Bowen (ed.), *The Worlds of the East India Company* (Woodbridge: Boydell & Brewer, 2002), 111–7; David Veevers, '"The company as their lords and the deputy as Great Rajah": Imperial expansion and the English East India Company on the West Coast of Sumatra, 1685–1730', *Journal of Imperial and Commonwealth History* 41, no. 5 (2013), 687–709.

39 Mark Bailey, 'Historiographical essay: The commercialisation of the English economy, 1086–1500', *Journal of Medieval History* 24, no. 3 (1998), 297–311.

Part II

The limits of imperial control

4

The limits of royal control over migration to Spanish America in the sixteenth century

Eric Roulet (English translation by Agnès Delahaye)

The Castilian monarchy encouraged emigration to the Indies, in this case, the West Indies, or America, to secure its hold on the newly discovered and conquered territories over which it had been given sovereignty and possession at the end of the fifteenth century. More than 250,000 Spanish individuals crossed the Atlantic Ocean over the course of the sixteenth century, the majority of whom travelled during the second half of the period.[1]

Migrants were at first free to remove, but emigration was increasingly regulated and controlled by the Crown, who wished to dictate the manner in which the American continent would be populated. These regulatory efforts on the surface set the Spanish imperial policies at odds with the laissez-faire of the British and Dutch Empires in their first centuries, discussed in this volume by L.H. Roper and Susanne Lachenicht. The Spanish Crown favoured some publics while excluding others, and particular procedures were put in place to select suitable candidates for passage. Some of these dispositions were enforced throughout the colonial period, but some were changed significantly, particularly over the course of the sixteenth century. This chapter traces these changes through a close study of royal letters and instructions, to highlight the evolution of the Crown's migratory policy and the different requirements it sought to fulfil.

Migration has been widely dealt with in the literature on the Spanish Empire. Scholars first focused their attention on the numbers and nature of migratory flows through quantitative methods. They were able to assess the principal movements of people for each period, as well as their origins and destinations.[2] The registers of the *Casa de contratación* in Seville have often served as the basis for this research.³ By focusing on their connections at home and their motivations for departure, these studies have led to better and more precise profiles of migrants and to better understandings of the processes though which colonial societies were formed, in the Caribbean, New Spain and Peru. Since the 1990s, the development of global historical methods has led to a reconsideration of migratory flows from wider perspectives, leading to the publication of new synthetic works measuring the impact of European migration to the New World on a continental scale.⁴ Recent research has also focused on the nature of the relationship between overseas territories and their metropole, or the imperial question, thought of in turns along the periphery and centre model or as a mosaic of interrelated territories with their own specific status.⁵ The very notion of empire is not only understood as an extension or projection of sovereign power over new territories but it also interrogates the manner in which men emigrating out of the Iberian peninsula remained part of the imperial constitution.

However, certain aspects of the migratory policy of the Spanish monarchy have been less studied, most notably, the manner in which imperial authorities enforced the legislation. This chapter studies the measures the Spanish monarchy put in place in the sixteenth century to control migratory movement on both sides of the Atlantic, in Spain and in America, to measure the extent to which the monarchy understood the scope and nature of illegal transport and emigration, and the actions it took to stem them. As Elizabeth Heijsmans and Rafaël Thiebaut argue in the case of the Dutch Empire in this volume, centralised imperial policies could run against the imperatives of colonisation. The desire of the Spanish Crown to use migration as the next step in taking control of its overseas dominions, many of them hostile and unattractive, and many more still unknown, ran against a desire to control who was allowed to people them.

The licensing system

At the end of the fifteenth century, emigration to the Indies was unrestricted, but nevertheless reserved for the subjects of the kingdoms of Castile and Aragon, that is, the provinces of Castile,

Aragon, Léon, Valencia, Catalonia and Navarre, and the islands of Majorca and Minorca. In September 1501, the instructions sent to the governor of Hispaniola Nicolas de Ovando added another restriction, strictly barring foreigners from passing to the Indies.[6] Deemed foreign were all those who held a nationality different from Spanish.[7] The monarchy also reserved the right to give leave or to restrain the departure of ships transporting migrants across the ocean.[8]

These restrictions emanated partly from a desire to preserve the morality of the societies under formation in the Americas, which required that certain minorities or social categories be prevented from leaving the metropole. The royal provision of 1501 barred moors, heretics and converts from migrating to the Indies and conditioned passage on the granting of a licence.[9] Since 1492, Spanish Jews had been forced to convert to Christianity or leave the kingdom. The policy of forced conversion was extended to the Muslims of the former kingdom of Granada in the sixteenth century, who continued to be suspected of adhering to their former faith.[10]

The *Casa de contratación* founded in Seville in 1503 was at the heart of the migration system, in charge of organising and controlling the migratory flow to the Indies, and, from there, to the American continent. It supervised convoys, collected taxes and checked the ships' cargoes. Its orders of 1505 and the instructions given to its officers in 1510 explicitly forbade the passage of any unauthorised person.[11] The royal patent of 9 September 1511, however, showed more flexibility, allowing passage without a licence but ordering that passenger names be duly recorded in a register.[12]

This relatively liberal system did not last. Legal dispositions were reinforced from 1518 onwards, making a licence granted by the authorities mandatory for all migrants seeking passage to America.[13] Licences were delivered by the *Casa de contratación* to anyone who applied for one in their own names and for a precise destination. They were to be used within two years of delivery but could be valid for up to three years when the territory mentioned was particularly distant, such as Chile or the Philippines.[14] After 1522, all passengers were required to present both their licence and the document attesting to their identity before boarding their ship.[15] There were a few derogatory dispositions to this stricter system for shipping crews such as captains, seamen and soldiers, or for biracial men, born of a Spanish father and an Amerindian mother, who wished to return home after their studies.[16]

The groups of people who had already been barred from emigrating in the fifteenth century continued to be excluded from the licensing system. The list of publics targeted by the ban also expanded over the course of the century to include heretics, converts and reconciled men and women, along with their sons and grandsons, on both sides of each family.[17] Later, Romani, prostitutes, sodomites, criminals and 'delinquents' of all sorts were added to the list of those barred from migration. The purpose of these bans was to protect the Crown's overseas territories against any risk of heretical contagion made greater by the strengthening of the Protestant reformation in Europe, and against greedy exploiters attracted by the promise of quick wealth in America. Passage to the Indies was therefore reserved for old Christians only. Even though it was often mentioned in the documents, the migrants' actual morality does not seem to have impeded their removal. Indeed, the bishops of New Spain often complained about the quality of the priests sent to them, who were failing their evangelising duties.[18]

At times, the granting of a licence was dependent on certain conditions. In 1530, for instance, married men were obliged to remove accompanied by their wives and single women were barred altogether. Women consequently represented about 15.3 per cent of the migrating contingents over the course of the century, even if this proportion increased over time, from 10 per cent between 1509 and 1538 to 23 per cent in 1575.[19] Men wearing the habit of San José and San Esteban were only allowed passage with a royal licence clearly stating their clericature, while curators and tutors of wardships were only given a licence if they had returned their accounts.[20]

Foreigners were generally barred from taking part in the trade with the Indies, due to the international context and the relations between Castile and the European states from which they came.[21] For instance, after 1530, foreign clerics were forbidden to travel to America, even with a licence.[22] However, merchants and seamen serving on board the royal fleets could be exempted, and foreign merchants seem to have been particularly tolerated between 1525 and 1538 for their role in dynamising transatlantic trade. The Cortés of Castile repeatedly objected to this toleration to the King and Emperor, and a new royal cedula abolished this special regime in 1538.[23]

A few particular groups of Spanish men enjoyed special dispositions. Merchants and their factors could be granted a licence for a limited time, generally three years, to do business.[24] Similarly, the Crown's officials travelled to the Indies with a licence for the time of their commissions.[25] Licences given to clerics received particular attention, since evangelisation and the supervising of Christians were fundamental aspects of the Spanish mission. The Crown retained the authority to deliver clerical licences already conditioned on the written permission from the superior of each priest's convent.[26] The Bishops of New Spain, therefore, asked in 1540 for more leniency, so that more priests could come over to evangelise the peoples of America.[27]

The Crown also reserved the right to grant licences to certain people who were barred *a priori* from removal because of their social or religious conditions. Special dispositions could thus be accorded to single women or newly converted individuals.[28] The law also required an explicit royal licence for the passage of enslaved people leaving the peninsula (*Negros ladinos*).[29]

It became the responsibility of various authorities in Spain, in the Americas and on board the ships to check the licences shown by the passengers. These authorities included the officers of the *Casa de contratación*, ship captains and the *gobernadores, justicias, ciudades* and *villas y lugares* in America.[30] However, the efficiency of these measures remains questionable.

The limits of royal migratory policy

Despite the many measures put in place, considerable numbers of passengers boarded outgoing ships undocumented or illegally. Living conditions in the peninsula pushed many inhabitants to try their luck in the New World, by every means possible.[31] These candidates for emigration took advantage of the faults in the system, undeterred by the repressive arsenal put in place to find out 'illegal' migrants and those who helped make their passage possible. The extent of migratory fraud is difficult to assess but judging from letters written by the officers and the many repetitions in the legislation, it seems to have been quite significant. The Crown's migratory policy was not as efficient as it would have liked.

There were, indeed, many ways to cheat the system. People could simply board a ship without a licence, for instance, after an inspection had been completed.[32] Effective control was made difficult because boarding points were numerous, ship captains neglectful and the officers of the *Casa de contratación* complaisant.

In 1508, residents of the Canary Islands were authorised to trade with the Indies, which made it possible for some Spanish travellers to transform their stopover on the islands into passage to America.[33] In 1519, the Crown allowed ships bound for America to leave from Cádiz and in 1529, nine additional ports were listed as departure points to America, including A Coruña, Bayonne, Aviles, Laredo, Bilbao, San Sebastian, Cartagena, Malaga and Cádiz.[34] Other ports sending ships to the Americas were required to register their migrants and send copies of their registers to the *Casa de contratación* in Seville, but the more boarding points there were, the harder they were to control, preventing officers from concentrating their efforts on a single location. In addition, not all officers were diligent in checking both goods and people leaving for the Indies, unless it was of interest to them. There was obviously much corruption, which is not the same as negligence, for sometimes the officers acted with much zeal. For instance, when in 1544 a cleric called friar Dionisio was barred from passing to the Indies by the King, all the people bearing that name were also forbidden to migrate, to ensure the friar in question would be arrested.[35]

Cheating the licensing system was commonplace. Licences for passage to the Indies were often trafficked and many fake licences circulated, public writers advertising their ability to forge these documents on the streets of Seville.[36] Other licences were bought, sometimes many times over, or were obtained through false testimonies. A few churchmen kept their profession hidden to embark more freely, giving up their frocks and dressing up in civilian clothing.[37] People also spoke of identity theft, often by a relative, to describe how the names of recipients were fraudulently altered. This was particularly prevalent for licences written out for servants (*criados*) accompanying their masters. In 1549, the Crown was visibly worried about this problem, for it asked the *Casa de contratación* to investigate the sale of these particular licences and to bar passage to individuals and their servants carrying them. These licences had to be seized and inquired into.[38]

Strengthening control

The Crown eventually realised the extent of fraud and in the middle of the sixteenth century decided to strengthen controls.[39] In 1562, Philip II established a new procedure making preliminary information mandatory prior to authorisation. Passengers seeking a permit or a licence from the *Casa de contratación* were required to confirm their identity and destination. After that date, candidates to emigration to the Indies were to follow a five-step process: they were to apply for a licence (*petición de licencia*), have their file examined, get their licence granted in Seville, be registered in a passenger register and, finally, be checked for conformity to the terms of their licence on arrival in the Indies. Each candidate also had to justify their interest in the New World, for instance, by producing letters of recommendations from friends and family in America, along with testimonies proving their identity and morality.

The amount of information required by the authorities increased over time and its validity was to be certified by the authorities of the localities from which the travellers originated. After 19 July 1569, passengers to the Indies were also required to appear in person for verification in front of the officers of the *Casa de contratación*.[40] The Crown recommended that the information provided by the applicants be checked, and specifically required that those calling themselves merchants be proven to be so.[41] Officers were to pay particular attention to changes in people's situations. Therefore, after 1567, the *prohibidos*, who were forbidden to migrate under the new rules but may have held an earlier licence, could no longer hope to renew it.[42] Officers were to verify the nature, status and dates of all licences and consult the passengers' list on the day of a ship's departure, the latter being required by law to provide the names, conditions and destinations of all persons on board.[43] Officers were forbidden from delivering additional licences or any other documents, while the Crown encouraged informants with rewards of up to one fifth of a fraudster's goods.[44]

Penalties against offenders were severe. Any person proven guilty of fraud was fined 100,000 silver *maravedis* and sentenced to ten years of banishment if they were members of the nobility, or to one hundred lashes if they were commoners. After 1560, any property acquired in the Indies by an offender was to be seized.[45] Foreigners who tried to pass over without a licence were punished through the confiscation of all their goods for the benefit of the King.[46] People caught on board the ships without a licence could be immediately put to death, without due process, and if they were arrested in the Indies, they were sent back to Spain.[47] From 1604 onwards, clandestine passengers were sentenced to the galley for four years, while ship captains caught helping them were fined one thousand ducats. After 1607, they even risked the death penalty.[48] Generals and admirals were held accountable for licence control and officers guilty of neglecting their duties could lose their commissions.[49]

Controlling immigration in New Spain

Checking passengers in their ports of departure was just one step in the long chain of control over migratory movements to the Indies. On arrival, passengers were also required to show the licences granted in the metropole to port officers in Havana, Cartagena de Indias and Vera Cruz, where most migrants coming into New Spain landed, or they were not allowed to disembark.[50] In April 1553, port officers were made essential agents in the control of migratory flows through new dispositions set by the Crown. The latter also asked '*que en esa audiencia haya un libro en que se asiente los que pasaren de estos reinos a esta tierra*'[51] ('that the audience should keep a book in which all those who passed from the kingdoms on to these lands be recorded'). It was to be kept by the *fiscal* of the Audience of New Spain, to whom all the passengers disembarking without a licence were to be reported. Those passing through without a licence were not to be allowed in. In 1566, it was ordered they should be sent back to Spain as prisoners.[52] Officers in Vera Cruz had to check all the ship registers and send a summary of their findings and were to pay particular attention to the durations indicated in the licences.[53]

But, again, Crown policy ran against local circumstances. Jeronimo Valderrama, who visited Vera Cruz in 1563, reported that the officers did not do much more than simply check that the passengers carried a licence.[54] Valderrama blamed illegal migration on the negligence and complacency of officers and on ship captains, whom he argued should be punished harshly.[55] He regretted that officials in New Spain ignored the dispositions established in the royal cedula of 24 April 1553, even though they owned a rule book containing all the King's decisions.[56] Negligence was also at work in religious circles. The chapter of Guadalajara admitted not knowing whether the priests arriving in their diocese had held a licence on entering New Spain and shifted the responsibility for migratory controls on to the other bishoprics in Tlaxcala, Michoacán and Mexico, where passengers had first come through.[57]

Because the officers in Vera Cruz took the passengers' licences when they first disembarked, it was difficult to check their identities and professions thereafter. Valderrama believed it was imperative for the authorities in Vera Cruz to pass on this information to the officials in the localities listed by the passengers as their destinations.[58] But the Vera Cruz officers were content with issuing some passengers with a new document in the form of a *laissez-passer*, which people got rid of to confuse the authorities. The bishop of Guadalajara could not tell whether the priests arriving from Castile had come over with a licence, because they all claimed to have left them with the authorities in Vera Cruz.[59] To stop this confusion, Philip II forbade the seizure of licences in 1574 and ordered that passengers should carry the original documents with them throughout their travels.[60] Illegal immigration nevertheless continued in spite of the restrictions. There were fake licences and false identities, and many people leaving the ships and reaching the shore secretly. The arrival of these 'undesirables' could not be prevented, but the authorities on land were responsible for making sure they could not take up any public charge in the territory.[61]

The arrival of illegal clerics occupied the authorities almost exclusively because they risked jeopardising the Crown's plans for evangelisation and the spiritual management of all residents. The bishops of New Spain often remarked on the poor quality of the clerics who were coming to America illegally, while the good ones, who were mindful of the law and the established rules, relied on the good will of their sovereign and consequently failed to get permission to travel.⁶² In 1552, the Crown ordered that clerical authorities should turn back all priests entering the province illegally and ensure those already there did not accomplish any sacred acts.⁶³ It also expected all New Spanish authorities to reject any cleric who came over without a licence.⁶⁴ In spite of these rules, though, it seems that the bishops retained the secular priests who passed clandestinely into New Spain. Who else was willing to spread the gospel into the more remote or dangerous areas of the Spanish conquest? Whether good or bad, every priest who landed successfully was allowed to stay.⁶⁵ The bishop of Oaxaca, for instance, welcomed to his province men such as Cristobal de Torres and Barreda, whose morality was clearly in doubt.⁶⁶

The Crown intended to control the movement of people from province to province, to prevent instability and the depopulation of certain areas for the benefit of other more attractive zones. It therefore strictly forbade entrants from moving on freely from their original destination, considering their circulation an infringement on the terms of their licence, in which their place of settlement was registered.⁶⁷ In 1595, 1613 and 1615, the Crown warned its New Spanish governments not to let any traveller disembark if New Spain was not the destination noted in their licences. It also forbade American audiences to deliver licences to people seeking to travel through the empire. Passage from Venezuela to the Kingdom of New Grenada or from New Grenada to Peru was strictly forbidden⁶⁸ and, in 1596, similar restrictions were imposed between New Spain and Peru.⁶⁹

The Castilian monarchy made the ownership of a licence to travel to the Indies mandatory in an attempt to control migratory flows and make sure overseas territories would be suitably populated. However, many cheated the system. The Crown aimed to be firm on this issue and remained so throughout the century. In this respect, the years 1552–53 were a turning point in Spanish migratory policy, as the rise in prohibitions and sanctions testifies. The impact of this strengthening of the Crown's migratory policy is difficult to assess, but it is certain that illegal passage continued. The Crown reiterated the responsibilities of the authorities in both Spain and the Americas, but in a 1595 letter to Don Luis de Velasco, Viceroy of Peru, Philip II lamented 'the great numbers of people continuously crossing the Atlantic without a licence'.[70] His policies were insufficiently enforced and sometimes ignored, because people were needed to fill American territories and there were places with little appeal. Local authorities in the Americas could not afford to be too selective regarding the status of incoming migrants. This was particularly true for the peripheral regions, where few people offered to migrate. Colonisation required labour, which fit uneasily with the rules of the monarchy in the sixteenth century, and with its desire to build a virtuous society. Pragmatism was the rule, even if it was never outspokenly so, and even if the monarchy imposed increasingly constrictive rules. The expectations and the severity it professed were tempered on the ground by the realities of colonisation. Migratory flows remained strong, with more than 200,000 people coming to settle in the Indies in the first half of the seventeenth century.[71] The share of illegal migrants continued to be significant.

Notes

1 No efficient assessment of migratory flows can be made from existing official documents. They mention only 150,000 people, although there were many more according to Bernard Lavalle, *L'Amérique Espagnole de Colomb à Bolivar* (Paris: Belin, 1993), 143. Magnus Mörner, for instance, found only 15,480 authorisations for the period between 1509 and 1559 in the catalogue of passengers to the Indies, when in fact there were more than 100,000 crossing the ocean: Magnus Mörner, *Le Métissage dans l'Histoire de l'Amérique Latine*, trans. H. Favre (Paris: Fayard, 1971), 27. Licences and passenger registers convey a partial and imperfect view of migration to the Americas, a central issue of historians' debates in the 1960s and 1970s. For a historiographic approach, see Grégoire Salinero, 'Aux Indes! Motivations et Conditions des Migrations entre l'Espagne et les Indes, XVIe-XVIIe siècles', in C. Moatti, W. Kaiser and Ch. Pébarthe (eds.), *Le Monde de l'Itinérance en Méditerranée de l'Antiquité à l'Époque Moderne* (Pessac: Ausonius Éditions, 2009), 405–26.
2 Many regional studies have been conducted that cover most of the Spanish provinces. See Juan Andreo García and Lucía Provencio Garrigós, 'Pasajeros a América: aportación al estudio de la emigración del Reino de Murcia durante el S. XVI', *Anales de Historia Contemporánea* 8 (1991), 97–130; Rafael Anes Álvarez, *La*

Emigración de Asturianos a América (Colombres: Fundación Archivo de Indianos, 1993); José Manuel Azcona Pastor (ed.), *Identidad y Estructura de la Emigración vasca y navarra hacia Iberoamérica Siglos (XVI–XXI): Redes Sociales y Desarrollo Socioeconómico* (Cizur Minor: Thomson Reuters Aranzadi, 2015). Among the most recent synthetic studies of migration to the Americas are Pedro A. Ives, Pepa Vega and Jesús Oyamburu (eds.), *Historia General de la Emigración Española a Iberoamérica* (Madrid: Historia 16, 1992); Antonio Eiras Roel (ed.), *La Emigración Española a Ultramar, 1492–1914* (Madrid: Ediciones Tabapress, 1991); Carlos Martínez Shaw, *La Emigración Española a América, 1492–1824* (Colombres, Asturias: Archivo de Indianos, 1994); Germán Rueda Hernanz and Consuelo Soldevilla Oria, *Españoles Emigrantes en América (Siglos XVI–XX)* (Madrid: Arco, 2000); Alain Hugon, *La Grande Migration. De l'Espagne à l'Amérique, 1492–1700* (Paris: Vendémiaire, 2019).

3 The registers have been published as *Catálogo de Pasajeros a Indias durante los Siglos XVI, XVII y XVIII* (Sevilla: Imprenta editorial de la Gavidia, 1940–1980).

4 Ida Altman and James Horn (eds.), *'To Make America': European Emigration in the Early Modern Period* (Berkeley: University of California Press, 1991); Pieter C. Emmer and Magnus Mörner, *European Expansion and Migration: Essays on the Intercontinental Migration from Africa, Asia, and Europe* (New York: Berg, 1992); Nicholas Canny (ed.), *Europeans on the Move: Studies in European Migration, 1500–1800* (Oxford: Clarendon Press, 1994); Patricia Galeana (ed.), *Historia Comparada de las Migraciones en las Américas* (Mexico: UNAM, 2014).

5 J.H. Elliott, *Empires of the Atlantic World: Britain and Spain in America, 1492–1830* (New Haven: Yale University Press, 2006); Carlos Martínez Shaw and José María Olivar Melgar (eds.), *El Sistema Atlántico Español (Siglos XVII–XIX)* (Madrid: Marcial Pons, 2005).

6 Antonio García-Baquero González, *La Carrera de Indias. Histoire du Commerce Hispano-Américain (XVIe–XVIIIe Siècles)* (Paris: Desjonquères, 1997), 18. This indication was repeated in the ordinances of the *Casa de contratación* of 1505 and in the instructions to its officers in 1510 (*ibid.*, 19–20).

7 José Luis Martínez, *Pasajeros de Indias* (Mexico: Alianza Editorial, 1984), 38. A few royal cedulas, as in 1560, 1571 and 1608, contain the lists of nations then considered as foreign. These changed considerably. In 1614, the Portuguese were foreigners, in spite of the Iberian union (*Real cédula*, El Pardo, 14 December 1614, *RLI*, 9–27–28, 3: 332. In 1620, the children of foreigners born in the kingdoms

of the peninsula were deemed *'naturales de ellos'* (*Real cédula*, San Lorenzo, 14 August 1620, *RLI*, 9–26–27, 3: 332).
8 García-Baquero González, *La Carrera de Indias*, 18.
9 Grégoire Salinero, 'Sous le Régime des Licences. L'identification des Migrants vers les Indes Espagnoles, XVIe–XVIIe Siècles', in C. Moatti and W. Kaiser (eds.), *Gens de passage en Méditerranée de l'Antiquité à l'Époque Moderne. Procédures de Contrôle et d'Identification* (Paris: Maisonneuve et Larose, 2007), 345–67.
10 About the religious policy of the monarchy, see Joseph Pérez, *Isabelle et Ferdinand, Rois Catholiques d'Espagne* (Paris: Librarie Arthème Fayard, 1988); Henry Kamen, 'La política religiosa de Felipe II', *Anuario de Historia de la Iglesia*, 7 (1998), 21–33. The experiences of Moriscoes are studied in A. Domínguez Ortiz and Bernard Vincent, *Historia de los Moriscos. Vida y Tragedia de una Minoría* (Madrid: Alianza, 1978) and those of the Marani in Antonio Domínguez Ortiz, *Los Judeoconversos en España y América* (Madrid: Istmo, 1971). Suspecting converts was symptomatic of a period concerned with the purity of Spanish blood, Albert Sicroff, *Les Controverses sur les Statuts de Pureté de Sang en Espagne, du XVe au XVIIe siècles* (Paris: Didier, 1960); Juan Hernández Franco, *Cultura y Limpieza de Sangre en la España Moderna. Puritate Sanguinis* (Murcia: Universidad de Murcia, 1996).
11 García-Baquero González, *La Carrera de Indias*, 20. About the *Casa de la Contratación*, see Ernesto Shäfer, 'La casa de la contratación de Indias durante los siglos XVI y XVII', *Archivo Hispalense 5*, no. 13–14 (1945), 149–62; Antonio Acosta Rodríguez et al. (eds.), *La Casa de la Contratación y la Navegación entre España y las Indias* (Sevilla: Universidad de Sevilla, CSIC, Fundación El Monte, 2003); Francisco Fernández López, *La Casa de la Contratación. Una Oficina de Expedición Documental para el Gobierno de las Indias (1503–1717)* (Sevilla/Zamora: Editorial Universidad de Sevilla/El Colegio de Michoacán, 2018).
12 *Real cédula*, Burgos, 9 September 1511, in Diego de Encinas, *Cedulario Indiano*, 4 vols. ([1596] Madrid: Ediciones Cultura Hispánica, 1945), 1: 396.
13 Martínez, *Pasajeros de Indias*, 32; García-Baquero González, *La Carrera de Indias*, 20–1. See *RLI*, 9–26–1, 3: 307.
14 *Real cédula*, San Lorenzo, 28 August 1584, *RLI*, 9–26–15, 3: 309; Salinero, 'Sous le Regime des licences', 345–67.
15 García-Baquero González, *La Carrera de Indias*, 20–1.
16 *Real cédula*, Valladolid, 30 January 1559, *RLI*, 9–26–28, 3: 313.

17 *Real cédula*, Saragosse, 24 September 1518, *RLI*, 9–26–16, 3: 312; *Real cédula*, Valladolid, 15 September 1522, *RLI*, 9–26–15, 3: 312. This ban is found in other patents dated 1530 and 1539.
18 *Carta de los Obispos al Rey* (Mexico, 1540), in Francisco del Paso y Troncoso, *Epistolario de Nueva España 1505–1818*, 16 vols. (Mexico: J. Porrúa e hijos, 1939–42), 4: 11–12 at 11.
19 *RLI*, 9–26–24, 3: 314. E. Serra Santana, 'Mito y realidad de la emigración femenina española al Nuevo Mundo en el siglo XVI', in Claire Pailler (ed.), *Femmes des Amériques* (Toulouse: Université de Toulouse-le-Mirail, 1986), 31–42; Lavalle, *L'Amérique espagnole*, 144. About the condition of female migrants, see also Amelia Almorza Hidalgo, *'No se hace pueblo sin ellas'. Mujeres españolas en el Virreinato de Perú: emigración y movilidad social (siglos XVI–XVII)* (Madrid: CSIC, Universidad de Sevilla, Diputación de Sevilla, 2018); M. Anore Horton, *New Perspectives on Women and Migration in Colonial Latin America* (Princeton: Princeton University Press, 2001).
20 *Real cédula*, San Lorenzo, 7 September 1589, *RLI*, 9–26–13, 3: 311; *Real cédula*, 8 February 1535, *RLI*, 9–26–70, 3: 324.
21 García-Baquero González, *La Carrera de Indias*, 22. Foreigners travelling with a licence to the Indies could not disembark and sell their goods and enslaved persons in the ports where they stopped on their way to their destination (*Real cédula*, Valladolid, 17 May 1557, *RLI*, 8–27–4, 3: 327). In spite of this legislation, foreigners managed to be involved in trade. See Antonio García-Baquero González, 'Los Extranjeros en el Tráfico con Indias: entre el Rechazo Legal y la Tolerancia Functional', in M. B. Villar García and P. Pezzi Cristóbal (eds.), *Los Extranjeros en la España Moderna*, 2 vols. (Málaga: Universidad de Málaga, 2003), 1: 73–99.
22 Martínez, *Pasajeros de Indias*, 37.
23 García-Baquero González, *La Carrera de Indias*, 20. About foreigners, see Richard Konetzke, 'Legislación sobre immigración de extranjeros en América durante la época colonial', *Revista Internacional de Sociología* 11–12 (1945), 269–99; Jean-Pierre Tardieu, *L'Inquisition de Lima et les Hérétiques Étrangers (XVIe–XVIIe Siècles)* (Paris: L'Harmattan, 1995).
24 *Real cédula*, 19 December 1554, *RLI*, 9–26–32, 3: 316. See also the royal cedulas of 1550, 1561 and 1563, *RLI*, 9–26–29, 3: 315.
25 *Real cédula*, Madrid, 24 April 1553, in Alonso de Zorita, *Cedulario de 1574. Leyes y Ordenanzas de las Indias del Mar Océano* (Mexico: Secretaría de hacienda y crédito público/Miguel Ángel Porrúa, 1985), 332–3.

26 *Real cédula*, Toledo, 23 May 1539, *RLI*, 9–26–11, 3: 311.
27 *Carta de los Obispos al Rey*, 12. About the migration of priests, see Pedro Borges Morán, 'La Emigración de Eclesiásticos a América en el Siglo XVI. Criterios para su Studio', in Francisco de Paula Solano Pérez-Lila and Fermín del Pino Díaz (eds.), *América y la España del Siglo XVI* (Madrid: CSIC, 1982), 47–62; Manuel Hernández González, *Al Margen de la Corona. La Emigración del Clero Regular Canario a América en la Edad Moderna* (Tenerife: Ediciones Idea, 2018).
28 *Real cédula*, Valladolid, 15 September 1522, *RLI*, 9–26–15, 3: 312.
29 *Real cédula*, Seville, 11 May 1526, in Encinas, *Cedulario Indiano*, 4: 384. See also *RLI*, 9–26–17 and 18, 3: 312.
30 About this subject in particular, see the *Casa de contratación* ordinance of 1539 (*Ordenanza*, Toledo, 23 May 1539, *RLI*, 9–26–11, 3: 311).
31 The issue of the migrants' motivations will not be discussed here. They are explored in Salinero, 'Aux Indes!'; Enrique Otte, *Cartas Privadas de Emigrantes a Indias 1540–1616* (Mexico: Fondo de Cultura Económica, 1996); Martínez, *Pasajeros de Indias*; Antonio Eiras Roel, 'Sobre las motivaciones de la emigración Gallega a América y otros aspectos. Un enfoque comparative', *Revista da Comisión Galega do Quinto Centenario* 2 (1989), 57–72.
32 Lavalle, *L'Amérique Espagnole*, 143.
33 García-Baquero González, *La Carrera de Indias*, 27. The Crown ended up forbidding passage from the Canary Islands, but this rule was largely ignored (*Real cédula*, Madrid, 25 February 1568, *RLI*, 9–26–40, 3: 317).
34 *Real cédula*, Toledo, 15 January 1529, in Encinas, *Cedulario Indiano*, 4: 133–4.
35 AGI, gobierno, indiferente, 1093, ramo 3–23, *Carta de los Oficiales de Sevilla al Principe*, Seville, 4 March 1544, fo. 3r.
36 Salinero, 'Sous le Régime des Licences', 345–67.
37 *Carta de los Obispos al Rey*, 11.
38 *Real cédula*, Valladolid, 29 April 1549, in Encinas, *Cedulario Indiano*, 1: 404; *Real cédula*, 28 January 1560, *RLI*, 9–26–38, 3: 317; *Real cédula*, Valladolid, 25 September 1604, *RLI*, 9–26–36, 3: 316.
39 Bernard Lavalle has noted that licences were given relatively freely under Charles V and less so under Philip II. These shifts were driven by expansion and the discovery of new mines and new lands to cultivate: Lavalle, *L'Amérique Espagnole*, 143.
40 García-Baquero González, *La Carrera de Indias*, 21.
41 *Real cédula*, Valladolid, 5 July 1555, *RLI*, 9–26–31, 3: 315.

42 *Real cédula*, 23 June 1567, *RLI*, 9–26–34, 3: 316. On this issue, see Esteban Mira Caballos, 'Los prohibidos en la emigración a América (1492–1550)', *Estudios de Historia Social y Económica de América* 12 (1995), 37–54.
43 *Real cédula*, 14 October 1574, *RLI*, 9–26–5, 3: 309.
44 *Real cédula*, Madrid, 24 April 1553, in Zorita, *Cedulario de 1574*, 332–3; *Real cédula*, Bosque de Segovia, 19 June 1569, *RLI*, 9–26–9, 3: 310; *RLI*, 9–26–1, 3: 307 and 9–26–2, 3: 308.
45 González, *Carrera de Indias*, 21–2.
46 *RLI*, 9–26–1, 3: 307.
47 Martínez, *Pasajeros de Indias*, 38.
48 González, *Carrera de Indias*, 21–2.
49 *RLI*, 9–26–2, 3: 307–8.
50 About Vera Cruz in the sixteenth century, see Pierre Chaunu, 'Veracruz en la segunda mitad del Siglo XVI y primera del XVII', *Historia Mexicana* 9, no. 4 (1960), 521–57.
51 *Real cédula*, Madrid, 24 April 1553, in Zorita, *Cedulario de 1574*, 332–3. About the political role of the audience in New Spain, see Beatriz Badorrey Martín, 'La audiencia de México y el gobierno de Nueva España a través de las instrucciones y memorias de los vir reyes (Siglos XVI y XVII)', *Anuario de historia del derecho español* 88–89 (2018–19), 45–75.
52 Martínez, *Pasajeros de Indias*, 34.
53 *Real cédula*, Madrid, 24 April 1553, in Zorita, *Cedulario de 1574*, 332–3.
54 *Carta de J. Valderrama al Rey*, Puebla, 25 August 1563, in Frances Vinton Scholes and Eleanor Burnham Adams (eds.), *Documentos para la Historia del México Colonial*, 7 vols. (Mexico: José Porrúa e hijos, 1961), 7: 26.
55 'di aviso del mal orden que hay en las visitas de los navios en lo que toca a los pasajeros', *Carta de J. Valderrama al Rey*, February–March 1564, in *ibid.*, 38.
56 *Ibid.*, 38. Many manuscript cedulas circulated in those days and some were even printed. The ordinances of the Viceroy Antonio de Mendoza were published in 1548: Antonio de Mendoza, *Ordenanzas y copilación de leyes* (Madrid: Ediciones Cultura Hispánica, 1945). One cedula redacted by auditor Vaso de Puga was published in Mexico in 1563, containing many royal cedulas about migration: Vasco de Puga, *Provisiones, cédulas, instrucciones para el gobierno de la Nueva España* (Madrid: Ediciones Cultura Hispánica, 1945).
57 *Carta de J. Valderrama al Rey*, Puebla, 25 August 1563, in Scholes and Adams, *Documentos*, 7: 26; *Carta de J. Valderrama al Rey*, Mexico,

February–March 1564, Scholes and Adams, *Documentos*, 7: 38; *Informe al Rey por el Cabildo Eclesiástico de Guadalajara*, Guadalajara, 17 September 1569, in J. García Icazbalceta (ed.), *Colección de Documentos para la Historia de México*, 3 vols. (Mexico: Porrúa, 1982), 2: 497.
58 *Carta de J. Valderrama al Rey*, Puebla, 25 August 1563, in Scholes and Adams, *Documentos*, 7: 26.
59 *Informe al Rey por el Cabildo Eclesiástico de Guadalajara*, Guadalajara, 17 September 1569, in Icazbalceta (ed.), *Colección*, 2: 497.
60 *Real cédula*, Aranjuez, 24 January 1574, *RLI*, 9–26–46, 3: 318.
61 Martínez, *Pasajeros de Indias*, 33.
62 '*y estos siempre son los peores porque los buenos no se ponen en tales ofrentas ni atravimientos*', *Carta de los Obispos al Rey*, 11.
63 *Real cédula*, 31 May 1552; *Real cédula*, 4 August 1574, in *RLI*, 1–7–8, 1: 55.
64 AGI, gobierno, Audiencia México, 1088, book 3, *Real cédula*, Valladolid, 26 February 1538, fo. 2v; *Real cédula*, Madrid, 31 May 1544, in Joaquín García Icazbalceta, *Don fray Juan de Zumárraga. Primer Obispo Yarzobispo de México*, 4 vols. (Mexico: Porrúa, 1947), 4: 83; *Real cédula*, Madrid, 31 May 1552, in Genaro García, *Documentos Inéditos o muy Raros para la Historia de México* (Mexico: Porrúa, 1982), 445.
65 AGI, gob., A. Mex., 19–13, *Carta de Luis de Velasco al Rey*, Mexico, 7 February 1554, fo. 2r.
66 *Carta de Zumárraga al Emperador*, Mexico, 17 April 1540, in Icazbalceta, *Don fray Juan de Zumárraga*, 3: 201.
67 *Real cédula*, El Pardo, 19 October 1566; *Real cédula*, 6 October 1578, *RLI*, 9–26–40, 3: 317.
68 *Real cédula*, 4 August 1574, *RLI*, 9–26–50, 3: 320; *Real cédula*, 4 August 1561, *RLI*, 9–26–51, 3: 320. The King forbade the *Alcalde Mayor* of San Felipe de Porto Bello from issuing licences to travel to Peru or New Grenada (*Real cédula*, Valladolid, 3 April 1605, *RLI*, 9–26–52, 3: 320). The Rio de La Plata governor had to make sure people did not attempt to go elsewhere, *RLI*, 9–26–53, 3: 321.
69 *Ordenanza*, Toledo, 25 May 1596, *RLI*, 9–26–61, 3: 322.
70 *Instruction*, 22 July 1595, in Lavalle, *L'Amérique Espagnole*, 143.
71 Mörner, *Le Métissage dans l'Histoire de l'Amérique Latine*, 27; Salinero, 'Aux Indes!', 405–26.

5

Imperial struggles, colonisation and the Dutch slave trade in seventeenth-century New Netherland

Anne-Claire Faucquez

Recent research has demonstrated how New York developed as an enslaving society in the seventeenth and eighteenth centuries.[1] Less clear are the processes that brought the first enslaved Africans to this remote North American colony soon after its foundation and planted the seeds of slavery in that infant settlement. The Dutch trade was predominant in the Atlantic world during the Golden Age, to the extent that Dutch historians Pieter Emmer and Wim Klooster have described it as 'an empire without expansion', meaning by that that Dutch people were interested in commerce rather than colonisation.[2] Yet, through a close study of the slave trade in New Netherland (1624–64), I would like to argue that the Dutch managed to pursue *both* trade and colonisation during this period. Enslaved Africans were used *both* as trading goods to supplement commercial exchanges and as instruments to further the exploitation of the land in America. Dutch and colonial merchants effectively colonised the Atlantic world, that is, appropriated markets and spaces, by inscribing their presence, weaving networks, establishing ports, exchanging goods and developing slavery. If Dutch participation in the slave trade was deeply impelled by European wars and was at first commanded by European political interests, records show that the Dutch progressively embarked on a series of colonial ventures in which private and personal interests reigned supreme. As the colony of New Netherland developed, colonial merchants started to take the upper hand over the monopoly of the Dutch state, embodied by the Dutch West India Company, breaking the golden rule of mercantilism which stipulated that colonies served to generate wealth for the mother country. Studying the slave trade in the Atlantic world will allow us to highlight tensions between the interests of states, colonies, companies and individuals, all of whom instrumentalised slavery to serve their own interests, namely self-enrichment. The new Dutch Republic, despite being a federal state, acted as other early modern states discussed by Susanne Lachenicht and L.H. Roper in Chapters 1 and 3 of this volume, and managed to build its empire through tight economic and political connections between patria and its colonies.

As potent as these political influences could be, though, the Atlantic area became a battle scene between competing interests. European states tried to impose imperial frameworks, governing their set of faraway territories from a distance, trying to have these new societies modelled after the old ones. Yet, as John Elliott put it in his classic comparative study of European empires, 'nature as well as nurture had formed these new colonial worlds', the old environment combining with the new one without the mother country being able to control it. As German scholar Claudia Schnurmann has asserted, to understand these phenomena, we need to 'denationalize the Atlantic Ocean', to show how colonies responded to their own logic, far from the control and interests of European states, operating autonomously and responding to the needs of their immediate environment. Colonial societies therefore saw the emergence of transnational connections and communities, of which New York was the perfect example, with the overlapping of Dutch and English Empires. These 'cross-national' links, according to Christian Koot, were built 'as a strategy for commercial success', to which we can add the slave trade, as the main commercial incentive for the pursuit of these global connections.[3]

While the introduction of slavery was the result of the imperialist policies of European states (the Spanish, British, Dutch and French), colonists entered into competition when they saw the benefits that they could derive from the slave trade. In the context of the imperial wars that punctuated the seventeenth century, the quest for 'black gold' became inseparable from the illegal practices of smuggling, privateering and piracy. Enslaved Africans, who comprised the bulk of some cargoes, were targeted commodities for whom everyone, from European or colonial merchants to international traders, from privateers to pirates, was ready to challenge regulations to enrich themselves. Piracy was condemned by European states but it could, for instance, be encouraged and protected by colonial governors.

As Douglas Burgess put it: 'the colonial record reveals an extraordinary complete account of attempts by successive administrations to safeguard privateering, which they viewed as not only an essential element of colonial commerce but a defensible prerogative of the governor himself'.[4]

The example of the slave trade in the Dutch colony of New Netherland (1624–64) allows us to look at the interplay between state and private interests in the colonial era, and to argue that the merchants did colonise space in the Atlantic. First, we will show that the involvement of the Dutch in the slave trade was a clear result of European imperial conflicts, a reaction against their archenemy, Spain, and how the Dutch went from condemning Spanish participation in the slave trade to becoming major slave traders themselves, sowing the seeds for English New York to become an enslaving society in the eighteenth century. Second, we will see how the slave trade constituted the sinews of war for the Dutch West India Company, which had been granted a charter for trade monopoly by the Dutch state. Lastly, we will highlight the way the slave trade became a colonial venture, in which personal and private goals prevailed over European political interests.[5]

The aversion of Spain, the love of liberty and the rejection of slavery

On 23 January 1579, through the Union of Utrecht, the United Provinces, consisting of the seven northern provinces of the Spanish Netherlands (Holland, Zealand, Overijssel, Friesland, Groningen, Gelderland and Utrecht) declared their independence from the Habsburg monarchy, before constituting themselves into a new Dutch Republic in 1581. The Eighty Years' War (1568–1648) between the Republic and the Habsburgs was suspended for a Twelve Years' Truce between 1609 and 1621, but the Habsburgs did not officially recognise the independence of the Republic until 1648 and the Peace of Münster. This political, economic and religious struggle was reinforced by a patriotic sentiment that was needed to bind together these loosely federated provinces. If the idea of nationalism can be contested with respect to the seventeenth century, the presence of a confessional identity cannot be denied.

The militant Protestantism that emerged after the Reformation strengthened the sense of national belonging. The United Provinces were thus defined by their common hatred of Spain, which they saw as the centre of the Counter-Reformation, their contempt for 'popery' and the 'tyranny' of Philip II. Even if these zealous Calvinists formed a minority of the population, they were extremely influential, many of them being merchants who saw the Catholicism of Spain as the greatest danger to their religious convictions as well as their economic interests.[6]

Dutch identity was thus formed around the notion of freedom and in the rejection and fear of political slavery embodied by the Spanish occupation of the United Provinces, the deployment of the Inquisition and the sending of prisoners to the galleys of the monarchy. Many examples drawn from popular culture convey this idea. In 1615, in his popular play *Moortje*, the playwright Bredero vehemently denounced the slave trade in the Iberian colonies: 'Inhuman manners! Pagan swindle! Men are sold as horses would be sold! In our own city, there are some who, in Pernambuco, practice this kind of commerce; but nothing escapes the sight of God'. Similarly, the jurist Ulric Huber (1626–94) extolled the practice of free labour in the United Provinces: 'We employ as servants only free persons, men or women, who rent their services for a specific wage, for a predefined duration, and under certain conditions that they are entitled to claim; thus, the master and his wife are bound as servants to the conditions of employment'.[7] We might, thus, wonder why the Dutch, who glorified themselves as the champions of liberty and the despisers of servitude, eventually decided to enter the transatlantic slave trade.

The development of the Atlantic slave trade was largely entangled with imperial expansion. The practice of slavery came to be justified by the jurist Hugo Grotius, who wrote in his *De jure belli ac pacis* (*On the Law on War and Peace*), published in 1625, that it was legal in times of war as 'the victors had a natural right to the possessions and labour of the defeated'. As the United Provinces were not at war against any African nations but against the Habsburgs, pillaging Iberian goods – Portugal being a constituent of the monarchy until 1640 – was perfectly justified.[8] The Dutch provinces thus embarked on the conquest of the Atlantic as a response to their desire to attack the Iberians. One of the first pamphleteers to develop that argument was Willem Usselincx, an exiled Antwerpian who, during a stay in Spain, discovered how that kingdom drew its wealth from its American colonies. In 1591, he returned to the United Provinces with a project for colonisation of the American continent, which, by the fight against the Habsburgs, would weaken the enemy's metropolis. According to the British historian Jonathan Israel, 'only expansion across the oceans and in the Indies, and above all the planting of colonies, would place the countries' trade and industry on a sound basis'. The historian and economist Jan de Vries has described how merchants and reformers envisioned this Dutch Atlantic dream, mixing a thirst for evangelisation and economic expansion, to create 'a new world free from the Spanish/Catholic yoke, populated by Dutch settlers and Calvinist Indians, forming a productive and profitable part of a global trading economy'.[9]

Yet, weary of these years of struggle, having just overthrown Spanish tyranny, the young Republic had neither the ideological propensity nor the surplus of population sufficient to establish an empire. So, what really pushed the Dutch out of their borders was the prospect of a lucrative trade, especially against Spain and Portugal (united from 1580 to 1640) and their Catholic monarchies, which continued to threaten Dutch independence. To counter the Iberians, the Dutch had two choices: attack their American colonies or their Portuguese posts in West Africa. In 1623, they established the Grand Design (*Groot Desseyn*), according to which the Dutch West India Company (WIC) would take charge of seizing the possessions of the Iberian Union. The WIC obtained from the Dutch state a monopoly of trade and navigation with the Americas and West Africa and was granted the rights of conquest, colonisation and exploitation of all the territories which came under its control and on which it enjoyed many military, legal and administrative privileges. Its charter dated 3 June 1621 was valid for twenty-four years, after which period it was regularly renewed until 1674, when it was dissolved and replaced by a second West India Company which survived until 1791.[10] Historian Jaap Jacobs has described it as a 'belligerent Company', 'a privately financed weapon in the fight against Spain'. Indeed, extra clauses were added in its 1621 charter, absent from the Dutch East India Company charter, which promised the WIC state support in the shape of fortresses and soldiers.[11]

The first target was Portuguese northern Brazil. As part of a plan devised in 1623 by the Dutch West India Company to attack Portuguese interests in Africa and the Americas, Admiral Jacob Willekens led an expedition of twenty-six ships and 3,300 men to Salvador, the capital of Brazil and the centre of a captaincy attractive for its sugar production. The Portuguese Governor Diogo Tristão de Mendonça Furtado surrendered to the Dutch as soon as they arrived on 8 May 1624, but one year later, on 30 April 1625, the Portuguese colonists recaptured Salvador with the help of a combined Spanish and Portuguese force.

The Dutch did not stop there, however. In 1628, Dutch admiral and privateer Piet Heyn managed to seize an enormous Spanish silver convoy in Matanzas Bay, on the northern coast of Cuba, which was said to have almost caused the bankruptcy of Spain. It certainly helped the Dutch to fund another attempt at Pernambuco, the largest and richest sugar-producing area in the world. The WIC managed to gain control of Olinda on 16 February 1630, and Recife, the capital of Pernambuco, on 3 March. In 1637, the WIC transferred the governing of the new colony of New Holland to Johan Maurits van Nassau-Siegen (John Maurice of Nassau). Soon after his arrival, he captured the province of Ceara, thanks to alliances with Native American tribes, and in 1641, the province of Maranhão. Dutch control now extended across the entire coastline between the Amazon and São Francisco Rivers.[12]

This colonial endeavour, though, proved brief, as the Portuguese planters rebelled and managed to take over the *Nordeste* region and the capital of Recife in 1654.[13] Notwithstanding, the Dutch presence in Brazil triggered the Dutch entry into the slave trade. If the shareholders of the Company had first questioned the desirability of taking part in the slave trade, the need for enslaved labour in the sugar plantations was such that they finally recognised that the company could meet this demand. In 1638, Johan Maurits declared: 'It is impossible to do anything in Brazil without slaves ... and if anyone thinks that is bad, it is a futile scruple'.[14]

The second target of the WIC was the Portuguese trading posts in Central Africa. In 1637, the governor of New Holland organised an expedition from Recife to Elmina on the Gold Coast in present-day Ghana. In 1641, the Dutch seized the ports of Luanda and Benguela, thus gaining control of the Angolan and Congolese slave trade that threatened the loss of the Spanish Empire in America, since Portugal had been providing the Spanish planters with essential enslaved African labour pursuant to the 1494 Treaty of Tordesillas.[15]

In 1634, the Dutch had already captured the Spanish island of Curaçao that became, because of its proximity to the Venezuelan coast, a centre of trading for forty years. The natural harbour of Willemstad became an ideal place for trade and permitted commerce, shipping and piracy to flourish on the island. Salt mining was also developed and served as an export commodity to Europe and for the intercolonial trade. From 1641, Curaçao therefore served as a warehouse for enslaved Africans before they were sent to New Holland, New Netherland, the French and English colonies in the Windward Islands and the South American continent. Some enslaved Africans remained on the island, working either as servants for WIC employees or harvesting crops used to feed the enslaved in transit. Curaçao was strongly connected to New Netherland as Petrus Stuyvesant served as director-general of the two colonies from 1642 to 1654. Between 1659 and 1664, no fewer than 438 enslaved people were exported from Curaçao to New Netherland.[16]

The WIC and the slave trade

This struggle between European powers, putting Protestants against Catholics, also manifested itself in the practice of privateering. The privateer differed from the pirate in the legitimate character of his activity. He received from the sovereign or a delegated authority a commission of war, also referred to as a letter of marque. The recipient was allowed to carry on all forms of hostility permissible at sea by the usages of war, which included taking foreign vessels and crews as prizes. He thus worked in the name of the state when it was officially at war with an enemy country, and he offered the state services and equipment. If the privateer continued his activity after the cessation of hostilities, he became a pirate. The pirate, meanwhile, ran the seas without authorisation; he was a criminal who worked for his own profit exclusively.

Before 1632, the West India Company was a veritable *kaapvaartcompagnie*, a company of privateers. Articles 42 and 43 of the

Company's charter provided for the right to use force and privateering. As a governing body, the WIC could issue its own letters of marque to captains while the States General supplied the warships and appointed the admirals. Unable to control the entire Atlantic basin alone, the WIC received authorisation from the States General in 1632 to grant privateering commissions to individuals and would in turn collect a percentage of the loot. On 6 December 1646, to develop and coordinate privateering in Brazil more specifically, the Dutch state formed the *Brasilse Directie*, an ad hoc structure composed of directors and privateer shipowners, which instituted its own prize court in Recife in 1653 to adjudicate its captures. On 15 September 1653, the directors of the Company met in The Hague to encourage the selling of enslaved Africans emanating from privateering. It thus allowed independent vessels, once emptied of their cargo and enroute to the United Provinces, to capture and loot foreign ships transporting goods within the Company's monopoly jurisdiction.[17] As Gregory O'Malley puts it, looting Spanish goods had always been a target for European powers:

> The primary hope of English (and Dutch and French) privateers was always to snare a Spanish treasure ship ferrying Peruvian silver to Europe, but the corsairs and buccaneers rarely hesitated to prey upon the Spanish American economy in other ways as opportunities presented themselves. Of these secondary opportunities, slavery and the slave trade were among the most profitable. Because enslaved people sold for high prices relative to the amount of space they required aboard a ship, a vessel full of them carried two or three times the cash value as that same vessel transporting colonial produce or other vendible commodities, excepting only gold or silver. In the labour-starved Americas, exploitable workers were the next best thing to coin.[18]

The first enslaved Africans who are said to have been brought to North America in 1619 came on a Dutch privateer bound for Point Comfort, Virginia. Whether they actually were the first enslaved people or not in the English colonies is not my interest here. Instead, I would like to stress the fact that these were randomly disembarked from a Dutch 'man of War' which had stolen them from the Portuguese slave ship *São João Bautista* coming from the Angolan port of Luanda and on its way to Vera Cruz, Mexico. They were part of a group of two hundred captives, taken as a war prize off the Yucatán coast. It is estimated that between a quarter and a third of the enslaved workers imported to America by the Dutch were brought by privateers. Indeed, between 1623 and 1636, Dutch privateers attacked 547 Spanish and Portuguese ships with cargoes valued 118 million guilders and generated 81 million guilders in revenue for the WIC.[19]

Sometimes, the Dutch Republic would use foreign privateers to reach its target. In 1642, the French privateer *La Garce* received a commission from the governor of New Netherland to attack Spanish ships in the West Indies. The vessel arrived in New Amsterdam with a group of 'Spanish negroes', namely, Spaniards who had been captured because of their swarthy skin and had been mistaken for African people. We can wonder if this was a true blunder or whether the Dutch had done it on purpose to incarcerate Spaniards.[20]

The West India Company had entered the slave trade in order to counter the Iberians, but ironically, when the Eighty Years' War ended in 1648, the WIC officially became the first supplier of enslaved workers to the Spanish colonies in America. Indeed, as Spanish merchants could not traffic in enslaved Africans directly, the Crown had to set up contracts called *asientos de negros*, granting a licence to individuals in exchange for the payment of a fee that allowed them to obtain enslaved persons from the Portuguese West African colonies. When they rebelled in 1640 to obtain their independence from Spain, the Portuguese lost the *asiento*, which was transmitted in 1662 to the Dutch, who retained it until 1713.[21]

During this intermediate period (1640–62), Dutch pirates and merchants engaged in illegal trade, supplying their colony of New Holland in Brazil in African captives, and, after 1654, the Spanish colonies – mainly modern Colombia, Mexico, Venezuela, Santo Domingo and Puerto Rico. Between 1648 and 1657, the Dutch managed to transport some 3,800 enslaved Africans to Curaçao and to the Spanish colonies. Most of these were captured from the Portuguese and transported on Dutch boats flying the Spanish flag.[22]

After 1662 and the signing of the *asiento* contract, trade between Dutch merchants and the Spanish colonies was legally pursued. Two private Genoese merchants, Domingo Grillo and Ambrosio Lomellino, were granted this privilege for seven years starting from 1 March 1663. Their contract required that they transported a total of 24,000 enslaved Africans over seven years, or 3,000 to 3,500 per year. Grillo and Lomellino then subcontracted with the West India Company to use WIC ships and transported enslaved people from company posts in Africa to Curaçao and the Spanish colonies. The WIC, which had shipped 2,029 enslaved persons between 1658 and 1662, took 23,466 to Curaçao between 1662 and 1674, to which one must add the 10,273 individuals whose destinations are unknown, for a total of 33,739 enslaved Africans. Alejandro Garcia-Monton analysed the data about the place of purchase for 16,345 enslaved people and concluded that prior to the Second Anglo-Dutch War (1665–67), Dutch merchants played a key role in supplying Grillo and Lomellino: 'Almost 89.5 per cent of those enslaved came from Curaçao. The rest came from Barbados (5.5 per cent) and Jamaica (5 per cent)'.[23]

After concluding peace with Spain in 1648, the United Provinces could no longer justify the actions of these privateers and condemned their activities as acts of piracy. In 1655 and 1657, two cargoes stolen from Spanish ships arrived in New Amsterdam. On each occasion, the directors of the Company wrote to Director-General Stuyvesant to express their concern that such behaviour would have serious consequences to diplomatic relations between the United Provinces, France and Spain. In the 1655 incident, the Spanish ambassador wrote a letter of grievance to the States-General concerning an act of piracy allegedly committed in 1652 by Captain Sebastian De Raeff and his lieutenant Jan van Campen. They had captured the Spanish ship *St Anthoni* off the Jamaican coast and resold the entire cargo, including nine enslaved Africans belonging to Juan Gallardo Ferara and thirty-six others belonging to Antonio De Rivera. The two Dutchmen were arrested, imprisoned for four or five months in Amsterdam before being released and returning to New Netherland. Juan Gallardo could only obtain a promise from the Sieur Grand Escoutette, magistrate at Amsterdam, that the pirates would be charged upon their return. Warned by their relatives, Sebastian De Raeff and Jan van Campen never returned to the colony. Moreover, since the enslaved had been sold several times, it would have been impossible to take them back from their new enslavers without offering them financial compensation.[24]

If Dutch mariners could no longer attack Iberian shipping, they found a new target: England. Privateering thus resumed against

English ships, as the case of the ship *'t Wapen van Amsterdam* shows. This vessel was originally an English ship called *The Merchant's Delight*, owned by John Bonner and X. Young, but it was captured off the coast of Guinea by the Dutch ship *Amsterdam*. The crew was brought to Elmina where the coat of arms of the King of England was erased and replaced by that of the city of Amsterdam, and the ship renamed 'the arms of Amsterdam'. The boat was then sent to Loango (Central Africa) on 21 February 1663, to acquire timber and 101 enslaved Africans for the Curaçao Deputy Director-General Matthias Beck. On 26 June, short of resources, the ship had to stop at Cayman Brac in the Cayman Islands. There, it was attacked by five ships, four sailing under the English flag and one, the *Mary*, under the Portuguese flag piloted by the English pirate Robert Downman. The latter exclaimed 'Coup for the King of Portugal' and fired weapons that killed two Africans and injured a Dutchman. He then took possession of *'t Wapen van Amsterdam* and headed for Virginia, which he reached on 10 September. On 6 October, the Dutch captain Paulus Hayn Ridder fled to New Netherland. On 20 October, Stuyvesant informed Sir William Berkeley, the Governor of Virginia, that he was going to send a delegation to recover the ship and its cargo.

This story shows the complexity of these imperial struggles, in which loyalties to European empires were constantly made and unmade, according to individual will and whims, and at the heart of which were enslaved Africans. Here, the irony of the story lies in the fact that the Dutch governor sought to claim from the English governor a 'commodity' that the Dutch had themselves stolen from the English, proving how subtle and complex these national lines could be.

From a European to a colonial venture: the role of merchants in the slave trade

As the case of piracy has shown, private interests were a key motive in the choices of the actors who shaped the Atlantic world. If the slave trade was initiated by European decision-making in the midst of Atlantic competition between early modern states, these political and religious interests emanating from the metropolitan centres of imperial nations gradually came into conflict with those of the settlers and the private traders who were looking for their own economic benefits. The monopoly of the merchant companies was progressively undermined by the merchants living in the colonies as well as the privateers turned pirates who shared the same objective – to enrich themselves.

New Netherland colonists continuously challenged the monopoly of the West India Company in which the authority of the Dutch Republic was embodied. First, the Company suffered from a lack of unity of purpose and policy, which could be felt between the different chambers that comprised its directorate: the high authority of the WIC, the Nineteen Directors (*Heren XIX*) and the Zeeland chamber tended to defend the Company's monopoly, while the Amsterdam chamber often advocated its curtailment and favoured free trade. This desire to open colonial markets to independent merchants was also encouraged by the financial difficulties the Company habitually faced.[25]

Gradually, the Company was forced to make concessions. In 1650, a new Charter of Freedoms and Exemptions granted the inhabitants of New Netherland the privilege of exporting their products free of charge to all the territories controlled by the WIC, except the coast of Guinea. On the other hand, they would have to pay customs duties on goods exchanged and imported into the colony – for example, twenty guilders per imported enslaved person. On 4 April 1652, the directors of the WIC presented to the States-General a new plan for colonisation and trade, emphasising the fact that the inhabitants were now free to supply themselves with enslaved labourers. A note specified that the merchants embarking in this trade could not go 'further west than Ardre or Popo Sonde and were excluded from the Gold Coast, Cape Verde, Sierra Leone on the Côte de Poivre and the Côte Qua on pain of having their boat and cargo confiscated'. Enslaved individuals were 'taxed at 15 guilders per head, payable in tobacco or beaver furs'.[26]

Enslaved workers from Guinea, though, could only be transported by merchants who received a licence from the Company. On 19 November 1654, the Company's directors agreed to grant certain privileges to a group of independent merchants travelling on the *Witte Paert* (the White Horse). Jan de Sweerts and Dirck Pietersen had asked permission from the assembly to go to the African coast to buy enslaved people and bring them to New Netherland. If the assembly recognised that such a measure would increase the African population of the colony, it still wanted to impose a tariff amounting to 10 per cent per enslaved person payable to the WIC. That way, they managed to bring the largest cargo ever recorded in the history of the colony: 397 individuals. Eventually, on 9 March 1660, the Company's directors agreed to open the slave trade to all the inhabitants of New Netherland but refused to lower the tariff.[27]

The private traders' participation in the slave trade needs to be emphasised. As French historian Pierre Gervais wrote about the eighteenth century: 'merchant activity was a central element in the networks and webs of relationships over the Atlantic ... When closely analysed, however, daily merchant practice does not fit easily into regional categories, whether Atlantic or Imperial'. Similarly, Catia Antunes and Filipa Ribeiro da Silva, in an article on the role of Amsterdam merchants in the Atlantic, have claimed that individual Dutch ventures always played an essential role in global trade. According to them, between 1580 and 1674, private entrepreneurs were responsible for just under half of the total investment in Dutch trafficking in enslaved Africans, with 12 per cent of such voyages having been managed by the WIC. Johannes Postma came to the same conclusion when he asserted that the WIC surrendered its monopoly on the slave trade in New Netherland because it was insignificant.[28]

Indeed, looking more closely at the different vessels that arrived in New Netherland, the majority is shown to have been commanded by free traders. Out of the eleven ships that came between 1627 and 1664, only two were owned by the WIC: the *Musch* in May 1664 brought forty enslaved Africans from Curaçao and the *Gideon* left Guinea and Angola with 421 African people, of whom only 291 were disembarked in August 1664. One vessel was a privateer – *Den Bruynvisch* in 1627, who captured twenty to thirty enslaved persons from a Portuguese ship – and two were pirate ships – the *St Anthoni* that brought enslaved Africans from Jamaica in 1652 and the *Tamandere* which imported fifty enslaved people of unknown origin, so we can assume it was a pirate ship, in 1646. The remaining four vessels were free traders: the *Witte Paert* disembarked 397 enslaved workers in 1655; Jan Pietersen of Dockum, skipper of the

Sphera Mundi, transported five enslaved Africans in 1659; then the *Eyckenboom*, commanded by Captain Henrick Schaeff, arrived in 1660 with twenty Africans on board after having journeyed from Amsterdam to Guinea and Elmina, then to the Dutch West Indies (Curaçao, Aruba and Bonaire) and New Netherland; finally, in August 1660, Dirck Jansen van Oldenburgh, captain of the *Nieuw Neederlandtsen Indiaen*, imported ten black men whom he had acquired from Governor Beck.[29] Gregory O'Malley focuses on the importance of these second trips in terms of the continuity of the infamous 'passage of the middle', which he calls 'final passages'. If the transatlantic trade was managed by large traders, this intercolonial trade also benefited small traders, who were most often more aware of the realities of prices and markets, since long-range traders often came to America with commercial estimates more than one year out of date due to the length of the crossing. Small traders could thus manage the distribution of enslaved people in the secondary ports and avoid the saturation of more limited markets. Indeed, the four free traders who brought enslaved persons to New Amsterdam had departed from Curaçao, thereby feeding this intercolonial trade.[30]

The merchant community in New York had gained considerable importance when the English took over New Netherland in 1664. In the Articles of Capitulation, English governors understood their importance and enabled them to maintain their commercial relations with the Dutch Republic and with other Dutch colonies, thereby bypassing the Laws of Navigation. Many prominent slave traders were descendants of old Dutch families, such as Frederick Philipse, who arrived in New Netherland as a carpenter in 1653 and died in 1702 as the wealthiest merchant and the largest trafficker of enslaved people in New York. The first enslaved Africans he imported to his estate, Philipsburg Manor, arrived from Barbados in June 1685 aboard the *Charles*, which Philipse had sent to Amsterdam to trade furs for muskets, textiles, chains and barrels, that is, a whole series of objects essential for a successful slaving voyage. After paying customs in England, the ship set off for Angola, where the crew acquired 140 (or 146) Africans before departing for Barbados. On the way to New York, fourteen out of twenty-three captives remaining on board died and nine were sent to his manor. In June 1685, Philipse was sued for importing these enslaved Africans illegally into the colony, but he was acquitted thanks to his many political connections. Slave trading had thus become more than an economic activity involving actors in each corner of the Atlantic space. It was a real colonial venture, in which traders were ready to go against the prescriptions of European states and colonial authorities in order to pursue their personal enrichment and political power.[31]

Conclusion

The Dutch entered the slave trade in the context of imperial struggles forged in Hispanophobia and anti-Catholicism. We can underline the irony here because it was by wanting to free itself from the yoke of the Habsburg monarchy, by denouncing its political tyranny and by despising its barbaric practices, that the Dutch Republic found itself involved in the importation of Africans to the New World and even became the official supplier for the Spanish Crown. The establishment of slavery in New Netherland was therefore the result of an imperial struggle in which European political powers played a leading role. By founding merchant companies and commissioning privateers to import enslaved Africans to develop their colonies in the Atlantic world, the Dutch Republic had the sole purpose of expanding its empire in order to reduce Spanish presence in America. As historians Heywood and Thornton have written, 'this initial illicit trade opened the opportunity for the Dutch to establish a permanent presence in the Americas, and it also established a precedent for using enslaved Africans as labor in the new colonies'. Accordingly, if the Dutch Empire was in no way comparable to the British Empire as we envision it in the nineteenth century, the Dutch were able to make themselves indispensable to the Atlantic world. The colonial merchants in New Netherland managed to develop a tight network of intercolonial trade that gave them control over the region and enabled them to realise their colonising ambition. They managed to leave their mark on many colonies from Brazil, Curaçao, Suriname to New Netherland, which still celebrate their Dutch heritage today, a legacy which is, however, intrinsically linked with slavery.[32]

Notes

1. See Andrea Mosterman, *Spaces of Enslavement: A History of Slavery and Resistance in Dutch New York* (Ithaca: Cornell University Press, 2021); Anne-Claire Faucquez, *De la Nouvelle-Néerlande à New York: La Naissance d'une Société Esclavagiste 1624–1712* (Paris: Les Indes Savantes, 2021); Thelma Wills Foote, *Black and White Manhattan: The History of Racial Formation in New York City, 1624–1783* (New York: Oxford University Press, 2004); Leslie Harris, *In the Shadow of Slavery: African Americans in New York City, 1626–1863* (Chicago: University of Chicago Press, 2003).
2. Pieter C. Emmer and Wim W. Klooster, 'The Dutch Atlantic, 1600–1800: Expansion without empire', *Itinerario* 23, no. 2 (1999), 48–69. The great work on the Dutch trade is Jonathan Israel, *Dutch Primacy in World Trade, 1585–1740* (Oxford: Oxford University Press, 1989). See also Catia A.P. Antunes and Jos L.L. Gommans (eds.), *Exploring the Dutch Empire: Agents, Networks and Institutions, 1600–2000* (London: Bloomsbury, 2015).
3. J.H. Elliott, *Empires of the Atlantic World: Britain and Spain in America, 1492–1830* (New Haven: Yale University Press, 2006), xiv; Claudia Schnurmann, 'Atlantic trade and American identities: The correlations of supranational commerce, political opposition, and colonial regionalism', in Peter A. Coclanis (ed.), *The Atlantic Economy during the Seventeenth and Eighteenth Centuries* (Columbia: University of South Carolina Press, 2005), 186–204; Christian J. Koot, *Empire at the Periphery: British Colonists, Anglo-Dutch Trade, and the Development of the British Atlantic, 1621–1713* (New York: New York University Press, 2011), 11–18.
4. Douglas R. Burgess Jr, *The Politics of Piracy: Crime and Civil Disobedience in Colonial America* (Lebanon: University Press of New England, 2014), 8. See Chapter 9 by Charlotte Carrington-Farmer in this volume on the role played by pirates in undermining colonial trade.
5. Anne-Claire Faucquez, 'La Compagnie des Indes occidentales néerlandaises en Nouvelle Néerlande', in Éric Roulet (ed.), *Les premières compagnies dans l'Atlantique 1600–1650, I. Structures et modes de fonctionnement* (Aachen: Shaker Verlag, 2017), 13–34.
6. Susanne Lachenicht explains in the first chapter of this volume how composite the notion of 'state' was and that colonisation had been made possible thanks to 'private investors'; Jonathan Israel, *The Dutch Republic: Its Rise, Greatness, and Fall, 1477–1806* (New York: Oxford University Press, 1995), 179–230; Virginia W.

Lunsford, *Piracy and Privateering in the Golden Age Netherlands* (New York: Palgrave Macmillan, 2005), 79; Simon Schama, *The Embarrassment of Riches: An Interpretation of Dutch Culture in the Golden Age* (New York: Alfred A. Knopf, 1987), 84–91; Johannes Postma, *The Dutch in the Atlantic Slave Trade, 1600–1815* (Cambridge: Cambridge University Press, 1992), 8.

7 Simon van Leeuween, *Commentaries on the Roman-Dutch Law* (London, 1820), 28, 66. Bredero cited in Pieter C. Emmer, *Les Pays Bas et la Traite des Noirs* (Paris: Karthala, 2005), 34.

8 Pieter Emmer, *The Dutch Slave Trade, 1500–1800* (New York: Berghahn Books, 2006), 56.

9 Israel, Dutch Primacy in World Trade, 84; Jan de Vries, 'The Dutch Atlantic economies', in Coclanis (ed.), *The Atlantic Economy*, 1–29.

10 Ernst van den Boogaart and Pieter Emmer, 'The Dutch participation in the Atlantic slave trade, 1596–1650', in Henry A. Gemery and Jan S. Hogendorn (eds.), *The Uncommon Market: Essays in the Economic History of the Atlantic Slave Trade* (New York: Academic Press, 1979), 353–71; Pieter C. Emmer, 'The West India Company, 1621–1791: Dutch or Atlantic', in Leonard Blussé and Femme Gaastra (eds.), *Companies and Trade: On Companies during the Ancien Régime* (The Hague: Nijhoff, 1981), 71–96.

11 Jaap Jacobs, *The Colony of New Netherland: A Dutch Settlement in Seventeenth-Century America* (Ithaca: Cornell University Press, 2009), 28; 'Charter of Privileges and Exemptions the Dutch West India Company. June 7, 1629', *DRCHNY* 2: 553–7.

12 Postma, *The Dutch in the Atlantic Slave Trade*, 18–21. The booty seized by Heyn's fleet amounted to 11.5 million guilders in gold, silver, indigo and cochineal.

13 Lou Roper's chapter in this volume addresses these colonial failures in the first half of the seventeenth century.

14 Quoted in Harvey M. Feinberg, *Africans and Europeans in West Africa: Elminans and Dutchmen on the Gold Coast during the Eighteenth Century* (Philadelphia: American Philosophical Society, 1989), 31, and Charles Ralph Boxer, *The Dutch in Brazil, 1624–1654* (Oxford: Clarendon Press, 1957), 83. There were Dutch plantations in Guiana using enslaved Africans by the first decade of the seventeenth century.

15 Ray A. Kea, *Settlements, Trade, and Polities in the Seventeenth-Century Gold Coast* (Baltimore: Johns Hopkins University Press, 1982), 38–50, 133–4.

16 Cornelis Ch. Goslinga, *The Dutch in the Caribbean and on the Wild Coast, 1580–1680* (Assen: Van Gorcum, 1971), 264–75. Jaap Jacobs

believes that if Curaçao began to play a role in the slave trade in 1641, it was hardly a warehouse at that stage and played a major role only after 1665.
17 'Resolution of the West India Company to Encourage Privateering', *DRCHNY* 14: 214; Roberto Barazzutti, 'La guerre de course hollandaise sous Louis XIV: essai de quantification', *Revue Historique de Dunkerque et du Littoral* 37 (2004), 269–80.
18 Gregory E. O'Malley, *Final Passages: The Intercolonial Slave Trade of British America, 1619–1807* (Chapel Hill: University of North Carolina Press, 2016), 86.
19 Linda M. Heywood and John K. Thornton, 'In search of the 1619 African arrivals: Enslavement and middle passage', *Virginia Magazine of History and Biography* 127, no. 3 (2019), 200–11. We have not found yet any source relating this event but as the Company never expressed its intention to import enslaved people, we can suppose they came from privateers. Historians have agreed on this arrival date of the first enslaved individuals as those who petitioned for freedom in 1644 claimed they had been in the colony for eighteen years: Edna Greene Medford, *The New York African Burial Ground History Final Report* (Washington: Howard University Press, 2004), 12; Robert J. Swan, 'First Africans into New Netherland, 1625 or 1626?', *de Halve Maen* 6 (1993), 75–82; Johannes Postma, 'A monopoly relinquished: The West India Company and the Atlantic slave trade', *de Halve Maen* 70 (1997), 81–8.
20 David T. Valentine (ed.), *Manual of the Corporation of New York, 1841–70* (New York, 1860), 764. This practice happened repeatedly with English people as well. In 1711, Governor Hunter had to make his apologies to the Lords of Trade for having arrested and imprisoned 'Spanish Indians', *DRCHNY* 5: 342.
21 Postma, *The Dutch in the Atlantic Slave Trade*, 31.
22 *DIHST* 1: 138–40; Wim Klooster, *Illicit Riches: Dutch Trade in the Caribbean, 1648–1795* (Leiden: KITLV Press, 1998), 106; Postma, *The Dutch in the Atlantic Slave Trade*, 32.
23 Gregory E. O'Malley and Alex Borucki, 'Patterns in the intercolonial slave trade across the Americas before the nineteenth century', *Tempo* 23 (2017), 314–38 at 325; Wim Klooster, *The Dutch Moment: War, Trade, and Settlement in the Seventeenth-Century Atlantic World* (Ithaca: Cornell University Press, 2016), 181–2; Alejandro Garcia-Monton, 'The cost of the asiento: Private merchants, royal monopolies, and the making of the transatlantic slave trade in the Spanish empire', in Amelia Polonia and Catia Antunes (eds.), *Mechanisms of Global Empire Building* (Porto: CITCEM, 2017), 11–34 at 17.

24 DRCHNY 1: 577, 581, 617; 2: 1–4, 23–43; *DIHST* 3: 415–19.
25 Postma, *The Dutch in the Atlantic Slave Trade*, 23.
26 DRCHNY 1: 364, 404; 14: 166.
27 DRCHNY 14: 162; *DIHST* 3: 415; Gregory E. O' Malley, 'Beyond the middle passage: Slave migration from the Caribbean to North America, 1619–1807', *WMQ* 66, no. 1 (2009), 125–72; Cathy Matson, *Merchants and Empire: Trading in Colonial New York* (Baltimore: Johns Hopkins University Press, 1998), 334.
28 Pierre Gervais, 'Neither imperial, nor Atlantic: A merchant perspective on international trade in the eighteenth century', *History of European Ideas* 34, no. 4 (2008), 465–73; Catia Antunes and Filipa Ribeiro da Silva, 'Amsterdam merchants in the slave trade and African commerce, 1580s–1670s', *Tijdschirft voor Economisch en Sociale Geschiedenis* 9, no. 4 (2012), 3–30; Postma, *The Dutch in the Atlantic Slave Trade*, 25.
29 *DIHST* 3: 444.
30 O'Malley, *Final Passages*.
31 Robert C. Ritchie, 'London merchants, the New York market, and the recall of Sir Edmund Andros', *New York History* 57, no. 1 (1976), 4–29 at 8–9; Peter R. Christoph (ed.), *The Dongan Papers, 1683–1688* (Syracuse: Syracuse University Press, 1993–96), 171–2, 268–73; Kenneth Scott, *New York City Court Records, 1684–1760: Genealogical Data from the Court of Quarter Sessions* (Washington: National Genealogical Society, 1982), 2.
32 Quoted in Linda M. Rupert, *Creolization and Contraband: Curacao in the Early Modern Atlantic World* (Athens: University of Georgia Press, 2012), 58.

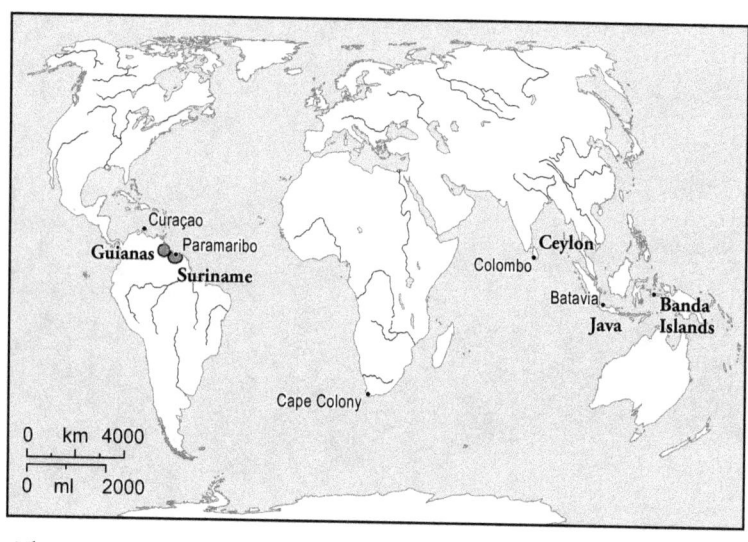

The Dutch colonies involved in the development of unfree labour within the Dutch Empire, eighteenth century

6

The control of unfree labour across the Dutch Empire in the eighteenth century

Elisabeth Heijmans and Rafaël Thiebaut

The early modern Dutch Empire extended from Asia to the Americas and, as the previous chapter has shown, was intrinsically linked with slavery. During the eighteenth century, these extra-European territories were almost all administered by trading companies that were private enterprises, principally the Dutch East India and West India Companies.[1] The delegation of sovereign rights – such as issuing legislation and implementing justice – by the Dutch Republic to these companies had significant social implications. Both companies became increasingly involved in the governance of ethnically, religiously and socially diverse societies, in which the need to control labour was amplified by the institution of slavery and the fear of slave revolts and social unrest. Legislation regulating labour served the colonial purpose of ensuring the resilience of the different colonial labour regimes (and, in particular, the institution of slavery) and enabled the extractive capacity of companies. However, as shown in the laws and proceedings of criminal courts, this process was not exclusively top-down. In practice, company-led colonial administrators had to adapt their laws and prosecution to local power dynamics featuring a variety of actors, free and unfree.

Among the free population of the colonies, the interests of colonial administrators and freemen (*vrijburgers*) did not always align. They did not constitute strictly distinct groups: freemen were slaveowning planters, merchants and entrepreneurs, while some administrators also owned plantations and enslaved people.[2] However, they had diverging concerns. Private commercial interests dictated the political lines of human traffickers, but colonial administrators had to balance their policies between the interests of the Dutch State-General, the Company itself and the influence of the local colonial elites, who challenged the restrictions imposed by the metropole.[3] Lastly, while being devoid of political power, the unfree population was the basis of the colonial system and could exercise some influence through mass desertion or revolts.

Much has been written about the diversity of colonial societies and about the institution of slavery within them.[4] Yet, the historiography has been divided between the Indian Ocean and the Atlantic worlds, and forms of labour control in these separate spheres have not been compared. In the Atlantic, the preponderance of European-controlled plantation slavery and the racialisation of enslaved societies have dominated historical debates.[5] This stands in contrast with the apparent diversity and openness of the Indian Ocean world, where labour conditions were heterogeneous and the presence of strong states in South, Southeast and East Asia led to the development of an intricate economic system.[6] Building on the recent historiographical trend partially refuting this dichotomy, we take a comparative approach to the control of unfree labour in the early modern Dutch Empire. This global perspective enables us to point to similarities and differences in the strategies of company-led colonial institutions in their separate contexts. While we are aware that forms of coerced labour varied greatly throughout the empire, we focus here particularly on slavery.[7] The worlds of free and unfree labourers were not strictly separated and overlapped continuously, in spite of legal efforts to disconnect them as much as possible. Nevertheless, we consider enslaved labour a relevant entry point into the strategies of labour control by the Dutch colonial administration at global level.

This chapter explores how the Dutch colonial governments regulated the behaviour and living conditions of enslaved people in various Dutch settlements stretched over the Atlantic and Indian Oceans in the eighteenth century, which represents a period of consolidation of colonial possessions.[8] By doing so, we shed light on what the editors of the volume call the 'diversity of imperial experiences', by focusing not only on the European colonisers and legislators but also on the colonised and enslaved.

We use locally issued by-laws compiled in *plakaatboeken* from Batavia (present-day Jakarta), Suriname and the Cape, but also Ceylon (present-day Sri Lanka), the Guianas (Berbice, Essequibo and Demerara) and Curaçao. We have systematically analysed court records from the colonial criminal courts of Batavia and Suriname for case studies involving enslaved individuals.[9] We focus particularly on Suriname and Batavia, which were pivotal possessions in their respective regions, and on the Cape Colony, an enslaved society at the edge of two worlds. We start by providing some contextual information about slavery in the Dutch early modern colonies and its legal context. We analyse Dutch legislation issued by company-led colonial authorities and court cases relating to the control of enslaved people. We then delve into the regulation regarding enslavement and analyse whether these regulations were implemented in practice.

Slavery, law and the Dutch Empire

Enslaved individuals accomplished a wide range of tasks and were of crucial economic importance in Dutch colonial societies. Slavery in the Atlantic world has been characterised as a large-scale, agricultural and cash-crop production economy.[10] It was also the case in some parts of the Indian Ocean world, like the Cape Colony and the plantations on Ceylon, Java and the Banda Islands, but the enslaved also worked in mines, construction and ports, and performed many domestic tasks.[11] Dutch reliance on unfree labour in the colonies is reflected by the tens of thousands of enslaved workers present there. In the Atlantic world, there was a steady increase in numbers directly linked to the transatlantic slave trade. The situation in the East was different as there was easier access to other forms of labour like *corvée*,[12] contract and wage labour. Nonetheless, enslaved persons still accounted for an impressive part of the population in different port cities like Batavia and Colombo,[13] or in plantation colonies like the Guianas and the Cape.[14] While in the Atlantic world, the Dutch instated an enslaved society and its supply nearly *ex nihilo*, the VOC used and developed social systems and trade networks already present in the region.[15] In this environment, the Dutch or European minority lived in constant fear of rebellion and other subversive acts, such as the desertion of the coerced population on which their power was based. Dutch colonial authority soon felt the urgency to control enslaved individuals through legislation.

The Dutch Government had delegated the government and administration of justice in overseas settlements to chartered companies through the foundational monopoly charters of 1602 and 1621 for the VOC and WIC respectively.[16] These companies authorised company administrators, who constituted the colonial Government in the settlements, to draft their own legislation locally. In matters involving enslaved individuals, colonial officials used colonial ordinances issued locally (*plakaten*), influenced and complemented by Roman law. In the Indian Ocean, the colonial legislation about slavery was compiled in 1642 in a book of statutes (*Statuten van Batavia*) to be used in all Dutch settlements of the region.[17] By contrast, in the Dutch settlements of the Atlantic, no overarching 'slave code' can be found.[18] Nevertheless, the legislation enacted locally by colonial administrators throughout the empire is revealing of the different concerns of colonial governments in their attempts to control the labour force. It is also indicative of the lack of control of company administrators on the enslaved population and their enslavers, and of the need to adapt to existing practices and balance power locally.

In the Dutch colonies, criminal courts were closely connected to company-led colonial governments and their memberships overlapped. Access to colonial criminal justice was extremely limited for enslaved individuals, since, from a legal perspective, enslaved individuals were considered as property, not people.[19] For instance, in Curaçao, their testimony against white people was not accepted.[20] In general, it was difficult for enslaved people to file complaints to colonial authorities and even more difficult to build a case solid enough against whites.[21] An illustration of this is the fact that in Suriname, criminal court cases involving enslaved victims were disproportionally low compared to the number of enslaved people living in the colonies.[22]

As in other slave-based empires, multiple forms of resistance against the institution of slavery existed within the Dutch settlements, ranging from disobedience and desertion to physical violence and slave revolt. The enslaved, however, faced brutal torture and even death when they acted against the authority of their 'masters'. For instance, in Batavia in 1758, an enslaved man called Batjo was sentenced to be impaled until death followed for having tried to kill his 'mistress', while another named Panaij, who had attacked and wounded his 'master' (*lijfheer*), was wheeled.[23] In Curaçao, in 1716, enslaved people accused of the double murder of Jan Cornelisz and his pregnant wife were dismembered and tortured before being beheaded.[24]

Controlling public behaviour

Much of the colonial legislation about enslaved individuals in the Dutch Empire regulated their behaviour in public places. Some restrictions were directly related to the fear of revolt, like the ban on enslaved people carrying weapons.[25] The movement of the enslaved population in public spaces was limited in all the regions under Dutch control. Many ordinances forbade them to go out without written authorisation from their 'masters' or to walk the streets in the dark after sunset. Similar restrictions were issued in Ceylon, Suriname, the Guianas and the Cape.[26] In Curaçao, the same ordinance was reissued seven times over the course of a century, illustrating the difficulty in enforcing such a ban.[27]

Company administrators in the settlements also strongly regulated the way the enslaved could act in their spare time. For example, in the Western colonies with a high enslaved population like Curaçao, Suriname, the Guianas and the Cape Colony, they were not allowed to gather.[28] Other restrictions included bans on gambling and the interdiction for pub owners to serve them alcohol.[29] Multiple ordinances were concerned with limiting enslaved person festivities, which were outlawed in Suriname in the early eighteenth century.[30] For instance, the *watermamadans*, a ritual centred around the African water goddess or spirit, was particularly feared and repressed by the authorities,[31] as was black magic like *obeah*.[32] Cultural expressions in public were perceived as threatening to the colonial social order. Other restrictions involved less obviously threatening themes such as the way certain groups of enslaved people could dress, which varied according to the region and the ethnic diversity of the servile population present. In Ceylon, for instance, Muslim enslaved persons were not allowed to cover their heads, while in Suriname, the enslaved could not wear hats, shoes or stockings.[33] These restrictions were created to establish a hierarchy among enslaved people and those who enslaved them, as well as to make the boundaries between the free and the unfree more visible.

Maintaining colonial social order was a difficult task because of the high percentage of enslaved individuals in the population, the continuous interactions between free and unfree people and the conflicts between 'masters' and colonial authorities.[34] In Suriname, for instance, legal restrictions only had a limited impact on the movement of enslaved persons, and, consequently, their resistance remained important.[35] In some regions, rules on the behaviour of enslaved individuals were combined into one set of regulations.[36] Often prompted by continuous resistance, they reveal how ineffective control by colonial authorities actually was. An example of such a set of regulations was issued in 1754 in the Cape Colony 'because for some time slaves have shown more assurance and more rowdiness, and they have ignored the many orders placed against them in the ordinances'.[37]

A large number of these rules were concerned with controlling the movement of the enslaved, their behaviour in public and their cultural and social activities, in order to separate them from the rest of society. Others, such as the prohibition to buy goods from enslaved individuals, limited their economic independence, which could increase their chances of reaching freedom. This set of regulations reasserted the authority of 'masters' over enslaved people and protected the private property of enslavers. It is comparable to other sets of legislation in Dutch settlements where slave resistance was growing through armed resistance and the creation of maroon communities, especially but not exclusively in the Americas.[38]

For instance, the Cape Colony in the 1730s was subjected to multiple acts of resistance from maroon communities living in the countryside in the area of Table Mountain. In 1736, maroons were even suspected of having set fire to parts of the city of Cape Town.[39] As a result, social control intensified throughout the Cape Colony. In one court case, two free Blacks and three enslaved persons were found in the street after 10 p.m., and all five of them were brutally whipped and put in chains.[40] The distinction between free and unfree was increasingly blurred and punishment enforced along racial lines rather than along free or unfree status.

In the Indian Ocean, it is important to mention that a large part of the legislation regarding the enslaved regulated the private property of enslaved people through mandatory registration and forbade enslaving by specific groups. For instance, in Batavia in 1621, Christians were banned from selling their enslaved people to non-Christians.[41] In Ceylon, the same legislation was issued three times between 1650 and 1750, forcing 'Moors' and 'Pagans' to sell their Christian enslaved individuals to Christians.[42] The diversity of 'masters' in the East created different priorities for company-led legislators in the Indian Ocean as they attempted to limit the power of non-Christian 'masters'.

Living and working conditions of enslaved people

Another aspect regulated by company-led colonial administrators concerned living and working conditions of privately owned enslaved people. Recurrent by-laws were issued around the mid-eighteenth century in Berbice and Essequibo expecting plantation owners to provide enough food and clothes for their enslaved individuals.[43] In Berbice and Suriname, administrators also started regulating the quality and quantity of the plots of land assigned to the enslaved for their sustenance, also referred to as slave gardens or *kostgronden*, under the penalty of a fine for plantation owners.[44] Colonial authorities further controlled the planters through 'inspections and visitations' by local authorities, for instance, in 1664 and 1773, to implement the rules. The issues remained unsolved as a new by-law of 1780 ordered 'masters' to give a clear and specific report of their enslaved persons' gardens.[45] Similarly, in Berbice, an ordinance of 1740 ordered planters to provide garden plots for their enslaved people. However, administrators later stated that they found those regulations were incorrectly attended to and further regulated on this issue in 1804 and 1806.[46] Additionally to this attempt at enforcing slave garden rules, legislation on the basic nutrition of enslaved people was continuously reissued in the Atlantic settlements until the beginning of the nineteenth century.[47] In Suriname in 1775, 'masters' were to be prosecuted in court if they did not provide 'enough' food, clothing and medical care to their enslaved labourers.[48] Whether the shift in punishment from a fine to prosecution in court was actually implemented is difficult to assess. In Curaçao, a by-law of 1795 reissued in 1812 forbade 'masters' from deducting rum, sugar and tobacco from food rations, revealing attempts by 'masters' to evade regulation on the basic nutritional provisions of the people they enslaved. In addition, in the last quarter of the eighteenth century and the beginning of the nineteenth century, throughout the Dutch Atlantic colonies, authorities tried to regulate in detail the maximal length of workdays and to forbid 'masters' from making their enslaved individuals work on Sundays and holidays, except for 'house slaves' and 'urgent cases'.[49] The ordinances regulating the working days and hours which 'masters' could impose upon slaves had to be reissued, and in Berbice, for instance, legislators once again stated explicitly that such legislation was easily ignored.[50]

The regulation on the living and working conditions of enslaved people throughout the colonies testifies of an awareness of the Dutch colonial authorities that the entire colony's existence and development was based on the perpetuation of slavery. According to legislators in Suriname in 1784, it was for that reason that 'the situation for slaves should be bearable and in accordance with the reasons and obligations of humanity'.[51] However, rather than a 'humanitarian' goal, these laws were aimed at upholding the institution of slavery and, in particular, plantation slavery in the colonies. However, the repetitive issuing of the same by-laws testifies of the inability (or unwillingness) of administrators to enforce them on planters. In the different versions of the legislation through time, punishments remained relatively mild: enslavers were either fined or at times threatened with prosecution. In addition, the rules aimed at protecting enslaved persons did not improve through the different legislations. The terms used, such as 'enough food' or 'proper rations', remained vague and their correct implementation was therefore difficult to assess, leaving a wide discretionary power to enslavers. The position of colonial authorities was ambiguous. On the one hand, they sought to uphold the system of enslavement exposed by mass desertion, high mortality rates and rebellion, and, on the other hand, they were reluctant to interfere in the administration of plantations.

While an overwhelming number of criminal court cases in the colonies in the Atlantic Ocean dealt with the prosecution of slave desertion and resistance, some were concerned with the living and working conditions of the enslaved under their enslavers' authority. Maltreatment of enslaved individuals, if proven, was punishable. In one case in Suriname in 1775, an enslaved individual named Tam complained about seven years of ill treatment by his 'master' Treboulon, who forced him to work on Sundays and did not allow his enslaved people time to eat at noon. Treboulon was ordered by the court to treat his enslaved persons better (i.e. according to the existing ordinance) and an inspector was sent to the plantation Nieuw Timotibo to ensure that the workforce received enough food.[52]

Enslaved individuals took tremendous risks when they defied the authority of their enslavers and complained about them to the authorities.[53] The Governing Council (*Hof van Politie en Criminele Justitie*) did not always recognise their complaints were justified. In Suriname, in 1775, the enslaved individuals of the D'Eendragt plantation complained to the colonial authorities in Paramaribo that they were made to work on Sundays, received bad food and poor medical care and were abused, one enslaved woman having almost died from her punishment. However, the judges considered that the plaintiffs' pleas were based 'on frivolous excuses' and ordered they be beaten by *Spaanse bok* in the fortress of Paramaribo.[54] That same year, the enslaved people of the La Jalousie plantation came to their 'master' to complain about the harsh treatment of the plantation manager Beekman, who referred them to the public prosecutor (*fiscaal*). Interrogated by the Governing Council, Beekman tried to downplay the harshness of his actions and insisted the enslaved deserved being whipped. His fellow white officers supported him by arguing they knew nothing about his harsh treatment of his workers, but they could not deny his abusive methods. In the confrontation with the enslaved people, Beekman could not refute his treatment either and he was sentenced to pay 800 guilders as well as all the judicial costs.[55] However, it does not seem that Beekman was replaced.

We see similarities between the strategies of colonial authorities in Suriname, Batavia and the Cape. Indeed, they were designed to maintain the status quo, that is, to protect the dominant class from the servile population unless their misconduct was undoubtedly proven. In the Indian Ocean, the Statutes of Batavia (1642) contained a set of legislation regulating the living and working conditions of enslaved individuals. For instance, if a sick or impotent enslaved individual was mistreated by his or her 'master', he or she could be freed by the judge.⁵⁶ In the early eighteenth century, measures were issued to improve the working conditions of enslaved people at the service of the VOC.⁵⁷ However, the Statutes also stated that an enslaved individual who accused their 'master' falsely would be whipped and put in chains. In the Indian Ocean, court cases relating to enslaved people accusing their enslavers of maltreatment systematically referred to the ordinance of 17 October 1752 concerning the 'control of slaves', which punished defamation as 'the worst thing a slave could do to his master'.⁵⁸ Enslaved persons had to be certain of their case if they wanted to have a chance to succeed, as the slightest doubt would swing the balance in favour of their 'masters'.

In 1757, for instance, Astrea, the enslaved girl of Captain Pieter Pietersz, complained the 'master' had enchained her and her fellow enslaved without the necessary permission. However, inconsistencies were found in her story and her accusation was deemed unfounded. She was flogged publicly as an example and put in chains for ten years.⁵⁹ Some twenty years later, the excellent reputation of a man called Wimmercrantz played against the testimony of Aron, who accused him of maltreating his enslaved individuals, sometimes even causing their death. Other enslaved people were heard and Wimmercrantz's estate was inspected, but Aron's accusations were equated with defamation and he was hanged.⁶⁰ In 1748, Rudolf van Sant was accused of hitting his enslaved person Coridon van Bengale in the face several times with a *chiambok* (small cane) for having wrongly arranged some paintings in his house. But no proof could be found and Coridon was charged with wantonness (*baldadigheid*) and sentenced to being whipped, branded and put in chains for twenty-five years.⁶¹ In only a few rare cases was evidence found of enslavers punished for their cruelty.

The case of the Cape Colony is quite unique. While being judicially part of the East Indian empire of the VOC, it resembled the plantation societies of the Caribbean. Therefore, local authorities were concerned with the same issues as in the Americas and often opted for identical solutions while also applying the Statutes of Batavia. The ordinances issued in the colony itself are silent about the punishment of 'masters' who abused their enslaved individuals. A law stated that enslaved persons should be given new clothes twice a year because of the colder weather conditions than in Batavia, but this only applied to enslaved individuals owned by the VOC.[62] However, some court cases addressed the issue. In 1763, for example, Christina Strang was reported to the colonial authorities for abusive behaviour and was accused of having killed one of her enslaved persons two years earlier. It was only brought to the court's attention when some of her enslaved individuals went to Cape Town. Christina Strang tried to defend herself, but she was found guilty and had to pay a fine of fifty silver coins. The enslaved individual who had been central to her condemnation had to be sold and could never be in the possession of the Strang family again.[63] Even though two years had passed, the gravity of the incident shows that enslaved people were aware that the authority of their 'masters' was not without limits and was subjected to the rules of the local administration. Despite this, it is difficult to establish how seriously these accusations were taken.

Limiting domestic jurisdiction

An important factor of enslaved desertion, high mortality or revolts was the abusive treatment of 'masters', concerning not only nutrition and clothes but also physical punishments, enabled by the wide domestic jurisdiction they had over those they enslaved. Through domestic jurisdiction, plantation owners were allowed by the colonial authorities to punish enslaved people without reporting it to higher authorities, with the exception of the death penalty and extreme mutilations.[64] This naturally led to abuse: punishments on some plantations in Suriname were recognised to be extremely cruel.[65] Therefore, in the second half of the eighteenth century, legislation was created in the Dutch Atlantic to define and limit domestic jurisdiction.

In Suriname, legislation issued in 1759 forbade the use of a stick for flogging and 'limited' the number of lashes to eighty. If the plantation overseer wanted to administer a more severe sentence, he needed the authorisation of the plantation owner. The same by-law was reissued in 1784 and complemented the prohibition of existing practices of enslavers regarded as extremely violent.[66] The penalty for not respecting these laws was first a fine, and, in

1784, legislators added criminal court prosecution. Despite this change, these laws were not always respected in practice. In Berbice, regulation prosecuting 'masters' who inflicted cruel punishment on their enslaved people was issued in 1764; yet, four years later, another by-law stated that the punishment of the enslaved would be prosecuted if it led to the death of the victim after twenty-four hours.[67] In Demerara, laws were issued forbidding 'masters' from burying their enslaved persons after punishment in 1779, and again in 1784, testifying to the difficulties encountered by colonial authorities in preventing 'masters' from administrating penalties that led to the death of their enslaved individuals.[68] In 1771, Essequibo colonial authorities urged planters to punish enslaved persons in a 'Christian' and 'not cruel' manner.[69] Berbice followed much later in limiting the form and severity of corporal punishments. In 1810, domestic punishment was 'limited' to thirty-nine lashes per day.[70] The reissuing of the exact same legislation four years later points to the inefficiency of these limitations on domestic jurisdiction.

Legislation limiting domestic jurisdiction was often shunned by white employees and difficult for company authorities to enforce.[71] The laws limiting punishment were often vague and when they were precise, they still allowed for harsh sentences such as the eighty lashes in Suriname. In other colonies, like Berbice, these laws were issued much later or even not at all, like in Curaçao. Enslavers took advantage of these disparities and ignorance of the law was often used as an argument in maltreatment or the excessive punishment of the enslaved.[72] Plantation manager Du Peyrou, for example, punished three enslaved persons that were suspected of desertion instead of sending them to Paramaribo as the law required.[73] Excessive punishment was also often difficult to prove and only became visible in extreme cases, when the sentence administered by the 'master' or plantation manager resulted in death. These tragic incidents are related in the records. Next to the Orleanacreek in Commewijne, Suriname, was the Practica plantation, run by plantation manager Gerrit Hendrik Samuel. One day in 1762, Samuel severely punished the *kuyperneger* (coopernegro) Avantuur, whipping him with two different whips, beating him with a *Spaanse bok* and then a *tasstok*, resulting in his death.[74] Governor Nepveu condemned 'these methods of punishment' as being contrary to the Regulation of

Plantation Employees of 1759 (*Reglement voor plantagebedienden*) and lamented 'the killing of a negro in a cruel manner'.[75]

Another case occurred some thirteen years later, on the Clemensburg plantation near the Motcreek, where a man called Jan Hendrik Borghard was manager. He punished the enslaved woman Avia with the *Spaanse bok*, although plantation employees were only allowed to punish the enslaved with whipping. Avia died two days after her ordeal. Borghard was found guilty of breaching the same ordinance as the previously mentioned manager, Samuel. Borghard defended himself by saying that he ignored the content of the Regulation of Plantation Employees, that Avia had wounded a black officer with a sword and that it had therefore been necessary to make an example of her.[76] In both cases, the white manager was punished for *kastijding*, or excessive domestic punishment. Borghard was fined three hundred guilders, which amounted to the reimbursement of the 'price' of the enslaved person plus the costs of the trial. Samuel, on the other hand, was banished from the colony of Suriname and had to pay six hundred guilders to reimburse the cost of the enslaved individual he had killed.

The multiple attempts to curb domestic jurisdiction signal that local authorities were aware of the necessity to limit the harshness of punishments but not to suppress them altogether. In addition, sentences against individuals not respecting these limits were not consistent and, as in the case of Borghard, rather clement. In 1762, several enslaved workers of Hermanus Scheltus explained that the enslaved girl Francina had run away for a couple of days and, upon return, had been beaten by a *chiambok* for several hours until she fainted. This punishment lasted from Sunday until the following Tuesday with only short breaks, until she finally died. Her body was excavated to be inspected and bore the marks of severe beatings. However, because it could not be unconditionally proven that Francina had died from Scheltus' beatings, he was only charged for maltreatment and fined one thousand silver coins.[77]

These cases were not limited to the Atlantic enslaved societies. In 1747, two young enslaved individuals owned by Johan Frederik Wendschoe, assistant of the VOC in Batavia, presented themselves to the colonial authorities after repeated harsh punishments. A surgeon concluded after examination that the body of the boy showed multiple burns, while the girl was covered by marks from repeated beatings.[78] Three years later, Damon van Macassar was inspected by a surgeon who found several marks resulting from burning and binding. Damon explained that his 'master', Johannes Overman, had asked to see a small silver box that he had himself put in the pocket of Damon. Overman had tied Damon to torture him with a *dammer* and a candle until he would reveal where the small box was.[79] In both cases, the defendants called for their right of 'domestic punishment' (*domesticque correctie* or *straff*), which was allowed by the statutes in some circumstances. However, article six of the Statutes of Batavia explicitly forbade 'masters' to 'enchain, maltreat and even less torture them by burning or bleeding without the knowledge and consent of the judge'.[80] In both cases, proof of the abuse on the victims' bodies was overwhelming. Overman had a reputation for torturing his enslaved workers. In both cases, the enslaved people were confiscated by the local authorities and publicly sold and could never be owned by Overman again. However, the limits on the domestic jurisdiction of the 'masters' remained vague as to the difference between 'mistreatment' and 'domestic punishments'.[81]

The same ambivalence existed regarding the curbing of domestic jurisdiction as with the legislation on enslaved persons' working and living conditions throughout the empire. While laws limiting domestic jurisdiction and punishments by 'masters' were regularly issued in the second half of the eighteenth century, other ordinances reaffirmed the authority and extensive power of whites, 'masters' or plantation managers, over the enslaved population. In Suriname, if an enslaved person disrespected a white person, he could be beaten.[82] In Berbice, legislators urged planters to keep enslaved individuals in subordination, and, in Curaçao, a warning was issued to 'masters' to enforce discipline upon those they enslaved.[83] The combination of laws both limiting corporal punishment and urging planters and plantation managers to enforce strict discipline and subordination reveals the authorities' concern with upholding the colonial social order. In practice, even the less intrusive laws were difficult to enforce. Only the most excessive cases of repetitive corporal punishment, often resulting in death, were brought before the courts and led to the 'masters' being fined.

Conclusion

Although different in organisation and demography, the colonies of the Dutch Empire spread across the globe relied on slavery. Colonial authorities regulated the large unfree population through a wide range of laws serving two important purposes. First, they were meant to keep the enslaved population in check through a set of draconian measures that protected the white settler class and punished any social transgressions. Second, the administration attempted to avoid large-scale revolts, mass desertion and high mortality rates among those enslaved by protecting them somewhat from the excesses of their 'masters'. These colonial laws were characterised by a vague terminology and left 'masters' with wide discretionary powers. And, even in the cases where legislation was precise, it still gave tremendous power to the enslavers. In addition, the reissuing of the same legislation points to the difficulty of enforcing it.

Court cases also attest of the difficulty of law enforcement, especially when it interfered with the domestic jurisdiction of planters. Offences were almost exclusively reported by enslaved people, who took great risks because if the proof presented was considered too weak, they could be severely punished. When there was proof enough, offending enslavers received a fine and often had to let the enslaved persons under consideration go. In some cases, they could be banished from the settlement. Punishment for the abusive treatment of enslaved people was sometimes enforced but inconsistently so, and it never equated with the severity it was meant to condemn. By restricting the mobility of enslaved individuals, creating social distinctions and failing to enforce the law regulating the relationships between enslaved and enslavers with force and clarity, colonial authorities were attempting to make enslavement-based colonial societies resilient and sustainable without infringing too much on the privileges of 'masters'.

Notes

1 Femme Gaastra, *De geschiedenis van de VOC*, 10th ed. (Zutphen: Walburg Pers, 2002), 13–23; Henk den Heijer, *De geschiedenis van de WIC*, 3rd ed. (Zutphen: Walburg Pers, 2007), 13–34.

2 The plantation hierarchy was as follows: the owner could either live on the plantation or in Europe. In the latter case, he named an overseer or manager, also called a *Directeur* in Dutch, who was responsible for the exploitation of the plantation. He was often assisted by an accountant, a surgeon, different artisans and a person of colour called a 'Negro-officer' in the Dutch sources.

3 Pepijn Brandon, 'Between the plantation and the port: Racialization and social control in eighteenth-century Paramaribo', *International Review of Social History* 64, no. S27 (2019), 95–124 at 96.

4 Ulbe Bosma and Remco Raben, *De Oude Indische Wereld 1500–1920. De Geschiedenis van Indische Nederlanders* (Amsterdam: Bakker, 2003).

5 Peter Linebaugh, *The Many-Headed Hydra: Sailors, Slaves, Commoners, and the Hidden History of the Revolutionary Atlantic* (Boston: Beacon Press, 2000).

6 Remco Raben, 'Batavia and Colombo: The Ethnic and Spatial Order of Two Colonial Cities, 1600–1800' (Ph.D. diss., Leiden University, 1996); Matthias van Rossum, *Kleurrijke Tragiek: de Geschiedenis van Slavernij in Azië onder de VOC* (Hilversum: Uitgeverij Verloren, 2015).

7 Pepijn Brandon, Niklas Frykman and Pernille Røge, 'Free and unfree labor in Atlantic and Indian Ocean port cities (seventeenth–nineteenth centuries)', *International Review of Social History* 64, no. S27 (2019), 1–18.

8 Known as the 'Silver Century', where the colonial empire was not expanded but consolidated, Gaastra, *De geschiedenis van de VOC*; Jaap Jacobs, *Koopman in Azië: de Handel van de Nederlandse Oost-Indische Compagnie in de 18de Eeuw* (Zutphen: Walburg Pers, 2000).

9 Thanks to the NWO-funded 'Resilient Diversity' Project, we have created a database of more than 2,500 court cases for Batavia and over 1,500 for Suriname.

10 P.C. Emmer, *The Dutch in the Atlantic Economy, 1580–1880: Trade, Slavery and Emancipation* (Aldershot: Variorum, 1998); Wim Klooster, *The Dutch Moment: War, Trade, and Settlement in the Seventeenth-Century Atlantic World* (Ithaca: Cornell University Press, 2016).

11 Van Rossum, *Kleurrijke tragiek*, 93–115.

12 *Corvée* is a form of unpaid, unfree labour which is intermittent in nature and lasts for limited periods of time, typically only a certain number of days' work each year.

13 Van Rossum, *Kleurrijke Tragiek*, 63–6.

14 There were more than forty black enslaved persons for one white person in some regions, Brandon, 'Between the plantation and the port', 98; Van Rossum, *Kleurrijke Tragiek*, 8–9. The number of enslaved

people in the VOC possessions increased rapidly in the seventeenth century, attaining some 70,000 by 1700, before stagnating during the eighteenth century. The servile population in the Dutch Indian Ocean world outnumbered the enslaved population in the Dutch Atlantic until the second half of the eighteenth century.

15 In the Cape, the discussion about free or unfree labour lingered on up to the first quarter of the eighteenth century, when it was decided that forced labour was more beneficial to the VOC than wage labour, Pieter van Duin and Robert Ross, *The Economy of the Cape Colony in the Eighteenth Century* (Leiden: Centre for the History of European Expansion, 1987), 5–7.

16 Kate Ekama, 'Courting Conflict: Managing Dutch East and West India Company Disputes in the Dutch Republic' (Ph.D. diss., Leiden University, 2018), 19.

17 *NIP* 1: 572–6.

18 Jacob A. Schiltkamp, 'Legislation, government, jurisprudence, and law in the Dutch West Indian colonies: The order of government of 1629', *Pro Memorie: Bijdragen Tot de Rechtsgeschiedenis Der Nederlanden* 5, no. 4 (2003), 320–34 at 332.

19 Meindert Rutgert Wijnholt, *Strafrecht in Suriname* (Deventer: Kluwer, 1965), 31–2.

20 Han Jordaan, 'Free Blacks and coloreds and the administration of justice in eighteenth-century Curaçao', *New West Indian Guide/ Nieuwe West-Indische Gids* 84, no. 1–2 (2010), 63–86 at 68.

21 Karwan Fatah-Black, 'The usurpation of legal roles by Suriname's governing council, 1669–1816', *Comparative Legal History* 5, no. 2 (2017), 243–61 at 248.

22 In eighteenth-century Suriname, enslaved people accounted for 90 per cent of the total population but only 8 per cent of the victims of crime. Imran Canfijn, 'In Search for Justice: Legal and Judicial Inequality in Eighteenth Century Suriname' (M.A. thesis, Leiden University, 2018), 112, 200–2.

23 NL-HaNa, Schepenbank te Batavia, 1642–1801, 1.04.18.03, inv. 11963, fo. 30–45; Verenigde Oost-Indische Compagnie, 1602–1795 (1811) 1.04.02, inv. 9466, fo. 5–41.

24 NL-HaNa, Tweede West-Indische Compagnie, 1.05.01.02, inv. 215, fo. 328–31.

25 Ordinance of 1766-11-25, Curaçao, *CuP* 1: 1638–1782, 288; Ordinance of 1688-01-14, Cape Colony, *KP*, 1: 269. The ordinance was reissued in 1727.

26 Ordinance of 1743-01-13, Ceylon, *CP* 1: 269; Ordinance of 1760-12-12, Suriname, *SP*, 580, reissued in 1769; Ordinance of 1735-05-07, Berbice, reissues 1738, 1765, 1782, *PG* online. The *plakaatboek*

for Guiana is available online at http://resources.huygens.knaw.nl/retroboeken/guyana/; Ordinance of 1795-06-13, Demarary, *PG* online; Ordinance of 1697-04-13, Cape Colony, *KP* 1: 309-10. The ordinance was reissued in 1727, 1732, 1742, 1760 and 1791.

27 Ordinances of 1710-07-09, 1740-10-17, 1794-09-17, 1795-08-04, 1795-11-20, 1807-01-31, 1811-10-28, Curaçao, *CuP* 1: 67, 143, 2: 430, 435, 443, 587; 2: 677; Ordinance of 1750-07-24, Curaçao, *CuP* 1: 216.

28 Ordinance of 1720-04-25, Curaçao, *CuP* 1: 97. Further issues in 1741, 1756, 1785, 1799 and 1815; Ordinance of 1750-02-06, Suriname, *SP* 485; Ordinance of 1764-09-03, Berbice, Ordinance of 1811-05-02, Demarary, *PG* online; Ordinance of 1754-09-03, Cape Colony, *KP* 3: 1-7.

29 Ordinance of 1750-02-26, Suriname, *SP*, 556, reissued in 1759. Ordinance of 1780-01-10, Berbice, *PG* online; Ordinance of 1754-09-03, Cape Colony, *KP* 3: 1-7; Ordinance of 1676-09-02, Ceylon, *CP*, 126 (9); Ordinance of 1768-08-19, Essequibo, *PG* online.

30 Aviva Ben-Ur, 'Purim in the public eye: Leisure, violence, and cultural convergence in the Dutch Atlantic', *Jewish Social Studies* 20, no. 1 (2013), 32-76, 74-5. In Demarara, it was forbidden for enslaved persons to sing on vessels, Ordinance of 1779-10-19, Demarary, *PG* online.

31 Alex van Stipriaan, 'Watramama/Mami Wata: Three centuries of a water spirit in West Africa, Suriname and Europe', *Matatu* 27, no. 1 (2003), 323-37 at 324.

32 Ordinance of 1777-05-24, Suriname, *SP*, 766; Ordinance of 1801-07-21, Berbice, *PG* online.

33 Ordinance of 1664-05-19, Ceylon, *CP*, 75; Ordinance of 1769-05-17, Suriname, *SP*, 701.

34 Brandon, 'Between the plantation and the port', 113.

35 *Ibid.*, 116.

36 Ordinance of 1777-08-15, Suriname, *SP*, 778; Ordinance of 1784-10-01, Berbice, *PG* online; Ordinance of 1754-09-03, Cape Colony, *KP* 3: 1-7.

37 Ordinance of 1754-09-03, Cape Colony, *KP* 3: 1-7.

38 Revolts erupted in Suriname in 1750, in Berbice in 1763, in Curaçao in 1795 and at the Cape in 1808, Brandon, 'Between the plantation and the port', 110; Marjolein Kars, 'Dodging rebellion: Politics and gender in the Berbice slave uprising of 1763', *American Historical Review* 121, no. 1 (2016), 39-69; Matthias van Rossum, 'Running together or running apart? Diversity, desertion and resistance in the Dutch East India Company empire, 1650-1800', in Marcus Rediker,

Titas Chakraborty and Matthias van Rossum (eds.), *A Global History of Runaways: Workers, Mobility, and Capitalism 1600–1850* (Berkeley: University of California Press, 2019), 135–55.
39 Duin and Ross, *The Economy of the Cape Colony*, 54–72; Sentence, Cape Colony, 28–03–1737, WCA, CJ/786, fo. 88–93.
40 Nigel Worden and Gerald Groenewald, *Trials of Slavery: Selected Documents Concerning Slaves from the Criminal Records of the Council of Justice at the Cape of Good Hope, 1705–1794* (Cape Town: Van Riebeeck Society, 2005), 133–7.
41 Statutes of Batavia, *NIP* 1: 572–6.
42 Ordinance of 1657–12–28/29, Ceylon, *CP*, 29; Ordinance of 1704–04–25/08–14, Ceylon, *CP*, 205 (22); Ordinance of 1749–06–20, Ceylon, *CP*, 379.
43 Ordinance of 1740–12–17, Berbice; Ordinance of 1758–04–12, Essequibo, *PG* online.
44 Ordinance of 1759–12–27, Suriname, *SP* 1: 556.
45 Ordinance of 1780–08–24, Suriname, *SP* 2: 823.
46 Ordinance of 1804–04–30, Berbice. Another example is Demerara, where the legislation made slave gardens mandatory in 1788 and legislators regulated the size of plots assigned to enslaved individuals in groups of five: *PG* online.
47 For instance, in Demerara in 1768 and again in Berbice in 1784, the legislation on slave gardens was accompanied by another article on the food and clothing of the enslaved.
48 Ordinance of 1775–12–21, Suriname, *SP* 2: 761.
49 Length of workdays: Ordinance of 1774–01–01, Berbice, *PG* online; Ordinance of 1795–11–20 and 1812–12–08, Curaçao, *CuP*, 444, 687; no work on Sundays and holidays: Ordinance of 1701–10–18, Essequibo, *PG* online; Ordinance of 1779–10–19 and 1784–10–01, Demerara, *PG* online; Ordinance of 1810–11–14, Berbice, *PG* online.
50 Ordinance of 1814–10–04, Berbice, *PG* online.
51 'hun slaafsche staat zoo veel doenlijk en overeenkomstig de reden en pligten van menschelijkheid behoort dragelijk gemaakt te worden', Ordinance of 1784–08–31, Suriname, *SP*, 1066, cited in Canfijn, 'In search for justice', 99.
52 NL-HaNa, Hof van Politie en Criminele Justitie in Suriname 1.05.10.02, inv. 92; fo. 299; inv. 828, fo. 119–22.
53 Fatah-Black, 'The usurpation of legal roles by Suriname's governing council', 248.
54 This was a severe corporal punishment for enslaved persons, who had their hands tied and a stick put between the hands and the raised knees. The enslaved person's overseer struck the top side of the victim with

a rod of tamarind. If one side was beaten raw, the victim was turned over to receive the same punishment on the other side, NL-HaNa, *Hof van Politie en Criminele Justitie* (HPCJ), Suriname 1.05.10.02, inv. 827, fos. 293–309.
55 NL-HaNa, HPCJ, Suriname 1.05.10.02, inv. 827, fos. 119–34. By comparison, a sailor engaged in the VOC made between seven and twelve guilders per month, depending on his experience, Matthias van Rossum, *Werkers van de Wereld: Globalisering, Arbeid en Interculturele Ontmoetingen Tussen Aziatische en Europese Zeelieden in Dienst van de VOC, 1600–1800* (Hilversum: Verloren, 2014), 222.
56 Statutes of Batavia, *NIP* 1: 172–6.
57 Ordinance of 1809–12–12, Batavia, *NIP* 13: 636.
58 'naar den aard en gelegendheyd der zaken', Plakkaat of 17–10–1752, Batavia, *NIP* 6: 281–9.
59 NL-HaNa, VOC 1.04.02, inv. 9457, fos. 379–407.
60 NL-HaNa, VOC 1.04.02, inv. 9505, fos. 237–70.
61 NL-HaNa, VOC 1.04.02, inv. 9428, fos. 1002–15.
62 Ordinance of 1680, *KP* 1: 244.
63 Worden and Groenewald, *Trials of Slavery*, 399–405.
64 Natalie Zemon Davis, 'Judges, masters, diviners: Slaves' experience of criminal justice in colonial Suriname', *Law and History Review* 29, no. 4 (2011), 925–84 at 940.
65 *Ibid.*, 946.
66 Fatah-Black, 'The usurpation of legal roles by Suriname's governing council', 256.
67 Ordinances of 1764–09–03 and 1768–07–04, Berbice, *PG* online.
68 The legislation of 1784 also limited the number of lashes on the enslaved to a maximum of thirty-nine per day.
69 Ordinance of 1771–12–10.
70 Ordinance of 1810–11–14, Berbice, reissued in the set of regulations of 1814–10–04, *PG* online.
71 Brandon, 'Between the plantation and the port', 111–12.
72 Ordinance of 1814–10–04 concerning the treatment of the enslaved, *PG* online.
73 NL-HaNa, HPCJ, Suriname 1.05.10.02, inv. 44, fos. 217–9.
74 A stick that was used for punishments.
75 '*het ombrengen van voorst. Neeger op so cruelle wijse*', NL-HaNa, HPCJ, Suriname 1.05.10.02, inv. 806, fos. 425–69.
76 NL-HaNa, HPCJ, Suriname 1669–1828 1.05.10.02, inv. 828, fos. 446–53.
77 NL-HaNa, VOC 1.04.02, inv. 9473, fos. 179–245.
78 NL-HaNa, VOC 1.04.02, inv. 9414, fos. 963–6.

79 NL-HaNa, VOC 1.04.02, inv. 9428, fos. 589–92.
80 Statutes of Batavia, *NIP* 1: 172–6.
81 Statutes of Batavia, *NIP* 1: 572–6.
82 Ordinance of 1741-04-09, Suriname, *SP*, 400.
83 Ordinance of 1767-04-22, Curaçao, *CuP* 1: 290.

Part III

Local adaptations and developments

7

Settler colonialism and early American history

Trevor Burnard and Agnès Delahaye

Among the many agents of European imperial expansion, settlers occupy a particular place in British and American historiographies. They define a form of colonial agency that sets the British Empire apart from other areas of European overseas occupation. There is no word in the languages of the other imperial nations of the early modern era to define this particular type of colonist, who left 'home' in the metropole to take part in shaping the empire, built British 'communities' overseas and then never returned.[1] They form a particularly important group within the ambit of this volume, being quintessentially private agents promoting settlement and global expansion, and who had always a complicated and, at times, uneasy relationship to the imperial state, both advancing the interests of that state and also on many occasions acting in ways counter to imperial views, not least in respect to how they acquired and used land and to how they treated – often abominably – other peoples in the Americas. No other group was as important as settlers in what the editors of this volume call the 'engine room' of overseas endeavour, and no other group demonstrated so obviously various repertoires of power that were so successful, at least by the lights of settlers if not by other actors in global expansion, that in many places, not least in North America, the societies that were shaped by settlers became 'settler colonies'. English traditions of liberty and the rule of law were carried from Europe to settler empires by independent white men who emphasised liberty for themselves but denied it to others. The obverse of British freedom often turned out to be the subjection of others.[2]

Settler power was underpinned by settler prosperity: settler societies were marvellous machines of wealth creation, although only for the white independent males and their families permanently settled in extractive colonies from the seventeenth century to the start of the twentieth century. In the eighteenth century, white settlers created in North America societies that were richer and (for whites only) more egalitarian than anywhere else in the world, with extremely high living standards for the white population. White settlers in the eighteenth-century West Indies did not create such egalitarian societies but were richer by far than any group of people in the British Empire. By the 1820s, white settlers in Australia had taken over the mantle as the most prosperous and egalitarian group within the British Empire.[3] But their wealth was founded, as Ned Blackhawk notes, on the genocide, land dispossession and forced assimilation of indigenes, a fact often omitted in contemporary debates on the connections between slavery and capitalism, where slavery is seen as 'foundational' to American wealth creation.[4] Settler wealth, moreover, Brenna Bhandar contends, was inextricably tied up with emerging concepts of race and gendered racial difference contingent on particular features of labour and property relations captured by what Bhandar calls 'racial regimes of ownership'.[5]

Historians of the Anglo-World hold divergent views on the significance of settler contributions to the imperial projects they helped create, but they have recently asked more questions about their status and legacy. This questioning is especially true for the United States, where settlers have played a major role in commonplace representations of how the nation came to be. Consequently, the concept of settler colonialism has recently taken the academic world by storm, with many researchers now willing to view the United States as a settler colonial nation 'locked into a struggle over the meaning of place and belonging with the Native nations of North America'.[6] Others, however, object to the reductive blanket use of this concept to account for the complex history of American development.

This chapter argues for a takeover of the theory of settler colonialism by early Americanists, and for a more nuanced and multifaceted approach that adapts it to the rich and deep scholarship on early America produced in the last generation. We need, in particular, to move away from a simplistic notion of the Native being eliminated through sleight of hand.[7] What is clear is that throughout the colonial period, Native Americans were never removed from any part of colonial North America, even those parts that by the time of the Seven Years' War had been firmly placed under European settler control. As Chad Anderson notes, in regard to European attempts in mapmaking to erase Indian presence on the eastern seaboard in the mid-eighteenth century, 'by taking European rhetoric at face value about North America as an unsettled continent, we overlook a world where American Indians had the power to defuse the nature of settlement across much of North America – a power reflected in European maps'.[8]

Genealogy of the concept

In the last couple of decades, settler colonialism has been extensively mobilised by scholars determinedly committed to postcolonial studies. What do they mean by this concept? A useful explanation is provided by Alicia Cox in an entry on 'settler colonialism' for the *Oxford Bibliographies Online: Literary and Critical Theory*, which sees settler colonialism in entirely adversarial form, as a pernicious form of colonialism intended to dispossess Indigenous people of land, power and, eventually, identity. She defines settler colonialism as 'an ongoing system of power that perpetuates the genocide and repression of Indigenous people and cultures [which] includes interlocking forms of oppression, including racism, white supremacy, heteropatriarchy, and capitalism'. She refers to what she calls the 'ground-breaking' theory of the late Australian scholar Patrick Wolfe, and his expression of the 'logic of elimination' to 'show that settler colonialism is a system, not an historical event, and that as such it perpetuates the erasure of native peoples as a precondition for settler expropriation of lands and resources, providing the necessary conditions for establishing the present-day ideology of multicultural neoliberalism'.[9] Wolfe also has significant things to say about race, arguing that race is 'an "organising grammar" that divides humans into ethnic categories and normalises white supremacy to justify Indigenous genocide and settler colonialism'.[10]

Of course, early Americanists will have concerns about the utility of using settler colonialism as a concept, if it is restricted to the definition outlined above. It paints the opposition between settlers and Indigenous peoples in unduly stark terms that understate the complexity and fluidity of seventeenth- and eighteenth-century America. Indeed, the general response of early Americanists to calls for settler colonialism to be a dominant paradigm in the field has been lukewarm. In a recent forum in the journal of record for the subject, *The William and Mary Quarterly*, Allan Greer was particularly dismissive of the concept. Greer notes how the concept of settler colonialism developed from Wolfe's thinking about the case of Australia as a kind of ideal type of modern settler colonialism, 'a place where Indigenous resistance was weak, where the complexities of pre-Enlightenment territoriality were absent and where the brutal logic of appropriation could operate on what looked like (but was not) a clean slate'.[11] Greer argues that we need to be careful about transposing this Australian situation into the very different environment of seventeenth-century North America. He notes that Australia and America were not coterminous and that the Australian example works better for nineteenth-century America than for seventeenth-century North America, where Indigenous presence was powerful and inescapable, and where later ideas of Indians 'merely' occupying the land were never more than an occasional settler fantasy.[12]

Greer develops these thoughts in an extremely important book on property and colonisation, in which he demonstrates that while settler colonists in North America were heavily involved in the dispossession of indigenes and through this explicit manifestation of colonialism established effective European rule, this was not based upon a form of 'eliminationist logic', whereby settlers predetermined the utter destruction of indigenes through taking away their land and destroying their persons. What took place instead was a lengthy historical process in which Indigenous land tenure was very often part of empire-making, and in which settlers by no means always held the upper hand over Indigenous leaders. It was not until the nineteenth century that settlers endeavoured to liquidate indigenes by the destruction of their distinctive homelands. As Edward Countryman notes, in the late colonial period, 'European/African society crept westward. In the early republic, it surged'. The American Revolution played an important role in transferring power to settlers and speculators, facilitating both westward migration and extensive land-grabbing. Temporality, he insists, was very important. We have to be careful not to naturalise colonisation and 'treat "settlement" as an inevitable step towards the emergence of a future nation-state'. He notes that 'where landed property is concerned, there is still a tendency to equate colonization and modernization' and to 'see the European takeover of America as a vast modernizing operation' that kicked on 'the moment natives were displaced'. He warns against teleological explanation that ascribes Indigenous dispossession solely down to 'greedy and rapacious colonizers'. Some were, of course, and the effects of what they did resulted in Indigenous devastation, but it is hard to discern an intention to do such harm except in relatively few cases.[13]

It is also tempting to be sniffy, as an early Americanist, at settler colonialism emanating out of a particular narrow version of Australian scholarship. The concept came to Australia out of American scholarship, especially from the work of Frederick Jackson Turner, whose influence on Patrick Wolfe was especially profound, as noted in an important historiographical article by Erik Altenbernd and Alex Trimble Young.[14] Wolfe drew very much in his work in the 1990s from the ideas of Turner about the 'disappearing frontier' as it had been reinterpreted by Russel Ward in the 1950s and then, with due attention to the Aboriginal presence in colonial Australia, by the Tasmanian historian Henry Reynolds in the early 1980s. Turner exerted a powerful centrifugal force over twentieth-century Australian historians like Ward and Reynolds and is, as Altenbernd and Young note, the target behind the initial works of settler colonialism by scholars such as Wolfe. Reynolds in particular challenged Ward, and through Ward the legacy of Turner, in recasting the Australian frontier as a site of settler conquest and Indigenous resistance rather than a place of nation-building – it was nation-destroying, Reynolds asserted, more than nation-creating, once Aboriginal perspectives were taken into consideration.[15] By following Reynolds, Wolfe thus decisively rejected theories of Indigenous–settler relations that were fashionable in the 1990s within colonial North American scholarship, particularly the influential 'Middle Ground' paradigm put forward by Richard White.[16] Turner is a constant presence in Wolfe's work, even though Wolfe explicitly disavowed Turner's idea of the frontier as a site of dynamic pluralism in favour of seeing it as a one-way process of settler oppression and retreating Aboriginal presence. As Altenbernd and Young argue, Wolfe's analysis can sometimes be read as the ideological obverse of Turner's writing on the frontier, while remaining very dependent upon Turnerian categories for defining what a frontier is and how frontier history is, in Wolfe's famous formulation, a process, rather than a structure.[17]

The virtues of settler colonialism

But such carping from the sideline about the proper history of settler colonialism as a concept and its inadequacy to explain fully early American history is counterproductive. 'Settler colonialism' is the language increasingly used by people in connected fields. We may as well accept that it is here and deal with it, the inadequacies of the concept notwithstanding. Two immediate benefits present themselves for early Americanists in adopting some of the language of settler colonialism. First, as Jennifer Spear concludes in her contribution to the *William and Mary Quarterly* forum, settler colonialism is good to think with because it forces us to confront what it means – then and now – to live in stolen lands worked by stolen labour.[18] Second, settler colonialism connects early American scholarship to the scholarship of other places, especially within the colonies established by European empires in the Atlantic archipelago. It also allows early American historians to connect with colleagues who work in imperialism, colonialism, the American West, Indigenous history and settler relations during the 'settler revolution' of the nineteenth century.[19]

Nevertheless, early Americanists should not just work with the concept of settler colonialism as it is commonly presented but should adapt it to the particular situation of early American history, using the many insights from a historiography that is rich in how settler colonialism might have worked. We should use our especial expertise in continental/Native American history and in Atlantic/imperial history to adapt and change the concept of settler colonialism so that it is more sensitive to the varieties of settler colonialism in the many regions of early America. This variety of responses is less focused, as Greer argues, on 'the elimination of the native' and more interested in understanding changing patterns of land ownership and Native dispossession than at present. In short, early Americanists might use settler colonialism as a theory that can be adapted, and adapted critically and not without reservations, to the rich and deep scholarship that has come out of early American history in the last generation.

What are some of the advantages for early Americanists in adopting a version of settler colonialism as one paradigm for studying early American history? First, it adds a 'conquest' narrative to a more traditional narrative of early American history based around migration. Second, by making colonisation a key theme in early American history, it provides a means to connect the two most dynamic areas of early American historiography – continental and Atlantic history, fields which to an extent have been talking past each other.[20] Third, by focusing on colonisation as the structure within which not just settlers and Native Americans lived, it provides an entrée into imperial thinking and decision-making and the ways in which that thinking ran up against insistences by all parties for local autonomy and for local variations, as highlighted by Faucquez and Heijmans and Thiebaut in this volume. Fourth, a focus on settler colonialism allows us to pay attention to several ideal 'types' which can move discussion along. These types would include 'the settler', 'the Native American' and 'the African' in a new, revised and more geographically expansive understanding of traditional ideas of early American history being about the interaction of black, red and white. It can help us avoid simple racial identifications in favour of theories of how different groups related to imperial states involved in processes of colonisation.

The fourth discussion point is where early Americanists can most improve the concept of settler colonialism which, as critics have argued, is hindered by a reductive notion of all-powerful and undifferentiated 'settlers' imposing the will of imperial and colonial states in almost uncontested fashion upon Native Americans (and also, by implication, enslaved Africans) without much opposition from those being oppressed. That might have been the case for nineteenth-century Australia or parts of nineteenth-century United States of America, but it was certainly not true for seventeenth- or eighteenth-century early America, where states – notably France and Britain, as Lachenicht demonstrates in this volume – competed against each other relentlessly, allowing Native Americans multiple points whereby they could at the very least play one empire off another. And what is becoming increasingly clear in scholarship on Native America done by a multitude of scholars is that Native Americans were active agents in all aspects of early American history, including aggressively trying to 'eliminate' Native American enemies and occasionally deterring European settlement, as in the Natchez War in Louisiana in 1729 and around the *pays d'en haut* during the Seven Years' War.[21] Unlike the definition of settler colonialism proffered by Cox, which sees it as continuous, relentless and always oppressive, early Americans saw the relationship between Native Americans and settlers as constantly shifting and changing according to negotiation, conflict and occasional consensus.

Early Americanists have moved far away from the rather simplistic notion of intentional genocide transferred from Australian scholarship into realising that there was very seldom any intention by settlers or the imperial or colonial state to get rid of Native American peoples, even if settler presence was likely to lead to serious harm for Native American communities. This is a point that Allan Greer makes forcefully in his commentary in the *William and Mary Quarterly* forum. There is no doubt that settlers often expressed a desire for genocide and native dispossession. In 1666, for example, Governor William Berkeley of Virginia gloated that 'I think it is necessary to Destroy all those Northern Indians for twill be a great Terror and Example of Instruction to all other Indians'. As John Murrin comments, 'until the arrival of the Pacifist Quakers in the Delaware River after 1675, the English colonies were all founded by terrorists'.[22] In the colonial period, however, such wishes were seldom acted upon and were in any case impossible to achieve even for settler populations firmly opposed to Native American presence. An early American perspective helps us to move to new discussions about how settler colonialism structured modes of oppression and patterns of resistance.

Pocock's settler colonialism

The fifth reason why settler colonialism is useful is that it unites into one schematic theory histories from various places and times. There are sound reasons to push further with the idea of a British world as an interconnected zone of mutual interaction and to keep the colonising and the colonial world in a single world of vision. There

Settler colonialism 161

are also good reasons why it would be good to write greater British histories in terms of the intercultural story of conflict and crossbreeding between differently based societies. One theorist of settler colonialism – though he has never seen himself within this rubric, which is not surprising given his sympathy for insisting that the settler voice was one that needed to be heard in metropolitan Britain – is the distinguished intellectual historian and historiographer J.G.A. Pocock. In his surprisingly under-recognised *Discovery of Islands*, he called for a new kind of British history that recognised that settlers such as himself had a presence in British history.[23]

His views, expressed in his idiosyncratic and difficult prose and with a particular and perhaps peculiar vision of historiography and British history which he realised to great effect in the multi-volume masterpiece *Barbarism and Religion*, are sometimes seen, as Colin Kidd notes, as an early and sophisticated version of Euroscepticism.[24] It is worth paying attention to Pocock, however, when thinking about settler colonialism because it allows early Americanists to use settler colonialism as a way of thinking about colonisation without having to adopt the central contention of Wolfe, that settler colonialism is merely 'the elimination of the Native'.

Pocock insists that settler colonisation, drawing from his understanding of British, Māori and British settler history, is a historiographical contestation, first between 'native' and 'settler' histories, and then between different kinds of settler histories, not just in the British world but in worlds inhabited by several empires and then nation-states. For the first contestation, he notes that 'between *pakeha* [creole settlers from Europe in New Zealand] and *tangata whenua* [Māori inhabitants of New Zealand], there is a contest for authority between two alternative histories, which are not simply alternative accounts of the same events but alternative cultural codes which give conflicting accounts of what authority is'.[25] In regard to the second contestation, Pocock wants to see a place within British history for settler accounts, thus making settler colonialism not just a process whereby Britons (mostly the English) imposed themselves upon reluctant natives with a narrow and restrictive form of history but British history as the history of several nations interacting, and sometimes (as in British North America in the 1770s and Ireland in the 1920s) seceding from an association with an island state. His historical mission was 'to instruct the British peoples that they inhabit a history more complex than they could readily terminate'.[26] In short, what Pocock argues for is a related project to the 'elimination of the Native', which we tend to think is the main object of settler colonialism. He insists that the Native has not been eliminated and seeks to insist also that we cannot eliminate the settler from the histories of a British outward expansion which they helped to create.

Unlike an earlier mid-twentieth century historiography which showed little interest either in indigeneity or in the character and thought patterns of settlers establishing settler societies, Pocock's work foreshadowed work influenced by postcolonialism. As Saul Dubow writes about South Africa (one of Pocock's ancestral settler homelands), 'the static mechanical and spatial metaphors' that characterised imperial and colonial history in the mid-twentieth century 'along with the uni-directional outward diffusion of forces, ideas and people from the metropole contrast markedly with the resonating language of the postcolonial metaphorical repertoire: hybridity, fluidity, ambiguity and decenteredness'.[27] South Africa, like the West Indies, provides an interesting contrast to places like Australia, New Zealand and the United States in regard to settler colonialism, given the disparities in the numerical ratios between whites and non-whites and sizeable migrations of people from other parts of Africa, as well as the Indian Ocean world. Dubow argues that the concept of a British world in South Africa helps tease out a Britishness which was neither ethnic nor racial but which was 'a composite, rather than an exclusive form of identity'. It encompassed, in a way that resembles what Pocock insists for New Zealand, being South African as well as being British, this dual identity being a key part of settler identity in the colonial Anglo-World, which distinguished, Dubow thinks, concepts of identity within the British Empire, with 'British' being used in an 'adjectival' rather than a 'possessive' sense.[28]

Narratives and mythologies of settler societies

Pocock's understanding of settler colonialism as historiographic contest points to the important role of texts and ideas in shaping the diverse and complex histories of settler societies. Settlers were largely absent from early English promotion, in which 'planting' was first considered as a practical solution for enabling privateering in the North Atlantic and increasing returns on fishing expeditions.[29] This 'planting' was principally the work of 'private investors', as Lou Roper demonstrates in this volume, who 'possessed the fiscal and personnel resources that enabled them to bear the substantial risks and costs of long-distance ventures that the state could not absorb'.[30] Labourers at the bottom of the English social hierarchy who committed to a contract in the colonies were largely anonymous and were regularly made collectively responsible for the violence, the precariousness and the financial losses with which colonial ventures were associated.[31] As settlement projects took over exploration and seasonal trade, however, the verb 'settle' was increasingly used to describe the processes through which Indigenous land was appropriated, to 'settle plantations' where English presence would become permanent.[32] It carried connotations of resolution and anchorage centred clearly on human agency and violence, as in John Smith's 1622 proposal to the Virginia Company to manage a hundred soldiers and thirty sailors in 'ranging the counties and tormenting the salvages', before they would 'settle themselves in some such convenient place' to grow their own food.[33]

Given that colonisation was a public act in which imperialists competed for land and resources not only within their own communities but also within rival imperial nations, settlers narrated their enterprises within the bounds of the long tradition of European transatlantic promotional literature. That tradition had existed since the age of exploration, where the ongoing struggle between civilisation and savagery had been normalised within print. Imperialists and promoters of European settlement in the Americas routinely and conventionally claimed to seek to convert Native Americans as active agents whereby the inevitability of European appropriation of Indigenous land could be confirmed.[34] But for the sake of credibility, they also recognised that they occupied a hybrid environment where their domination was never complete. Daniel Dulany, Sr, of Maryland, whom we cite at length below, for instance, did not accept in his writings that Maryland was 'a conquered Country'. If there had been a conquest, 'the Indians must be the Vanquished, and the English the Victors, and consequently, the Indians would be liable to the Miseries in which a Conquered People are involved'.[35] Indigenous peoples had not disappeared from their tribal lands and continued to resist the expansion of coastal settlements, in spite of the efforts of generations of settlers to write them off the historical record.[36]

Settlers followed two contradictory impulses. They promoted their contribution to the wider movement of Western expansion in the name of their sovereign and nation, yet they also described their actions as uniquely valuable and worthy of financial and political support, in spite of their marginality and the utter precariousness of their initial condition. Massachusetts governor John Winthrop, for instance, defended his exclusionary policies of the 1630s as rendered necessary in the 'the infancy of a plantation', as opposed to the constitutional maturity of 'a settled state', while Virginia governor Robert Beverley, three generations later, continued to blame the difficult beginnings of his colony on the actions of men who sought to 'fetch away the treasure from thence aiming more at sudden gain, than to form any regular colony, or establishing a settlement in such a manner, as to make it a lasting happiness to the country'.[37] Settler voices in British America thus accounted for the particularities of their social orders as heroic sacrifice in service to the King and nation, while claiming ownership of their settlements in exclusionary historical terms. Massachusetts leaders in 1678, for instance, petitioned for the preservation of their privileges and the freedom 'to enjoy ... the known and declared ends of the first undertakers, which hath hitherto been carried on at their own charge, both formerly and lately defended by a greater expense of blood and treasure than will easily be believed, whereof they cannot but desire to reap the fruits'.[38]

Settlement defined both the enterprising act of colonising and the end product of such efforts – the formation and ownership of self-governing social orders where settler interests prevailed. As Dulany wrote from Maryland in 1728, settlers had come to this strange and difficult land and 'met with such Success, as to raise a Subsistence for themselves and to become very beneficial to their Mother-Country by greatly increasing its Trade and Wealth'. They were fully agents of the imperial project of the Crown and the nation, but their experience set them apart from the Englishmen 'that never went from their own Homes, or underwent any Hardships'.[39] The experience of colonisation itself defined the settlers as the rightful owners of their lands and the riches they yielded.

By the early national period, historians had come to use settlement extensively to refer to the historical process of colonisation that preceded independence, through which they accounted for the distinct character of each area of the new Republic. 'In each colony', David Ramsay wrote in his preface to his 1810 *History of the United States*, 'its history took a colouring from the first time and circumstances of its settlement, source of population, form of government, laws, religion, soil, agriculture and climate'.[40] *Settlers* and *settlement* occur over 380 times in the course of that particular and popular volume, attesting to the normative use of these terms in American perceptions of past developments. Adjectives were needed to distinguish 'the first permanent settlement of civilized inhabitants'[41] from, on the one hand, the series of failures that preceded it, and, on the other hand, the expansion that followed under constituted colonial governments, conceived as the prolongation and continuation of these momentous beginnings. The settlers were those among the colonists who were defined by their actions – entering a space unoccupied by Europeans and appropriating it through the cutting of trees and the formation of delineated homesteads through husbandry. The next generation of local historians throughout the United States took up this narrative structure extolling the enduring achievement of the founders, writing the history of their state as the end point of the process of expansion and the consolidation of original structures.[42]

Published at the end of a century of westward expansion under the guiding principle of 'manifest destiny', Frederick Jackson Turner's theory of Americanisation through westward expansion articulated these processes of appropriation as a 'common sequence of frontier types (fur trader, cattle-raising pioneer, small primitive farmer, and the farmer engaged in intensive varied agriculture to produce a surplus for export)', whose chronological succession on the western margins of American expansion marked the 'economic and social consolidation' of settler societies.[43] Turner conditioned the 'striking qualities' of the 'American intellect' not on the elimination of the Native but on the continuous confrontation of these manly men with the 'Indian question', locking settlers on the frontier into a permanently transitional state, between two distinct spaces with antithetical characteristics and between two periods of Eurocentric American development. Settlement ended when property lines and racial boundaries were clearly delineated, and territories became colonies and evolved into fully integrated states, imprisoning its actors in the mythical time of perpetual beginnings and making it particularly amenable to stories of collective heroism and American exceptionalism.

These stories are interpreted by settler colonialism scholars as illustrative of the 'historylessness' of settler societies – a 'historiographical order' torn between 'an utopian drive to build an ideal society' and the denial of Indigenous existence and settler conquest.[44] Exceptionalism is a creative act of interpretation and historiographic selection that relies on a few key texts and images in isolated or idealised contexts. The arbitrary and ahistorical nature of 'exceptionalism' has led historians to reject these 'foundational pieties', and to consequently associate the historical value of settlement to the demographic 'settler revolution' of the nineteenth century, during which the 'Anglophones bred like rabbits' and their 'wealth and power grew to match' their exploding numbers.[45] The founding and colonial periods so central to settler histories and narratives of the early national era are now relegated to 'the genealogy and prehistory of settler colonialism', a nineteenth-century phenomenon dependent on the constitution of established nation-states after the Age of Revolution.[46] US history monographs with settler colonialism in their title consequently tend to begin with antebellum Western expansion and the consolidation of state and federal policies of land management and development in the territories, leaving out the settler histories of the colonial period.[47]

The *longue durée* of settler colonialism in American history: Jeremy Belknap and Edward Long

In this final section of the chapter, we want to compare two settler historians writing in the eighteenth century to illuminate some of the complexities of the settler experience and the wealth of its historiography, which functioned from the onset of colonisation as the place where the purpose and means of settlement were discussed. One of these writers is Edward Long, whose most important work,

The History of Jamaica (1774), is a long but not uncritical paean of praise about the settlers of British descent in Jamaica. They had created, Long insisted, a truly British place in the tropics, despite the very different tropical environment they found themselves in after migrating from Britain, and even more so despite their manifest failure to do the thing that settlers did best, which was to populate new lands with numerous colonists of British inheritance. Long is also worth reading as a historian whose subject matter was a place in which the Native had indeed been eliminated as a result of the Columbian encounter, an erasure to which Long devoted little attention. The colony he wrote his panoramic history about was one in which a few very wealthy settlers of British heritage presided over a monstrous but highly profitable plantation system in which the great majority of the work was done by other settlers, in this case, Africans imported through the Atlantic slave trade and their descendants.[48] Our second case study is Jeremy Belknap, who wrote about a very different place – colonial New England – whose climate and topography was closer to the home country, yet in which settlement had led to the formation of societies Belknap described as the epitome of British liberty. Both writers were creole intellectuals aiming to take part in the transatlantic discussions about the legitimacy and means of successful imperial expansion discussed by Lachenicht and Roper in this volume, and to argue for the legitimacy of the labour and property regimes they bore witness to.

Although Edward Long (1734–1813) spent most of his life in southern England as a gentleman dependent on abundant income from large Jamaican estates, living in Jamaica for less than a decade in the 1750s and 1760s, he came from a distinguished Jamaican heritage. His family had come to the island in the Western Design in 1655 and his great-grandfather had been a prominent politician, speaker of the house in tumultuous years in the 1670s where he successfully challenged attempts by the Crown to increase its prerogative powers. Long represented almost perfectly the viewpoint of the white Jamaican planter class, as evidenced in his several writings, especially the three-volume *History of Jamaica*, probably the most ambitious and successful creole production ever completed in British America.[49] Belknap also had prestigious colonial ancestry and he enjoyed a delayed, yet successful, career at the heart of Boston, where he combined ministerial and historical pursuits in service to his Government and birthplace. His three-volume *History of New Hampshire* was not a publishing success, in spite of repeated praise by American intellectual elites, but his overall historical project, including the creation of the Massachusetts Historical Society, was central to the articulation between colonial and national historiographies of the United States.[50] Both writers invoked their roots and their knowledge of local practices and landscapes to argue for the value their colonial environment brought to the British imperial project.

Both Long's *History of Jamaica* and Belknap's *History of New Hampshire* were hugely impressive achievements, but they were not conventional histories. Rather, they were part narrative of past development and part extended commentary on contemporary Jamaica and New England, with a strong emphasis on social structures, physical geography and economic orientation, in direct continuation of promotional writing. What concerned Long, much more than the 'elimination of the native' during the Spanish period of Jamaican history, was rebutting attacks from metropolitan critics about white Jamaicans as irredeemably cruel. Such accusations were made by writers such as Adam Smith, who lamented how Africans – 'a humane and polished people' – had been entrusted to 'the refuse of the jails of Europe ... whose levity, brutality and baseness, so justly expose them to the contempt of the vanquished'.[51] Long countered such slurs by heaping praise upon Jamaica as a place of great beauty and celebrated the productivity of its white residents in creating 'a constant Mine whence *Britain* draws prodigious Riches', and thus making Jamaica 'the most advantageous and profiting colony to *Great Britain*, of any of his Majesty's Dominions'. These advantages, he insisted, arose from the industry of its settler population, whose efforts had led Jamaica to become an 'improved' place, although Long did not use the language of improvement specifically in describing these developments.[52] Improvement was also central to Belknap's understanding of historical development within the empire. He refrained from fantasies of terra nullius and embraced the mythology of English nationalism and exceptionalism to create continuity between the great figures of British expansionism and enterprise of the past and the growth of American power in the present.[53]

Both writers wrote in support of localised social orders that had been shaped by imperial competition, violence and precariousness on a global scale, and whose success – both sustainability and profitability – were dependent on settler commitment to defending their particular, local prerogatives. Long turned a blind eye to Jamaican settlers' brutal treatment of enslaved people, treatment so bad that the enslaved population did not ever achieve natural population increase, but he blamed the settlers for keeping, he believed, the island depopulated and reliant on importations of Africans through their weak attachment to family life and propensity to 'riot in the goatish embraces' of their 'coloured mistresses', preventing Jamaica from becoming a settler society on the North American model.[54] He faulted white Jamaicans in particular for their reflexive short-termism – in contrast to how French colonists behaved in neighbouring Saint Domingue, which he thought was a model of fruitful collaboration between a supportive government committed to long-term development of major infrastructure projects and a settler population willing to wait and plan for future success – and inattention to white settlement. Belknap also resorted to comparisons with other, foreign, forms of colonial occupation, particularly the French, and he abstained from judging his slaveholding counterparts too harshly.[55] He also consistently argued that town formation and corporate political structures in New England embodied the 'spirit of liberty' of the British constitution when unhindered by courtly and Parliamentary politics. Long set forward all sorts of plans, most of which were so costly as to be unrealisable, for attracting the 'right' kind of settlers to the island, who would cultivate as small proprietors the many empty areas of the colony while providing vital defence needs for a place threatened by both internal revolt from angry enslaved people and external attack from jealous European powers, eager to get the benefits of Jamaica for themselves.[56] For Belknap, town formation and corporate political structures throughout the entire history of settlement were the reasons why New England had been so stable and so prosperous, and he hoped to see them reproduced into the future as the continued expression of technological, economic and political progress.[57]

Neither abided by fantasies of *terra nullius* populated entirely by whites. Slavery and settler colonialism went together in Long's mind, for whom enslaved persons were essential for a fully functioning settler society in the tropic – '*inevitably* necessary' – as without adequate supplies of enslaved people, no one would stay on the island.⁵⁸ And, Long made clear, it was through slavery that Jamaica's massive contribution to the British economy was secured. It is not just modern historians following Eric Williams' *Capitalism and Slavery* who stress how much British prosperity owed to the plantation profits that were made by Jamaican settlers. That slavery was essential to British wealth and geopolitical power was an argument made over and over again by proslavers and by proponents like Long of Jamaican settler colonialism. Moreover, as Long insisted, these contributions to imperial wellbeing were not made by foreigners but by people who, although not resident in the British archipelago, were, as settlers, very much still British in identity and loyalty, just as Dulany had insisted for Maryland in 1728. Belknap not only acknowledged the impact of Indigenous presence on settler policies and progress: he argued that New England social orders were the product of settler adaptability to American land and Indigenous modes of land occupation and warship, creating both white solidarity and forms of hybridity central to the settlers' success.⁵⁹

Most importantly, both historians understood settler rights in relation to metropolitan traditions and the wider imperial project of the nation. Long argued that Jamaican settlers were 'freeborn Britons' or 'native subjects', most tellingly in his criticism of Lord Mansfield's judgement in *Somerset v Steuart* (1772) that James Somerset, even though enslaved, was a subject of the realm with as many rights to British justice as his 'master', Charles Steuart. Somerset, Long contended, was not a subject but 'merely a commodity' without any rights that Britons needed to care about. White Jamaicans, on the other hand, were part of a large and expanding British Empire with a significant investment in slavery and if they had rights in enslaved property, as Long was convinced they had, these rights were justified in numerous laws made by Britain and confirmed as lawful over many years. The British Empire was an interconnected world and if Britain insisted that Americans and West Indians had to obey parliamentary edicts, then Britain had to respect colonial settler rights, one of the most crucial of which was the right to own enslaved property.⁶⁰ Writing from New England during the Revolutionary War, Belknap went further, imputing the beginnings of settlement on 'an equal division of property among independent freemen' who 'held lordship and vassalage ... in abhorrence', but who pursued their 'love of liberty' abroad, where arbitrary monarchic rule nevertheless repeatedly hampered 'the spirit of the British constitution', in which liberty lay in the people, and not the King and his greedy and careerist envoys.[61] Both historians fed on their knowledge of the settler history of their native regions to argue for the legitimacy of settler rights, shaped by constant conflict and negotiations over the meaning of both Britishness and empire. Creole historiographies of settlement must be studied in the *longue durée* of European expansionism, for their contribution to shaping overseas political and social orders and their legacies in the postcolonial present.

Conclusion

The biggest strength of settler colonialism as a historiographical theory and practice is that it encourages us to place the structure of imperialism and the process of colonialism at the centre of European expansion outside their metropolitan homelands. Its two biggest weaknesses are its reductive notion of the logic of elimination and its lack of interest in explicating the 'ideal types' of indigene, settler and enslaved African. How might we improve this concept, so it is more analytically powerful for understanding early America? There are two themes that could be connected to settler colonialism which have so far been kept separate. These are the historiographies of the fiscal-military state – the state shaped the experiences of all three groups of colonial peoples in very profound ways – and how settler colonialism intersects with empire. Adopting a revised settler colonialism that pays attention to these two themes might have the added benefit of helping us transcend the 'slavery-to-freedom narrative' that so shapes both African American history and American history in general.

The Indigenous legal scholar Maggie Blackhawk makes this point when she argues that having a slavery-to-freedom narrative as the central dynamic of US legal doctrine excludes a different historical reality, that made by Indigenous historians about how Native Americans are central to the American experience and to the laws that govern the nation. She has written a lengthy article in the *Harvard Law Review* arguing for Native American law to be viewed as more central in constitution-making than it is at present, and argues that the USA's 'tragic history of colonialism and violent dispossession of Native American lands, resources, culture and children' has much to teach us about reimagining the constitutional history of the USA.[62] The slavery to freedom narrative is mostly unhelpful in understanding slavery in the colonial period when the slave trade was legal and flourishing, when slavery was fully accepted, and slave resistance was fiercely and successfully put down. The biggest problem with this narrative, as Robin Kelley, drawing on the work of Cedric Robinson, argues, is that it assumes that Africans were decultured people ripped from their past but fails to see that while Africans do not fit into an eliminationist narrative, they were assimilated or integrated as settlers and were placed within two very powerful structures – the plantation complex and the imperial state.[63] If disconnected from some of its more obviously untrue contentions, such as the 'elimination of the native', settler colonialism becomes more sensitive to the arguments and anxieties about establishing a settler presence in British America exhibited in writers like Long and Belknap, who understood the instability and transiency of 'settlers' when compared to 'subjects' or 'colonists'. As Eliga Gould and Rosemary Zagarri argue, 'Significantly, under English and Anglo-American law, European settlers and settlements were not in fact "settled" but could be forcibly removed, as happened repeatedly to Acadians in the borderlands between Nova Scotia and the United States'.[64] That settlers could always be removed somewhere else and indeed came from somewhere else can be an intriguing and useful way to think through some of the important dynamics of colonisation in the seventeenth- and eighteenth-century British Atlantic.

Notes

1 Robert Bickers, 'Introduction: Britains and Britons over the seas', in Robert Bickers (ed.), *Settlers and Expatriates* (Oxford: Oxford University Press, 2010), 1–17. One word that might work is 'creole', but it refers as much to a state of being as to a particular category of people: Richard Price, 'Créolisation, creolization and créolité', *Small Axe* 21, no. 1 (2017), 211–19.

2 Jack P. Greene (ed.), *Exclusionary Empires: English Liberty Overseas, 1600–1900* (New York: Cambridge University Press, 2009).

3 Peter H. Lindert and Jeffrey G. Williamson, 'American colonial incomes, 1650–1774', *Economic History Review* 69, no. 1 (2016), 54–77; Laura Panza and Jeffrey G. Williamson, 'Living costs and living standards: Australian development, 1820–1870', *European Review of Economic History* 24, no. 1 (2020), 80–97; Trevor Burnard, Laura Panza and Jeffrey G. Williamson, 'Living costs, real incomes and inequality in colonial Jamaica', *Explorations in Economic History* 71 (2019), 55–71.
4 Ned Blackhawk, 'The tracks of settler colonialism', *Reviews in American History* 47, no. 4 (2019), 564–71 at 568.
5 Brenna Bhandar, *Colonial Lives of Property? Law, Land, and Racial Regimes of Ownership* (Durham: Duke University Press, 2018).
6 Michael Witgen, 'A nation of settlers: The early American Republic and the colonization of the northwest territory', *WMQ* 76, no. 3 (2019), 391–8 at 398.
7 For a thoughtful treatment of Blacks in North America and the British Empire in the nineteenth century, set within the framework of settler colonialism, see Ikuko Asaka, *Tropical Freedom: Climate, Settler Colonialism, and Black Exclusion in the Age of Emancipation* (Durham: Duke University Press, 2017).
8 Chad Anderson, 'Rediscovering Native America: Settlements, maps, and empires in the eastern woodlands', *Early American Studies* 14, no. 3 (2016), 478–505.
9 Alicia Cox, 'Settler colonialism', in *Oxford Bibliographies Online: Literary and Critical Theory* (2017), www.oxfordbibliographies.com; Patrick Wolfe, 'Settler colonialism and the elimination of the Native', *Journal of Genocide Research* 8, no. 4 (2006), 387–409.
10 Patrick Wolfe, *Traces of History: Elementary Structures of Race* (London: Verso, 2016).
11 Allan Greer, 'Settler colonialism and empire in early America', *WMQ* 76, no. 3 (2019), 383–90 at 384. For a view similar to Greer, see Daniel Richter, 'His own, their own: Settler colonialism, Native peoples, and imperial balances of power in Eastern North America, 1660–1715', in Ignacio Gallup-Diaz (ed.), *The World of Colonial America: An Atlantic Handbook* (New York: Routledge, 2017), 208–33.
12 Greer, 'Settler colonialism'. For the application of settler colonialism to the nineteenth century, see Frederick E. Hoxie, 'Retrieving the Red Continent: Settler colonialism and the history of American Indians in the US', *Ethnic and Racial Studies* 31, no. 6 (2008), 1153–67. See also Jeffrey Ostler, *Surviving Genocide: Native Nations and the United States from the American Revolution to Bleeding Kansas* (New Haven: Yale University Press, 2019).

13 Edward Countryman, 'Indians, the colonial order and the social significance of the American Revolution', *WMQ* 53, no. 2 (1996), 342–62 at 348; Allan Greer, *Property and Dispossession: Natives, Empires and Land in Early Modern North America* (New York: Cambridge University Press, 2018), 3, 20, 22, 406. See also Stuart Banner, *How the Indians Lost their Land: Law and Power on the Frontier* (Cambridge, MA: Harvard University Press, 2005).

14 Erik Altenbernd and Alex Trimble Young, 'Introduction: The significance of the frontier in an age of transnational history', *Settler Colonial Studies* 4, no. 2 (2014), 127–50. For a somewhat different genealogy, which also places a lot of importance on Turner as an inspiration and opponent but which sees the concept of settler colonialism as emerging in stages, from being thought of as a subset of 'hypercolonialism' within a general theory of colonialism to being an autonomous scholarly field by the 1990s, see Lorenzo Veracini, '"Settler colonialism": Career of a concept', *Journal of Imperial and Commonwealth History* 41, no. 2 (2013), 313–33. Veracini and Gabriel Piterberg also trace the influence of another key thinker in Antipodean theories of colonialism – Edward Gibbon Wakefield – to Marxist ideas that combined into theories of settler colonialism, Lorenzo Veracini and Gabriel Piterberg, 'Wakefield, Marx and the world turned inside out', *Journal of Global History* 10, no. 3 (2015), 457–78.

15 Ronald Lawson, 'Towards demythologizing the "Australian Legend": Turner's frontier thesis and the Australian experience', *Journal of Social History* 13, no. 4 (1980), 577–87; Russel Ward, *The Australian Legend*, 2nd ed. (Melbourne: Oxford University Press, 1966); Henry Reynolds, *The Other Side of the Frontier: Aboriginal Resistance to the European Invasion of Australia* (Sydney: University of New South Wales Press, 1981).

16 Richard White, *The Middle Ground: Indians, Empires, and Republics in the Great Lakes Region, 1650–1815* (Cambridge: Cambridge University Press, 1993); Susan Sleeper-Smith (ed.), 'Forum: The middle ground revisited', *WMQ* 63, no. 1 (2006), 3–96.

17 Altenbernd and Young, 'Introduction', 131.

18 Jennifer M. Spear, 'Beyond the native/settler divide in early California', *WMQ* 76, no. 3 (2019), 427–34.

19 Another important survey of settler colonialism by an early Americanist that takes a similar position to that in this chapter and the *WMQ* forum is Charles Prior, 'Beyond settler colonialism: State sovereignty in early America', *Journal of Early American History* 9, no. 2–3 (2019), 93–117.

20 Trevor Burnard, *The Atlantic in World History, 1492–1830* (London: Bloomsbury, 2020).
21 Among a vast literature, see Elizabeth Ellis, 'The Natchez War revisited: Violence, multinational settlements, and Indigenous diplomacy in the Lower Mississippi Valley', *WMQ* 77, no. 3 (2020), 441–72; Michael A. McDonnell, *Masters of Empire: Great Lakes' Indians and the Making of America* (New York: Hill and Wang, 2015); Pekka Hämäläinen, *Lakota America: A New History of Indigenous Power* (New Haven: Yale University Press, 2019).
22 Sir William Berkeley to Major-General Robert Smith, 22 June 1666, in Warren M. Billings, 'Sir William Berkeley – Portrait by Fischer: A Critique', *WMQ* 48, no. 4 (1991), 598–607 at 601; John Murrin, 'Beneficiaries of catastrophe: The English colonies in America', in Eric Foner (ed.), *The New American History* (Philadelphia: Temple University Press, 1997), 3–30 at 4.
23 J.G.A. Pocock, *The Discovery of Islands: Essays in British History* (Cambridge: Cambridge University Press, 2005). For an important review of this book and how it connects to wider themes in British and intellectual history, see P. Glenn Burgess, 'From the common law mind to the *Discovery of Islands*: J.G.A. Pocock's journey', *History of Political Thought* 29, no. 3 (2008), 543–61.
24 J.G.A. Pocock, *Barbarism and Religion*, 5 vols. (Cambridge: Cambridge University Press, 1999–2011); Colin Kidd, 'Europe, what Europe?', *London Review of Books*, 30 (2008).
25 Pocock, *Discovery of Islands*, 231.
26 *Ibid.*
27 Saul Dubow, 'How British was the British world? The case of South Africa', *Journal of Imperial and Commonwealth History* 37, no. 1 (2009), 1–27 at 4.
28 *Ibid.*
29 For the genealogy of plantations, see Paul Musselwhite, '"Plantations," the public good and the rise of capitalist agriculture in the early seventeenth-century Caribbean', *Early American Studies* 20, no. 4 (2022), 597–618.
30 Lou Roper's essay in this volume.
31 See, for instance, William Stratchey, '"True reportory" from Virginia', in David B. Quinn, Alison M. Quinn and Susan Hillier (eds.), *New American World: A Documentary History of North America to 1612*, 5 vols. (New York: Arno Press, 1979), 5: 290.
32 Richard S. Dunn, James Savage and Laetitia Yeandle (eds.), *The Journal of John Winthrop, 1630–1649* (Cambridge, MA: Harvard University Press, 1996), 134; 'Governor Bradford's letter book', in *Collections of*

the *Massachusetts Historical Society*, 1st ser. (Boston: Massachusetts Historical Society, 1794), 56.
33 John Smith, *General History of Virginia, New England, and the Summer Isles* (London, 1624), 152.
34 Gary B. Nash, 'The concept of inevitability in European–Indian relations', in Carla G. Pestana and Sharon V. Salinger (eds.), *Inequality in Early America* (Hanover: University Press of New England, 1999), 267–91.
35 Daniel Dulany, 'The right of the inhabitants of Maryland to the benefit of the English laws (1728)', in Jack P. Greene and Craig B. Yirush (eds.), *Exploring the Bounds of Liberty: Political Writings of Colonial British America from the Glorious Revolution to the American Revolution*, 3 vols. (Indianapolis: Liberty Fund, 2018), 1: 649–76, 700.
36 Jean M. O'Brien, *Firsting and Lasting: Writing Indians out of Existence in New England* (Minneapolis: University of Minnesota Press, 2010).
37 Dunn et al., *Journal of John Winthrop*, 167; Robert Beverley, *The History and Present State of Virginia*, ed. Louis B. Wright (Chapel Hill: University of North Carolina Press, 1947), 55.
38 Courts addresse to his majestie, 2 October 1678, in Nathaniel Shurtleff (ed.), *Records of the Governor and Company of the Massachusetts Bay*, 5 vols. (Boston: Massachusetts Historical Society, 1854), 5: 197–8 at 197.
39 Dulany, *The Right of the Inhabitants of Maryland*, 687.
40 David Ramsay, *History of the United States, from their First Settlement as English Colonies, in 1607, to the Year 1808*, 3 vols. (Philadelphia: M. Carey, 1810), 1: iii.
41 Ibid., 11.
42 See, for instance, Hugh Williamson, *The History of North Carolina*, 2 vols. (Philadelphia: Thomas Dobson, 1812) or Benjamin Trumbull, *A Complete History of Connecticut, Civil and Ecclesiastical*, 2 vols. (New Haven: Maltby, Goldsmith and Co., 1818).
43 Frederick Jackson Turner, *The First Official Frontier of Massachusetts Bay* (Cambridge, MA: John Wilson and Son University Press, 1914), 254, and *The Significance of the Frontier in American History* ([1920] New York: Penguin Books, 2008), 14.
44 Lorenzo Veracini, 'Historylessness: Australia as a settler colonial collective', in Pramod K. Nayat (ed.), *Postcolonial Studies: An Anthology* (Hoboken: Wiley–Blackwell, 2016), 164.
45 James Belich, *Replenishing the Earth: The Settler Revolution and the Rise of the Anglo-World, 1783–1939* (Oxford: Oxford University Press, 2009), 4.

46 Susannah Shaw Romney, 'Settler colonial prehistories in seventeenth-century North America', *WMQ* 76, no. 3 (2019), 375–82 at 376.
47 Jeffrey Ostler, 'Locating settler colonialism in early American history', *WMQ* 76, no. 3 (2019), 443–50; Walter Hixson, *American Settler Colonialism: A History* (New York: Palgrave Macmillan, 2013); Bethel Saler, *The Settlers' Empire: Colonialism and State Formation in America's Old Northwest* (Philadelphia: University of Pennsylvania Press, 2015).
48 Trevor Burnard, 'Those other English colonies: The historiography of Jamaica in the time of James Knight', in Jack P. Greene (ed.), *The Natural, Moral, and Political History of Jamaica … by J[ames] K[night]* (Charlottesville: University of Virginia Press, 2021), 643–54.
49 Edward Long, *History of Jamaica*, 3 vols. (London: T. Lowndes, 1774). For an appreciation of Long's history as a text about settlers in Jamaica, see Elizabeth A. Bohls, 'The gentleman planter and the metropole: Long's history of Jamaica', in Gerald Maclean *et al.* (eds.), *The Country and the City Revisited: England and the Politics of Culture, 1550–1850* (Cambridge: Cambridge University Press, 1999), 180–96; Suman Seth, 'Materialism, slavery, and the *History of Jamaica*', *Isis* 105, no. 4 (2014), 764–72.
50 Jeremy Belknap, *A History of New Hampshire*, 3 vols. (Boston, 1812); Agnès Delahaye, 'Jeremy Belknap's *History of New Hampshire* in context: Settler colonialism and the historiography of New England', *Journal of Early American History* 8, no. 1 (2018), 60–91.
51 Adam Smith, *Theory of Moral Sentiments* (London, 1759), 402–3.
52 Long, *History of Jamaica*, 2: 262, 280.
53 Jeremy Belknap, *American Biography: Or, an Historical Account of Those Persons Who Have Been Distinguished in America*, 2 vols. (Boston: Thomas and Andrews, 1794, 1798).
54 Trevor Burnard, 'A failed settler society: Marriage and demographic failure in early Jamaica', *Journal of Social History* 28, no. 1 (1994), 63–82. For the centrality of population to discourses of settler colonialism, see Lorenzo Veracini, *Settler Colonialism: A Theoretical Overview* (Basingstoke: Palgrave Macmillan, 2010), 16–32.
55 Belknap, *History of New Hampshire*, 1: 65–6.
56 Trevor Burnard, *Jamaica in the Age of Revolution* (Philadelphia: University of Pennsylvania Press, 2020), Ch. 2.
57 Jeremy Belknap, 'Observations upon the question, has the discovery of American been useful or hurtful to mankind?', *Boston Magazine*, 1 May 1784, 280–6.
58 Long, *History of Jamaica*, 1: 413–4.
59 Belknap, *History of New Hampshire*, 2: 66–7, 226.

60 Planter [Edward Long], *Candid Reflections upon the Judgement Lately Awarded by the Court of King's Bench in Westminster-Hall, on What Is Commonly Called the Negroe-Cause* (London: T. Lowndes, 1772).
61 Belknap, *History of New Hampshire*, 1: 141, 173.
62 Maggie Blackhawk, 'Federal Indian law as paradigm within public law', *Harvard Law Review* 132, no. 7 (2019), 1787–877.
63 Robin D.G. Kelley, 'The rest of us: Rethinking settler and native', *American Quarterly* 69, no. 2 (2017), 267–76.
64 Eliga Gould and Rosemarie Zagarri, 'Situating the United States in vast early America: Introduction', *WMQ* 78, no. 2 (2021), 189–200.

8

Colonising the Cape of Good Hope: Company policy and settlers' interests in a contested space of European occupation in Southern Africa

Marilyn Garcia-Chapleau

The history of the gradual and conflictual growth of European settlement at the Cape of Good Hope illustrates the role settlers played in influencing the highly competitive world of colonial acquisition, which we consider too often as centred principally on the interests of the metropole. In the early seventeenth century, when European settlement began at the Cape, this outpost had an anchorage at the foot of what was to be called Table Mountain, a small massif with a flat top overlooking a thousand metres of narrow coastal plain already well known to Portuguese, English and French navigators. Dutch settlement was initiated in 1652, administered by the VOC. As numerous letters and documents exchanged between the VOC directors and the commanders at the Cape of Good Hope demonstrate, in the minds of the executive council of VOC directors in Amsterdam – the *Heren XVII* or Lords Seventeen – the Cape was an outpost in a place that offered no prospects in terms of spices, gems, gold or other valuable commodities.[1] It would serve as a harbour and a refreshment station supplying fresh water and food to the VOC fleets on their way to and from Asia, in order 'to promote the welfare of the United Netherlands, to secure and develop trade, and to operate for the profit of the Company and the inhabitants of the country', an approach that their officers on the ground duly executed. The Cape grew slowly until the British seized it in 1795, putting an end to almost 150 years of VOC rule. The British aimed to gain control over routes to the Far East to prevent all trade except their own. They withdrew from the Cape in 1802 pursuant to the

Treaty of Amiens, but they again took command, *manu militari*, in 1806, regained control and obtained lasting sovereignty on 13 August 1814. This chapter corrects the generally accepted view that the prospect of the Cape's natural riches and agricultural resources prompted the British takeover of the Dutch territory and explores the role of settler agency in influencing imperial plans. It argues that the different waves of European settlers to the Cape over the course of the eighteenth century had led to a settler population prone to invoking liberal continental influence, from the Netherlands and from 'Jacobinist' France in particular, that threatened British influence in this crucial location of its commercial empire.

The modest genesis of a supply station

The VOC was chartered in 1602 to trade east of the Cape of Good Hope and west of the Strait of Magellan. In two centuries, the VOC equipped some 4,700 ships, employed nearly one million sailors and soldiers, invested two billion guilders and sold shipments of spices, precious woods, porcelain and textiles for an even greater return. The VOC had sovereignty rights in its territories granted by the States-General, but it quickly freed itself from any control of the Dutch Republic.[2] It established itself as a thalassocracy, controlling a large expanse of sea, asserting its power in a commercial and military sense, arrogating to itself the right to dictate orders and signing treaties and declaring war according to its commercial interests. It was designed to be a powerful military and economic weapon. Such a 'military and naval power that imposes its unifying policy' was, therefore, in the words of the French navigator Louis-Antoine de Bougainville, 'more similar to a mighty republic than a merchant company' (*'plus semblable à une puissante république qu'à une société de marchands'*). Invested with the right to forge alliances, the VOC conducted its own shadow diplomacy and is customarily regarded as either a state within a state or as a multinational company with its military constituting a private force.[3]

Early European visitors at the Cape deemed the peninsula and coastal plain very inhospitable. Both were indeed populated by 'savage *Hautitants*' who, according to the 1645 observations of the French mercenary in VOC service Jean Guidon de Chambelle, 'if they found any isolated Christian, they would make a good meal of him' (*'S'ils trouvaient quelque chrétien à l'écart, en feraient un bon repas'*). The French adventurer also noticed 'many ostriches, lions, tigers, deer, panthers and small turtles' and had a vivid memory of 'a very barren country, bringing in almost nothing' (*'force autruches, lions, tigres, cerfs, panthères et petites tortues' ... 'pays fort stérile et ne rapportant presque rien'*).[4] Thus, the primary function of the Cape settlement was to feed and water crews on the long voyage to and from Asia and to service ships damaged by storms or attacks from Indian Ocean privateers. The directors of the VOC had no other ambition for the Cape as they were keen to benefit from Asia's great wealth. Between 1640 and 1700 and in the years 1700–95, the purchase prices of the return goods shipped home from Asia reached 205 and 667 million guilders respectively; the sale prices of these return wares were 577 million guilders in the first period and 1,633 million guilders in the second.[5]

Their letters to the local authorities were unequivocal: 'The establishment is to be kept down as much as possible ... The smaller the Cape station is kept, the more serviceable and profitable it will be for the Company,' they wrote on 17 December 1657. In a letter to Cape Commander Jan van Riebeeck, dated 23 August 1661, the Lords Seventeen again expressed their opposition:

> From your letters we have remarked that you are gradually tending towards the building of a town there and the enlarging of the colony; but as we look upon it here, this idea should be abandoned, and you should get along with the men and the freemen whom you have with you at present, without extending yourself any further. For what would it avail us to establish large colonies there if we are obliged to feed them successively from outside. Moreover, the men will be more required in India than at the Cape.[6]

'The Company', South African historian Hermann Giliomee has summarised, 'had envisaged a neat, compact settlement that would not extend beyond the shadow of the coastal fort'. Obviously, the Lords Seventeen wanted to reduce costs at the Cape and save manpower for their profitable operations in Asia. Thus, in 1657, they created a community of free farmers or free burghers, who had to produce refreshment foodstuffs for the passing fleets and were given military obligations to reduce the size of the garrison. The VOC, however, never managed to cut costs and had to run its operations at the Cape at a loss.[7]

An unpromising land neglected by the Dutch

Neither the limited interior explorations nor the installation of the first nine free burghers to the northeast of Table Mountain contributed to the development of the settlement, whose 'economic and political unimportance' was highlighted by Robert Ross. From 1657 onwards, ten reconnaissance missions failed to find any ivory, gold or precious stones in the hinterland. In October 1663, for instance, sergeant Jonas de la Guerre, a Frenchman from Le Havre de Grâce, acting under the instructions of Zacharias Wagenaer, Commander at the Cape, sought out Monomotapa, a legendary city rumoured to be rich in gold, but found nothing. Indigenous people encountered during these expeditions finally convinced the VOC local officials that the regions to the north of the peninsula lacked valuable commodities.[8]

On the other hand, the VOC accepted the installation of independent farmers on the land situated northeast of Table Valley, mainly to restrict the size of the company personnel and to increase local production of meat, wine and cereals. Former employees of the VOC, all European soldiers and sailors who had terminated their contract with the company, were made free burghers. Commander van Riebeeck granted thirteen *morgen*, or some ten hectares, to each of the first nine free burghers in February 1657 and to twenty-seven more burghers before his departure in 1662 (by that time, each burgher received fifty *morgen* of land). By 1706, the number of free burghers reached 568.[9] These migrants from Europe hoped to be 'burghers and citizens, not mere subjects or subordinates', but they were sworn subjects of the States-General and the VOC, to whom they remained bound by oath. For example, the Company reserved for itself the right and power to re-enrol them, as stated in the letters of freedom issued to former sailors and soldiers by the Cape commanders. As South African historian Yvonne Brink concludes: 'Becoming free did not mean freedom from VOC domination'.[10]

The VOC's labour policy aimed at reducing the number of company employees at the Cape, but it also promoted the settlement of

Colonising the Cape of Good Hope

French Protestant refugees, who came willingly and at their own cost, boosting European presence in the region but also transforming the original stock of Dutch settlers into a more diverse settler population. Two hundred and eighty Huguenots acquired lands of between sixty and 120 *morgen* (from fifty-five hectares to 110 hectares) in the Berg Valley, in the Drakenstein massif located about thirty miles from Table Valley, bringing valuable contribution to the development of viticulture and agriculture. VOC local authorities, however, were deeply suspicious of the Huguenots and encouraged their assimilation into the Dutch community. Huguenots, 'although settled here and well received are the least to be trusted,' Governor Simon van der Stel wrote in his instructions dated 10 March 1699 to his son Willem Adriaan. The conflicts between the French community and the Dutch authority demonstrate how weak and difficult local governance was when the settler population was hybrid and did not share the same motivation or incentives to obey orders.[11]

Simon van der Stel's animosity towards the French at the Cape began in 1688, when the Huguenot refugees asked to be resettled on other land than that given to them and required to be allowed to worship in their own congregation. When the matter came up at the meeting of the *Politieke Raad*, the 'Cape Political Council' that was the highest authority at the Cape of Good Hope, Van der Stel said that he experienced many difficulties from some of the 'so-called refugees' who had left France under the pretence of religious persecution by their King. The governor argued that the French Protestants settled in the Netherlands to live an idle and lazy life under the pretence of being devotees, members and supporters of the Reformed faith. He therefore 'decided to rein in the French impertinences, stop all conspiracies in time by giving them a thorough rebuke and to reprimand them seriously to do their duty'. They were also seriously warned to keep to the conditions of the contract under which they came to the Cape and to refrain in future from troubling the Commander with 'such impertinent requests'.[12]

During his governorship (1699–1707), Willem Adriaan van der Stel showed similar hostility towards the Cape Huguenots, especially those who sided with the burgher petitioners who in 1706 accused the governor of embezzlement and the clique of Cape officials of misconduct; 'Vergelegen, Willem Adriaan van der Stel's farm, had been developed in the grand style of European Estates.

The size of ten ordinary farms, it employed two hundred enslaved individuals and sixty white *knechten*, or overseers', Hermann Giliomee explains.[13] Most of the leading figures of the Huguenot community were thrown into jail as they expressed outrage for the Cape officials' nepotism and corruption and asked for the Governor to be recalled. Adam Tas, a Cape Dutch burgher who led the uprising against the unlimited power of the Governor and his aggrandisement and opulent lifestyle, called the French 'patriots'.[14] The VOC dismissed van der Stel, ordered his return to the Netherlands in 1707 and forbid VOC officials to own any land at the Cape of Good Hope. The Company had been forced under settler pressure to alter its policy.

Even though Nicolas Verburg, a senior VOC official, believed after his inspection of the Cape station in 1676 that it was 'highly necessary, now still more than before, that a good Dutch colony shall be planted and reared here', the small permanent establishment never underwent decisive expansion. It should be added that the local VOC officials could accumulate wealth only if they indulged in profiteering, which meant taking control of the local economy, creating and maintaining trade monopolies and relying on corruption. As Gerrit Schutte states, 'in a situation where everyone, from high to low, tried to enrich himself by more or less permissible means, excesses easily occurred'. The Cape Governor received a nominal salary of 2,400 guilders per annum, but subsistence allowances and payments in kind quadrupled this amount, while the tithe on wheat planted at the Cape ensured the governor of a supplementary income. Similar increases of salary occurred among the lower ranks.[15] The management of the refreshment station thus remained chronically in deficit, which further encumbered VOC revenues. The Fourth Anglo-Dutch War of 1780–84 and the Napoleonic Wars facilitated the downfall and bankruptcy of the Company, declared in 1799. The Dutch Government then assumed direct control of the VOC's affairs and assets, but it did not prevent the fall of the first multinational corporation in the world: the VOC collapsed on 14 April 1822.[16]

The VOC's governance had been increasingly challenged by the inhabitants of Cape Town, still exasperated by monopolistic practices and blatant corruption, and whose strong desire for emancipation inevitably grew. The burghers had no seat in the

Politieke Raad, and therefore no official voice in the running of the refreshment station, and they resented the 'deeply paternalistic attitude the Company displayed towards the colonists', as well as the hierarchical principles entrenched in the VOC administration. Corresponding distrust between local VOC officials and Cape burghers led to repeated complaints and conflicts, in 1706, between Governor Willem Adriaan van der Stel and the burghers, and in 1738–39, when Estienne Barbier, a French-born sergeant in the service of the VOC, incited people to disobedience and rebellion, and in 1778, when pamphlets circulated in Cape Town stating that the burghers had the duty to change the form of government.[17]

Containing Jacobinism and ousting the French

It was not so much the bankruptcy of the VOC that brought about the British intervention at the end of the eighteenth century but strategic considerations. The Cape of Good Hope was at the intersection between the Dutch, French and British Empires, and the Europeans of the Cape were calling for their emancipation. In the eyes of the British Government, the Cape's strategic importance grew, considering the limits of St Helena, the usual port of call in the South Atlantic where the East India Company had set up a post. But this small and barren island was not suitable to serve as a refreshment station for large fleets and was unable to produce enough provisions for the EIC's fleets heading to and from India.[18] Moreover, the British Government showed great concern about the growing threat to EIC ships by French privateers operating in the Indian Ocean since 1780, based in Ile de France (present-day Mauritius). Because of its location and supply capacity, the small Cape fort at the southern tip of Africa promised to become more than a stopover and serve as a stronghold for ensuring the safety of commercial vessels.

Meanwhile, Dutch governance at the Cape was increasingly unstable. The failure of the VOC, the profiteering of Cape officials and the endemic corruption within the company sparked a colonial rebellion. Burghers invoked their 'power' – their freedom and their duty – to change the form of government by violence if necessary, should the authorities no longer perform their natural task of 'standing for the people, and defending their lives, property, and liberty', wrote the Dutch historian Gerrit Schutte.[19] In the first months of 1778, two anonymous pamphlets were circulated in Cape Town denouncing the personal enrichment of high local officials and complaining that 'this languishing condition of the Cape citizenry and colonists is largely caused and further aggravated by the oppression under whose burden the entire citizenry must groan and the unauthorized private trade conducted by several of Your Honour's officials here'. Their elaborate petition, which criticised the arbitrary situation in Cape Town and the exorbitant monopolies held by a few civilian and military officials, was handed over to the Lords Seventeen by four burgher delegates on 16 October 1779.[20] The directors turned down this first petition, as they did the second one submitted in 1782, leading settler representatives to appeal directly to the States-General in February 1784. The petitioners warned the Dutch Government that 'discontent ha[d] become so prevalent among a considerable number of inhabitants of this colony that one ha[d] much ground for wondering whether public order [could] be maintained without disruption as necessary for the general welfare'.[21] This emergent free burgher minority – four hundred burghers signed the 1779 petition out of a total free burgher population of eight thousand, including families – was determined to make settler grievances and demands heard. They were certainly influenced by the Patriot movement in Holland which, at the time, was defying the authority of Prince William V of Orange and fighting against aristocratic privileges and for popular sovereignty. Besides, some dissidents did not hide their sympathy both for France, which came to the rescue of Cape Town in 1781, and for American republican ideals; thus, they sensed the rising tide of democracy and opportunities for self-determination in Europe and the Americas.[22] Located at a crucial intersection between European imperial interests, Cape settlers mobilised the language of rights and liberties at work in other imperial spaces to argue for their own particular settler prerogatives.

Settler interests, however, were complicated by the strategic position and advantage of their settlements. The Dutch colony was threatened by the British as the Fourth Anglo-Dutch War (1780–84) was raging from Europe to India. The need to reinforce the

French forces in the Indian Ocean and concern about the safety of the Cape had already received much attention in France before the outbreak of the war. Jean-Baptiste Charles Bouvet De Lozier, a former governor of Ile de Bourbon, had warned the Minister of Marine, the Marquis De Castries, that the Cape was 'the magazine of our islands of France and Bourbon' (*'le magasin de nos îles de France et de Bourbon'*) and that it would be difficult to maintain French claims to these islands and to wage the war in the Indian Ocean more generally without access to the Cape. In December 1780, news of a British plan to seize the Cape and a recognition of Dutch weakness compelled the French to act by sending a fleet of fourteen ships under Pierre André de Suffren and the Pondicherry Regiment with over seventeen hundred soldiers to hold the Dutch colony from 1781 to 1783. More troops, though, were needed to keep the British at bay: in 1781, the VOC contracted the Luxemburg Regiment of over eleven hundred soldiers and the Legion of Baron of Waldener, a battalion of five hundred men. The De Meuron Regiment was also contracted but its eleven hundred mostly Swiss soldiers arrived at the Cape only in 1783, to replace the Luxemburg Regiment that had left for Ceylon.[23]

With each new wave of military or strategic occupation, relations between settlers, occupiers and colonial authorities became more complex. The French presence coincided with two years of prosperity to Cape Town, with house property, enslaved people and horse values rising 50 to 100 per cent, as French officers bought mansions and horses and needed servants. It also brought two years of 'extravagance and frivolity' which saw Cape Town become a 'little Paris', according to the very Calvinist governor Jacob de Mist. On 25 August 1783, the French festival of Saint-Louis was celebrated at the Cape, with the VOC hosting a grand ball in the Castle. The French, Governor Mist recorded, 'entirely corrupted the standard of living at the Cape, and extravagance and indulgence in an unbroken round of amusements and diversions have come to be regarded as necessities'. On the other hand, the French presence also encouraged exchanges of ideas between Cape Europeans and French literate officers from the Pondicherry Regiment, like future French revolutionary leader Paul Barras, but also from the De Meuron Regiment, like Louis-Michel Thibault, a Freemason officer and future chief military engineer of Cape Town.[24]

In 1783, as the French contingent was returning to Europe, *L'Afrique Hollandaise ou le tableau historique et politique de l'état originaire de la colonie du cap de Bonne-espérance comparé avec l'état actuel de cette colonie* was published in Holland. The author was anonymous but presented himself as an 'educated observer' (*'observateur instruit'*). Indeed, the writer appeared to be very familiar with the history of the Cape station, its governance and the prevarication mechanisms of the VOC, whose excesses, he pointed out, had become 'unbearable' (*'insupportable'*). The text, more than an expression of discontent, was a call for sedition by empowered settlers against this 'horrible and destructive regime' (*'le regime affreux et destructeur'*). The author recalled that the Cape garrison had only five hundred soldiers, while the burgher militia, which was tasked to protect the Cape inland, had six thousand. By that time, the number of free burghers exceeded the number of VOC officials by fifteen to two.[25] This burgher militia had been created as a first burgher *kommando* in 1715, to supplement the small garrison at the Cape. It drew all men into military service to protect the colony from Khoikhoi attacks on farms and to prevent cattle theft, and grew into a regional system for the defence of European settlement. The writer warned that the people of Cape Town had the means to 'one day decide to take revenge' on the colonial Government.[26]

In early 1795, while those known as the Cape Patriots and many free burgher farmers displayed their pro-French and pro-revolutionary sentiments, the VOC, entangled in its cash flow problems, decided to increase local taxes. As Giliomee explains, 'the farmers were increasingly reluctant to pay because they had to travel a long way to do so and because the Company as they thought offered virtually nothing in return for the tax'.[27] A revolt immediately broke out in the new districts, east of Cape Town. In Graaff-Reinet in February 1795, and then Swellendam in June, farmers refused to pay taxes, expelled VOC officials and took power before setting up a 'national convention' as a new governing body that would secure their political rights and protect their economic interests as a National Constituent Assembly along the French model. In a September 1795 *Memorandum* on the condition of the Colony, J.F. Kirsten – a senior Company official who became a free burgher in 1792 – declared: 'This colony has for several years been on the decline, and rapidly approaching its annihilation. ... I may venture to say that nothing less than a revolution could have saved it'.[28]

Some of the seditious burghers even wore the tricolour cockade, the official symbol of the French Revolution, or the Dutch tricolour. This led the British General James Henry Craig, commander of the British Expeditionary Force sent to the Cape, to claim that it was 'certain that the great body of the people [were] at the moment infected with the rankest poison of Jacobinism'. The same general, in a letter dated 29 June 1795 to the *Politieke Raad*, warned, somewhat disingenuously, that if France took over Cape Town, the establishment would be ruined, the abolition of slavery imposed and human rights granted to Indigenous people. General Craig knew that manpower shortage at the Cape was acute and that Dutch colonists everywhere relied on enslaved people for labour, as shown by Elisabeth Heijsman and Rafaël Thiebaut in Chapter 6 of this volume. That year, when two thousand VOC officials and roughly twenty thousand burghers were counted, 'the Cape's reported enslaved population of 16,839 consisted almost entirely of private enslaved individuals, the Company possessing only 3 per cent of this figure'; 62 per cent of urban free burghers were enslavers in 1800.[29]

Enter the British

The rebellions of Graaff-Reinet and Swellendam were short-lived, for a British fleet anchored behind Table Mountain in False Bay on 9 July 1795 heralded the deployment of troops to seize the Cape. The British Admiralty had been ordered to neutralise the anchorages of the newly formed Batavian Republic, especially those likely to fall into the hands of the French Revolutionary Navy or to harbour French privateers. As Theodorus Daniel Potgieter explains, 'control of the Cape provided naval control of the southern oceans and the opportunity for maritime interdiction ... It was of value to Britain not only because of the sea route to India and as a place of replenishment, but also as a base which could act as an operational staging post for military operations in the South Atlantic and in the Indian Ocean'. Thus, 'British decision-makers were convinced that if France had control of the Cape, the feather in the hands of Holland would become a sword in the hands of France'. After almost a month of unsuccessful negotiations between the British and the VOC officials at the Cape, British troops landed, pushed out local defenders during the Battle of Muizenberg and took control of the Dutch territory on 16 September 1795.[30] France – and Jacobinism – had been ousted from the Cape. In his 1804 *Account of the Cape of Good Hope*, British Captain Robert Percival pondered:

> What would their situation have been at the Cape if the British forces had not arrived at the time they did; a period truly critical and teeming with tragical events. The sanguinary principles of Marat and Robespierre were by that time not only sown but growing to maturity amongst them. Jacobinism was ready to involve the colony in destruction and the cloud was on the eve of bursting when we appeared.[31]

But the British invasion had another consequence. It brought the era of the VOC to an end, in accordance with the aspirations of the Cape Patriots and burghers. The British era began in the name of His Britannic Majesty King George III, which, on the other hand, was not to please the local autonomists; some of them, in March 1796, refused to pledge allegiance to the Crown and even tore off the British flag.[32]

Like the VOC before them, the British underestimated the cost of maintaining the colony. Defences were improved, a large garrison of five thousand men was kept in Cape Town and a naval squadron of seven ships of the line, seven frigates, four smaller warships and a supply ship were stationed in Table Bay. All this proved quite expensive to the Crown, especially since the Cape was not commercially viable. In a letter to Secretary of State Henry Dundas, the Governor of the Cape Colony, Earl Macartney, confirmed the importance of the Cape for the security of India, yet, he recognised that defending it required 'a very great expense [and] not a little embarrassment'; Macartney mused that Ceylon might be retained instead if a choice had to be made regarding India's defence. However, the colony was returned to Dutch control in 1802, the resumption of the Napoleonic Wars renewed the concerns about French influence at the southern tip of Africa and the British seized control of the Cape again in January 1806.[33]

Unsurprisingly, the British at the Cape, especially Governors Craig and Macartney, sought to win the confidence of their new subjects, maintaining the system of law and the institutions of their predecessors, including the Dutch Reformed Church. The British also clearly espoused the cause of employers and enslavers. As South African historian Jeffrey Peires has summarised it, from an imperial point of view, 'the main object of the government was to establish order and tranquillity' so that 'by 1814 the transitional governments had simply reaffirmed the essentials of Cape social structure as it had existed prior to 1795'.[34] Cape colonists had therefore no reason to fear any major transformation of colonial society. On the commercial side, there was no change either. Thus, during the first British occupation, it was considered for a time to entrust the management of the Cape to the EIC. But as the colony could not contribute to its financial well-being, the EIC lost interest in governing it.[35]

From 1806, the new British rulers gradually focused on establishing order and prosperity with the view of securing their authority. Stability had to be maintained at all costs, but discontent on the eastern frontier provoked a revolt among the burghers in 1813, which historians call the Slagtersnek Rebellion. The rebels' discontent had arisen primarily from the perception that the Khoikhoi had been given privileges by the British. The Hottentot Proclamation of 1809 had given more protection to servants and enabled magistrates to eliminate brutal abuse of servants and other African labourers by European colonists. An acute shortage of land also generated grievances. In 1812, only 18 per cent of European colonists owned farms, and landless white farmers wished to settle beyond the borders of the colony. Ongoing armed conflict with Xhosa inhabitants and losses in cattle and land due to vagrancy and constant cattle theft by Khoikhoi raiders aggravated the settlers' sense of grievance.[36] Assuredly, the Government, unable to provide additional military resources, wanted to avoid clashes with Indigenous people. Exasperated frontier settlers then rose against colonial authorities. The 1816 crushing of the Slagtersnek Rebellion, though, demonstrated that the British would not tolerate insubordination from the colonists and would defend the Khoikhoi much more vigorously than the VOC had ever done. The British considered the Cape settlers immature men who needed to be governed by 'paternal despotism', as André du Toit and Hermann Giliomee put it.[37] British colonisation after 1814 therefore began with active restructuring, with the designation of English as the official language of the colony gradually imposed between 1822 and 1827 and rendered the only legally authorised language in courts and public offices in 1828. To be appointed to any official position, the applicant had to write competently and speak English fluently. So, plans to set up white English-medium schools throughout the colony were unveiled, where basic schooling was free and provided by English and Scottish teachers, some of whom founded the Athenaeum in 1829, which would become the University of Cape Town.[38]

To accelerate anglicisation, the British Government also decided to recruit British settlers to colonise the Eastern Cape. In addition to relieving the economic crisis in Britain after Waterloo, this measure was meant to provide a bulwark against attacks by African people, mainly Xhosa, pursuant to a scheme of assisted migration that involved eighty thousand candidates. On 9 April 1820, the first of these colonists landed in Algoa Bay, 470 miles east of Cape Town. Twenty other ships followed, carrying some four thousand people. The arrival of such a large contingent of British settlers profoundly affected frontier farmers in the Eastern Cape, whose lives in fact became harder, given that competition between Dutch, British, Khoikhoi and Xhosa people for grazing land had become even fiercer.[39]

This process of anglicisation also affected religious affairs. An attempt to anglicise the Dutch Reformed Church was made as the governor, Charles Somerset, recruited Scottish ministers to serve its parishes. The Reformed Church, nonetheless, remained an established church, together with the Anglican Church. However, as church membership reflected social status and the Anglicans were at the top of the social pyramid, part of the wealthy Dutch community moved over to the Anglican Church. As Robert Ross commented, 'by the mid-nineteenth century, most of the leading merchants in Cape Town were Anglicans, prepared to pay rents for the pews in the city's cathedral. It was a demonstration of the rank they had by then attained'.[40]

Lastly, regarding the administration of justice and the legal system, the British cautiously implemented a series of new labour regulation that was bound to put the basic structure of Dutch colonial society in jeopardy. Widely and deeply encouraged by English missionaries, the new measures were to regulate the employment of the Khoikhoi and prevent the abuse of free people of colour. In 1828, Ordinance 50 became law: it abolished passes implemented in 1809 to control the indenture system and the mobility of the labour force, proscribed the corporal punishment of labourers and granted Khoikhoi the right to land ownership. All in all, it curtailed the power that an employer had over his employees. Later legislation to abolish slavery came into force in 1834 at the Cape, resulting in the loss of 'human investment' and labour shortages and making manumission and labour critical issues among colonial enslavers and landowners.[41]

Some of the Dutch settlers, however, resisted these measures with their feet. In 1835, groups of Dutch farmers, called *Voortrekkers*, left the Cape Colony, crossed the colonial borders and headed for the hinterland of Southern Africa, in search of a 'promised land' where they hoped to restore economic, cultural and political unity beyond the reach of systematic imperial constraint on land ownership, labour relation and language. The Orange Free State and the Transvaal were established, in 1852 and 1854 respectively, by these migrants, but 'Britain had little to fear from these financially strapped republics', as Giliomee observed. In effect, the British Empire controlled the ports of Cape Town, Port Elizabeth and Durban, and the supply of ammunition to the landlocked republics. It is interesting to note that some *Voortrekkers* even established a republic, the Republic of Natalia, in 1839, which, however, was short-lived. The British would not recognise their independence, contrary to Boer independence in the Transvaal, for there was already a British trading community in Port Natal, now modern Durban.[42]

In spite of British input and British rule, the development of the Cape Colony remained slow. Robert Ross argues that in the mid-nineteenth century, 'the Cape economy was in all respect still puny', although over the course of two centuries, the production of wine, meat, wool and wheat had grown. By 1840, imports were still substantial, and the local economy continued to be heavily dependent on agriculture and livestock, leading to the disinterest of the Colonial Office, one of whose secretaries even wrote that 'it would be far better for this country if British territory in South Africa were confined to Cape Town and Simon's Bay'.[43] It took another twenty-five years for an economic boom to materialise in Southern Africa, beginning with the discovery of diamonds in 1867 in the Orange Free State and with the discovery of gold in 1886 in the South African Republic, or Transvaal. Two years later, forty-four gold mines were in operation, which constituted a mixed blessing: on the one hand, this meant great growth for the two independent states but, on the other hand, British companies and mining magnates quickly monopolised the sector, as they did with the commercial mining of coal begun in 1864.[44] Settler interests continued to jar with metropolitan imperial plans and economic interests.

Because of the sudden discovery of enormous mineral resources, in the late nineteenth century, the Colonial Office embarked on an imperialist enterprise, epitomised by the ambitions of Colonial Secretary Joseph Chamberlain, High Commissioner for South Africa Alfred Milner and mining magnate Cecil Rhodes, who wanted to secure economic and political power in the region.[45] This ultimate phase of British imperial grasp embedded violence at the heart of South African settler society. The advancement of British interests went against the resistance of local tribes, the Xhosa and the Zulu, who were definitively defeated in 1877 and 1887 respectively, and their lands annexed. It also pitted settler communities against one another: British encroachment was detrimental to the Boer republics, settled, organised and run by descendants of the seventeenth-century Dutch, French and German colonists. It took the deployment of more than 400,000 British soldiers and the deaths of 34,000 Boers, 22,000 British and 15,000 Africans for the Republic of the Orange Free State and then the Republic of South Africa to be annexed, at the end of the Anglo-Boer Wars in 1902.[46] The British at last gained control over South Africa's resources, but through a degree of violence, not only between settlers and Indigenous people but also between the settlers themselves, which reflected very negatively on the empire's outwardly benevolent purpose and efficiency.

Notes

1 www.historici.nl/Onderzoek/Projecten/DeVoc.BeschrijvingDoor PieterVan-Dam1693–1701. The record of the VOC administration may be accessed through the early archive compiled by its attorney Pieter van Dam (1621–1706), *Beschrijvinge van de Oostindische*

Compagnie 1639–1701 (published in 1902), http://resources.huygens. knaw.nl/retroboeken/vandam/#page=0&accessor=toc&view=home Pane; H.C.V. Leibbrandt, *Precis of the Archives of the Cape of Good Hope* (Cape Town: W.A. Richards and Sons, 1896–1906) covers seventeen volumes translated into English and is part of the VOC archives. Twenty-five million pages of VOC records have survived among the vast holdings in Jakarta, Colombo, Chennai, Cape Town and The Hague. In Cape Town, the full extent of VOC holdings is 322 metres. To preserve the VOC archives, the TANAP project was jointly developed in 1997 and 1998, www.tanap.net/content/activities/inventories/index.cfm. For the early VOC government of the Cape, see Femme S. Gaastra, *Bewind en Beleid bij de Voc. De Financiële en Commerciële Politiek van de Bewindhebbers, 1672–1702* (Zutphen: Walburg, 1989). For the Anglo-Dutch Treaty of London, also known as the Convention of London, which transferred the Cape to British rule, see 'The Prince Sovereign of the Netherlands agrees to cede in full sovereignty to his Britannic Majesty the Cape of Good Hope', https://hansard.parliament.uk/Commons/1815-06-09/debates/0e7491ad-421f-4e13-9843-e5a4e4591f6c/ConventionBetweenGreatBritainAndTheNetherlands. Until 1732, the Cape received instructions from both the Company's governing body at home and its seat in Batavia, whereby overseas affairs were controlled. Afterwards, the Lords Seventeen, all by themselves, controlled the vast Dutch colonial empire.

2 Femme S. Gaastra, *The Dutch East India Company: Expansion and Decline* (Zutphen: Walburg, 2003).

3 Marilyn Garcia-Chapleau, *Le Refuge Huguenot du Cap de Bonne-Espérance. Genèse, Assimilation, Héritage* (Paris: Honoré Champion, 2016), 52, 64–8; George Prévélakis, 'Les Diasporas comme Négation de l'Idéologie Graphique', in L. Anteby-Yemini, W. Berthomière and G. Sheffer (eds.), *Les Diasporas: 2000 Ans d'Histoire* (Rennes: Presses Universitaires de Rennes, 2005), 116; Tristan Mostert, 'Chain of Command: The Military System of the Dutch East India Company, 1655–1663' (M.A. thesis, Leiden University, 2007), http://vocwarfare.net/thesis/; L.A. de Bougainville, *Voyage autour du monde, par la frégate la Boudeuse et la flûte l'Etoile* ([1771] Paris: La Découverte/Poche, 1997), 277.

4 Dirk van der Cruysse (ed.), *Mercenaires Français de la VOC. La Route des Indes Hollandaises au XVIIe Siècle. Le Récit de Jean Guidon de Chambelle (1644–1651) et autres Documents* (Paris: Éditions Chandeigne, 2003), 100–1. 'Hautitants' was the seventeenth-century French word for 'Hottentot', a term used by Dutch settlers to describe the pastoral people of southern Africa, the Khoikhoi, who were nomadic pastoralists, and the San, nomadic hunter-gatherers.

5 The *Heren XVII*'s instructions stated in a letter dated 25 March 1651 that 'a permanent residency is intended to be made of the Cape as a refreshment station', Leibbrandt, *Precis, Letters despatched from the Cape, 1652–1662*, Part 1 (1897), 6, 10. For shipping figures, J.R. Bruijn, F.S. Gaastra and I. Schöffer, *Dutch-Asiatic Shipping in the Seventeenth and Eighteenth Centuries* (Den Haag: Nijhoff, 1979), 1: 165–7.

6 Leibbrandt, *Precis, Letters and documents received*, Part 2 (1898), 178.

7 Herrmann Giliomee, *The Afrikaners: Biography of a People* (Cape Town: Tafelberg, 2006), 7; Leibbrandt, *Precis, annual returns 1688–1792*, Cape Town Archives Repository, CAR-LM30, 1–38.

8 Robert J. Ross, 'The first two centuries of colonial agriculture in the Cape Colony: A historiographical review', *Social Dynamics* 9, no. 1 (1983), 30–49 at 32; G. Waterhouse, G.C. de Wet and R.H. Pheiffer (eds.), *Simon van der Stel's Journey to Namaqualand in 1685* (Cape Town: Human & Rousseau, 1979).

9 E.C. Godee-Molsbergen and Jon Visscher, *South African History Told in Pictures* (Amsterdam: S.L. van Looy, 1913), 133; Leibbrandt, *Precis, Riebeeck's journal*, Part 1 (1897), 47–8. The Company had the power to free burghers from their services, hence the phrase 'free burgher'.

10 Giliomee, *The Afrikaners*, 6; Yvonne Brink, *They Came to Stay: Discovering Meaning in the 18th-Century Cape Country Dwelling* (Stellenbosch: SUN Press, 2008), 73, 83, 101.

11 Garcia-Chapleau, *Le Refuge Huguenot*, Ch. 7; Leibbrandt, *Precis, Rambles through the Archives of the Colony of the Cape of Good Hope 1688–1700*, 10.

12 *Resolusie* C. 20, 76–9. The Resolutions of The Council of Policy of the Cape of Good Hope are available at www.tanap.net/content/activities/documents/resolutions_Cape_of_Good_Hope/index.htm; Pieter Coertzen, 'The Huguenots of South Africa in documents and commemoration', *Nederduitse Gereformeerde Teologiese Tydskrif* 52, no. 3–4 (2011), 301–24 at 303.

13 Giliomee, *The Afrikaners*, 24.

14 Leo Fouché (ed.), *The Diary of Adam Tas* (Cape Town: VRS, 1970), 390.

15 Donald Moodie, *The Record: or Series of Official Papers Relative to the Treatment of the Native Tribes of South Africa* (Cape Town: Balkema, 1960), Part 1, 340; Gerritt Schutte, 'Company and colonists at the Cape 1652–1795', in R. Elphick and H. Giliomee (eds.), *The Shaping of South African Society 1652–1840* (Middletown: Wesleyan University Press, 1989), 295.

16 Leibbrandt, *Precis, annual returns*, 1–38; Jan de Vries and Ad van der Woude, *The First Modern Economy: Success, Failure and Perseverance of the Dutch Economy 1500–1815* (Cambridge: Cambridge University Press, 1997), 446.
17 Brink, *They Came to Stay*, 39; André du Toit and Herrmann Giliomee, *Afrikaner Political Thought: Analysis and Documents* (Berkeley: University of California Press, 1983), 1: 252–3.
18 Robert Montgomery Martin, *Statistics of the Colonies of the British Empire* (London, 1839), 520–4.
19 Schutte, 'Company and colonists at the Cape, 1652–1795', 309.
20 Du Toit and Giliomee, *Afrikaner Political Thought*, 252–4.
21 *Ibid.*, 41–4.
22 *Ibid.*, for example, Anon., *L'Afrique Hollandaise ou le Tableau Historique et Politique de l'État Originaire de la Colonie du Cap de Bonne-Espérance comparé avec l'État Actuel de cette Colonie* (Amsterdam, 1783), 4–6.
23 G. Lagour-Gayeï, *La Marine Militaire de la France sous le Règne de Louis XVI* (Paris: Honoré Champion, 1905), 482; T.D. Potgieter, 'Defence against Maritime Power Projection: The Case of the Cape of Good Hope, 1756–1803' (Ph.D. diss., University of Stellenbosch, 2006), 158, https://scholar.sun.ac.za/handle/10019.1/50593.
24 Andrew B. Smith, 'The French period at the Cape, 1781–1783: A report on excavations at Conway Redoubt, Constantia Nek', *Military History Journal* 5, no. 3 (1981), 107–13, http://samilitaryhistory.org/vol053as.html; Robert Ross, *Status and Respectability in the Cape Colony, 1750–1870: A Tragedy of Manners* (Cambridge: Cambridge University Press, 1999), 11; E.A. Walker, *A History of South Africa* (London: Longmans, Green, 1947), 109.
25 Schutte, 'Company and colonists at the Cape', 295.
26 Anon., *L'Afrique Hollandaise*, 4, 6, 7, 99. This text has been sometimes attributed to François Bernard, but this teacher from Leiden appears to have only written the foreword, where he explained that he slightly amended the incipient manuscript and added footnotes. According to André du Toit and Hermann Giliomee, the author could have been Barend Jacob Artoys, one of the four burghers who went to the Netherlands to submit the petition to the Lords Seventeen in 1779, Du Toit and Giliomee, *Afrikaner Political Thought*, 256; Schutte, 'Company and colonists at the Cape', 295.
27 Giliomee, *The Afrikaners*, 72.
28 Cited in Du Toit and Giliomee, *Afrikaner Political Thought*, 90.
29 Giliomee, *The Afrikaners*, 56; G. McCall Theal, *Records of the Cape Colony 1793–1831 Copied for the Cape Government from the*

Manuscript Documents, 36 vols. (London: Swann Sonnenschien, 1902), 1: 95; James Armstrong and Nigel Worden, 'The slaves, 1652–1834', in R. Elphick and H. Giliomee (eds.), *The Shaping of South African Society* (Middletown: Wesleyan University Press, 1989), 129.

30 Potgieter, 'Defence against Maritime Power Projection', 329, 332, 373–427. The Batavian Republic was proclaimed on 19 January 1795 after the French revolutionary army's intervention and the collapse of the forces of the *stadtholder* William V and his Austrian and British allies. William V was forced to flee to England.

31 Robert Percival, *An Account of the Cape of Good Hope* (London, 1804), 307.

32 Du Toit and Giliomee, *Afrikaner Political Thought*, 269. The VOC was dissolved in 1798.

33 Potgieter, 'Defence against Maritime Power Projection', 492.

34 Du Toit and Giliomee, *Afrikaner Political Thought*, 11; J.B. Peires, 'The British and the Cape, 1814–1834', in Elphick and Giliomee (eds.), *The Shaping of South African Society*, 472–521 at 472.

35 William Freund, 'The Cape under the transitional governments', in Elphick and Giliomee (eds.), *The Shaping of South African Society*, 324–57 at 329.

36 Giliomee, *The Afrikaners*, 84–6. The Xhosa are a Bantu ethnic group settled on the east coast of southern Africa, more precisely, in the coastal plain and inland mountain region.

37 H. Giliomee, 'The Eastern Frontier 1770–1812', in Elphick and Giliomee (eds.), *The Shaping of South African Society*, 421–70 at 444; Du Toit and Giliomee, *Afrikaner Political Thought*, 12.

38 James Sturgis, 'Anglicisation of the Cape of Good Hope in the early nineteenth century', *Journal of Imperial and Commonwealth History* 11, no. 1 (1982), 5–32 at 11; E.G. Malherbe, *Education in South Africa (1652–1922)* (Cape Town: Juta, 1925), 58.

39 The Colonial Office proposed the idea in July 1817: H.J.M. Johnston, *British Emigration Policy, 1815–1830* (Oxford: Clarendon Press, 1972), 27–33. The four thousand emigrants remained British subjects, J.H. Clapham, 'The economic condition of Europe after the Napoleonic Wars', *The Scientific Monthly* 11, no. 4 (1920), 320–5.

40 Giliomee, *The Afrikaners*, 199; Ross, *Status and Respectability*, 107.

41 Under the Earl of Caledon, first civilian governor of the Cape Colony, the Hottentot Proclamation decreed that 'every Hottentot (or Khoikhoi) was to have a fixed "place of abode" and that if he wished to move, he had to obtain a pass from his master or from a local official', Brian Lapping, *Apartheid: A History* (London: Grafton Books, 1986), 36.

42 Giliomee, *The Afrikaners*, 175.
43 Robert Ross, 'The Cape of Good Hope and the world economy, 1685–1835', in Elphick and Giliomee (eds.), *The Shaping of South African Society*, 248–54, 271; Robert Ross, *A Concise History of South Africa* (Cambridge: Cambridge University Press, 1999), 75.
44 Giliomee, *The Afrikaners*, 236.
45 By the end of the nineteenth century, the mines in the Johannesburg area were producing a quarter of the world's gold, R. Ally, *Gold and Empire* (Johannesburg: Witwatersrand University Press, 1994), 1–28.
46 The First Boer War (December 1880–23 March 1881) was short-lived, but the Second Boer War (November 1899–May 1902) took the British three years to win.

9

Shipping mules in the eighteenth century: New England's equine exports to the West Indies

Charlotte Carrington-Farmer

In 1787, planters in the Dutch trading hub of St Eustatius had a problem; specifically, they had an equine labour supply problem. And, they knew exactly who to blame: equine breeders along the east coast of North America. In an anonymous letter, one St Eustatius planter lamented how he simply could not get the kind of equine labour that he wanted. Put bluntly, he wanted more mules and less horses. The letter was reprinted in countless newspapers as far north as Vermont and as far south as South Carolina (and everywhere in between) in the spring of 1787. The letter addressed how 'the major part of the planters in these islands' in and around St Eustatius wanted breeders on the east coast of North America to breed more 'mules for exportation' and to stop shipping 'parcel[s] of old horses'. To add insult to injury, the horses were often 'not worth the trouble nor expense of exportation' as they were not 'fit for the mills'. The planters in St Eustatius were willing to pay good money for the equine labourers they actually wanted, offering 'eight or ten joes for a good mule', while horses were valued at half that amount.[1] According to the letter, imported horses did have a place on the island as riding horses fit 'for the saddle', but not as draught animals nor in the quantities that east coast merchants were sending them.[2]

Many sugar planters around the West Indies agreed that for their strength, longevity and drudgery, mules were 'far superior to horses', requiring 'one-fifth the keeping' and surviving 'upon the very refuge of the farm'.[3] While planters, Atlantic merchants and east coast equine breeders clearly knew the nuanced differences between various equids, not all of their contemporaries were so savvy on the 'genus *Equus*'.[4] As one observer wryly noted in

1787, US city-dwelling politicians and most likely 'three fourths of both houses' had rarely heard of, let alone seen, 'such creatures' as mules and jackasses.[5] Luckily for them, contemporary mule experts explained how mules were a 'hybrid off-spring' that were a cross of a mare (female horse) and jackass (male donkey).[6] Mules were generally sterile; thus, while eighteenth-century horse breeders could continuously propagate horse stock from a stallion (male, ungelded horse) and a mare, mules were different. Once you had a mule, that was it – you could not breed from it. This was one of the reasons why breeding mules was more challenging than breeding horses.

West Indian planters did not suddenly decide on the superiority of mules overnight, but many of them did seek more mules from the get-go. Equids were central to ensuring that sugar plantations worked, and in spite of all of the dangers in crossing the Atlantic, it made sense to import them. The soil in many of the islands in the West Indies was not as well suited to raising animals, and if planters had spare acreage, they planted sugar or other cash crops.[7] Raising equines required time too; horses were not ready for work until they were four years old, while mules were ready at two. Most planters did not want to waste valuable acreage and time raising equines when they could import mature, work-ready animals. Even in Jamaica, where there was a thriving pen economy that bred equine and bovine workers, breeding efforts were never enough to keep up with the demand.[8] Thus, planters around the West Indies relied on importing animals.

New England's efforts to export mules were part of a wider chain of equid labour supply and demand around the Atlantic world. Rival empires fiercely guarded the animals that powered their sugar mills and profits. Spain dominated the mule-breeding industry and set tight restrictions on the export of both jacks and mules to rival colonial powers. Mules were also bred in Portugal, which also tightly regulated its exports. While the Iberian mule trade was never legalised, in reality, there was a vibrant trade across empires around the West Indies, which was supplemented by an indirect trade with the Dutch. While some merchants sought out alternative supply sources for jacks, notably, the 'Barbary coast', the 'Spanish Main' and 'Spanish Coast' were the principal trading hubs. The illicit smuggling of mules was a hotly debated topic due to challenges to rival empires. As early as the 1660s, Jamaica's Governor

Thomas Modyford encouraged a clandestine Anglo-Spanish trade by granting licences to traders to sell enslaved captives and commodities to Spanish America and to import livestock. While Spain repeatedly refused to sanction freedom of trade, the Free Port Act of 1766 opened up the trade to some extent.[9] The very existence of the Spanish trade was a controversial issue both in the mother country and British West Indian colonies. According to the principles of mercantilism, the colonies were meant to be supply sources for the metropole, while the colonies were meant to import their necessities from the mother country. The aim of national self-sufficiency meant that valuable commodities were subject to strict commercial control, which could effectively exclude foreign trade. But in reality, New England's equine breeding and trading negotiations were conducted outside empires and even sometimes against empires. A trip to the West Indies from Europe took twice as long as the voyage down from New England, which meant direct animal exports were limited. Even if direct trade from England had been easier, England did not have a large supply of jacks or mules to export to the colonies.

Given the high demand for mules around the West Indies and New England's long-term trading connections with the region, it is unsurprising that West Indian planters were keen for New Englanders to expand their equid breeding to include mules. As the eighteenth century progressed, farmers who bred quadrupeds along the east coast of North America were well aware that mules were 'the most lucrative animals they [could] generate'.[10] However, breeding mules for exportation had never been New England's original plan. In the seventeenth century, New Englanders (like their English counterparts) did not consider mules a priority. In England and New England, oxen and horses respectively were the choice draught animals. But, as West Indian sugar production took centre stage in the economic battle for empire, efforts to breed the animals that planters deemed superior increasingly informed equine breeding practices around the Atlantic world. New Englanders had long supplied horses to the sugar colonies, but after the Revolutionary War, they increasingly tried to diversify their equine exports to include mules.[11] While New England's foray into mule-breeding never reached the dizzying success of its horse enterprises, the efforts to breed mules for exportation underscore the extent to which New England's economy was driven by markets in the West Indies. Both before and after independence, equine breeders and merchants in New England bred and exported the animals that were most lucrative for them, and the trade often transgressed imperial frontiers. New Englanders struggled between prioritising profitable, non-British, West Indian markets and national interests, which led to reprimands and even conflict. Tracking the movement of mules around and across colonised spaces reveals that equine breeding efforts in New England were driven by overseas interests and commercial structures on West Indian sugar plantations. Mules were part of an essential non-human animal labour force that metaphorically and literally powered European overseas empires in the West Indies.

Equine empires

Providing human and non-human animal labour to power sugar plantations was at the heart of rival empire-building in the eighteenth century. As Antiguan planter Samuel Martin observed, 'negroes, cattle, mules, and horses are the nerves of a sugar plantation'.[12] Thus, New England's efforts to breed mules must be understood against this wider backdrop of Atlantic commerce. New England's equine breeding and trading negotiations were conducted outside empires and even sometimes against empires. Tracking the destination of New England vessels carrying equine cargo is complicated by the fact that ships often flitted between different islands trying to get the best price for their wares. In one voyage, merchants regularly traded with English, French and Dutch West Indian islands. For example, in 1768, the *Grace* departed New Haven, Connecticut bound for Martinique. After selling its wares, the vessel headed to Georgia, where it picked up rice and mules. Following a storm, the *Grace* took refuge in St Eustatius before heading to the French West Indies to deliver the rice and mules.[13]

Prior to the Revolutionary War, New England's horse exports were the subject of fierce debate on both sides of the Atlantic, and countless pamphlets, speeches and parliamentary debates addressed the implications of supplying non-British sugar colonies. The mother county was convinced that if New Englanders stopped sending horses to the French and Dutch colonies, then the British sugar colonies would thrive. They were certain that the French and Dutch could not get horses elsewhere with 'the Navigation of Canada being so difficult and dangerous'. British leaders claimed that the Spanish horse trade was limited, and Spanish mules always had very 'high Prices' and were only supplied 'by contraband Trade'.[14] In 1732, the anonymous *The British Empire in America* argued that the Dutch had no spare horses, as they would not trade with a 'foreigner' unless they imported 'a certain number of horses in proportion to the burthen of his vessel' in Suriname.[15] The report noted that while Spain had mules on the Continent, it was 'hardly more than sufficient for their own Service, and they set a very great Value on them, much more than they do on Horses'. Moreover, planters in Barbados would 'gladly prefer' mules to New England horses if they could get them 'upon any reasonable Terms'. However, any trade in Spanish mules was done 'by Stealth' in a 'clandestine Way' that was 'extremely hazardous' and 'chargeable'. The mules came via the 'Wind-ward as Martinique, or other Caribbee Islands'. The author only knew of six mules in Barbados during the last thirty years, while there had always been at least six thousand horses on the island.[16] Others explored how Barbadians tried to get mules from Puerto Rico, Curaçao or the Spanish Main, and usually paid between £20 and £28 per mule.[17]

The French sugar islands relied on the Spanish trade too, which was 'at best clandestine and precarious, and so very expensive', according to British sources seeking to prove the importance of New England's equine trade. The French were so desperate to get mules from the Spanish that some traders started to lower the price of their rum at Curaçao, 'where it is much wanted for the coasting Trade with Spain to get Mules from thence'. All of this meant that if the French and Dutch could not get equines 'at a reasonable and living Price', they would not be able to 'improve nor preserve their Sugar Settlements'. If the French, Dutch and English colonies could not get mules easily, they had to rely on their second choice of equine labour: New England horses. By this logic, the British colonies would be 'plentifully supply'd' and able to make sugar, rum and molasses 'in such Quantities' that by the time that the French and Dutch scrambled to acquire equines elsewhere, it would not be 'worth the while ... to vye with ours'.[18] The message from the mother country was simple: New England had to stop supplying horses to non-British colonies.

Unsurprisingly, many New Englanders disagreed. New England merchants countered that without the French and Dutch trade, their horses would be of little or no use elsewhere. Merchant Thomas Bannister summed up the position in 1715. He lamented that New England's equine trade to Suriname was being 'openly attacked' by planters in Barbados and officials in England.[19] He countered that the trade with Suriname took 'off a great number of small Horses (commonly called Surinams)', which were 'fit for no other Market'. In many ways, Bannister was right, and certain merchants such as James Brown and his son Nicholas Brown, in Providence, Rhode Island, specialised in shipping 'Surinam horses'.[20] Bannister expounded that any profit made on exporting horses to Suriname came back into New England, as merchants exchanged the horses for molasses, which were then brewed and distilled and 'thereby raise many good Livings; and ... one of the most profitable Trades'.[21] Other New Englanders defended their equine trade, arguing that they could not carry on their 'Indian Trade and Fishery' without the French rum and molasses it provided.[22]

In contrast to leaders in London and British sugar planters, New Englanders also believed they were not the sole suppliers of equines to the French and Dutch. By their calculations, the French could get horses and mules from the coasts of 'New-Spain and New Andalusia, and from the Dutch island of Curaçao', and the 'French colony at Canada' could with 'very little encouragement' furnish the French sugar islands with horses.[23] While it was 'difficult and uncertain in the winter time', the French could transport the horses 'in the proper season, and lodging them at their own settlement at Cape Briton, from whence they could easily be transported to their sugar islands at all seasons of the year'. According to New England merchants, any horses they shipped to the French were for 'luxury' purposes and no 'real use' in the plantations.[24]

There was some truth to what New Englanders were saying, and their efforts to breed and export equines to the West Indies were part of a larger trading enterprise around the Atlantic world. In some respects, the claim from England that the Spanish mule trade was 'extremely hazardous' was likely a case of special pleading. A number of accounts testify that Curaçaoan merchants used their already-established contacts on the Spanish Main to ship mules to the French colonies.[25] By the mid-eighteenth century, the Dutch island of St Eustatius served as an unofficial distribution centre between the islands, with mules arriving from Tierra Firme in Curaçoan vessels.[26] The hills around Coro in Venezuela were a major breeding site for mules, which were then shipped from the port cities Tucacas and Coro.[27] As early as 1723, the governor of Coro complained about the annual export of fifteen hundred mules to the Caribbean islands. Throughout the 1730s, mules and horses were also sent from Cumaná in Venezuela in exchange for rum and other goods.[28] The Orinoco region was also a hub for mules, and by the mid-eighteenth century, countless traders went 'up the Orinoco' river for scores mules.[29] Mules that were bred in Puerto Rico were exported as far south as Guadeloupe and as far west as Saint-Domingue, while eastern Hispaniola and eastern Cuba had their own mule circuits.[30] New England's mule-breeding efforts never seriously challenged the Spanish dominance of the trade, which flourished in many parts of the West Indies, even if systematic bribery did push prices up.

In Jamaica, there was an effort to breed their own animals, and by the early eighteenth century, certain parts of the island were noted hubs of animal breeding.[31] However, even though Jamaica had a thriving pen economy, planters continued to import equines. Yu Wu estimates that, in 1762, Jamaica annually imported 771 mules and 292 horses.[32] At £28 per head, planters needed to spend £109,200 each year on mules to power their plantations. In 1768, Edward Long calculated that planters needed a minimum of 3,900 mules to power the 651 sugar plantations; however, there were only 200 pens at the time.[33] Life in the sugar colonies was hard and loss of mules, horses and cattle frequent. In Suriname, Governor Nepveu reported that an estate usually lost fifty to sixty draught horses per year.[34] New England's equine breeders and merchants were well aware that sugar planters constantly needed more animals to work on the plantation, and by diversifying their breeding and export business, they sought to meet that demand.

Breeding equines

By the time that the St Eustachian planters penned their demands for more mules in 1787, New England merchants had been shipping horses to the West Indies for well over a century. In 1647,

Massachusetts Bay colonists William Brenton and William Coddington identified that New England was perfectly poised to send both saddle and draught horses to Barbadian planters. As England sought to replenish the horses that had been lost in the Civil War by setting a duty on horse exports in 1654, New England was able to exploit the lucrative market for exporting horses to the sugar colonies. Writing in 1660, Samuel Maverick observed how horses had not only changed the New England landscape but how they were part of the region's burgeoning trade: 'As for the Southern part of New-England. It is incredible what hath been done there ... in the yeare 1626 or thereabouts there was not a ... Horse ... in the Country ... and now it is a wonder to see ... the great number of Horses ... many sent to Barbados and other Carribe Islands'.[35] Just as Samuel Maverick had predicted, there was a ready market and money to be made in exporting horses. Rhode Island even developed its own type of horse, the Narragansett Pacer, which was shipped to the West Indies as a saddle horse for riding.[36] By the mid-eighteenth century, New England was a pivotal provider of horses to the West Indies, both for draught work and riding.[37]

As the eighteenth century progressed, New Englanders slowly started to diversify their equine breeding efforts to breed mules for export. As early as 1753, Antiguan planation manager William Mackinen knew that mules were being bred in New England. Writing to Abraham Redwood, the plantation owner, who was based in Newport, Rhode Island, Mackinen noted that 'there are mules bred somewhere near you'. Mackinen shrewdly advised Redwood that it would be worthwhile purchasing 'five or six [mules], so [as] to have ... here for about £20'. While Redwood only had one mule on the plantation at the time, it was clear that if they could be directly imported from Rhode Island, it made sense to increase the stock.[38] Getting hold of jacks to start the breeding programmes was central to New England's ability to export mules. New England ships brought back jacks for breeding from Iberia and North Africa as early as 1765, when Britain signed an agreement with the sultan of Morocco.[39] Exports of mules increased in the 1760s, and a shipping report from 1768 noted that Captain Emerson's vessel from Piscataqua, along the Maine and New Hampshire border, had arrived in Suriname 'loaded with mules ... after seventy days passage'.[40] In 1769, reports from Gibraltar revealed how 'several New England Vessels' were docked there after 'going on the coast of Barbary for mules'.[41] One of these vessels perusing the African coast for jacks might have had Ottoman onboard. Ottoman, who had 'lately arrived from Algiers', was owned by George Irish and covered mares during the spring and summer of 1774 at William Redwood's farm in Middletown, Rhode Island. Ottoman had a proven breeding record and was 'thought to be the largest and finest [ass] ever in America'. Ottoman's pedigree spoke for itself; Ottoman was 'got by Musti the favourite Ass belonging to the Dey of Algiers'.[42]

Irish's breeding practices illuminate the agency of private interests in the development of colonial trade. Irish knew that the 'raising of mules in this country' was 'very advantageous', and he was doing his fellow Rhode Islanders a favour by keeping Ottoman in the colony. Irish had been offered $500 for Ottoman 'in several other parts', but he wanted to 'give the preference to this colony'. Irish offered mare owners the price of '4 dollars for the season' with 'good pasturage, at a reasonable rate'. Those who wanted to put their mares 'to the ass by the leap' could make special arrangements with Irish. Irish's approach was typical for the time. The main breeding season was May and June, which meant that most foals were born the following spring, as a mare is usually pregnant for eleven to twelve months. Like Irish, many breeders assured mare owners that they had 'good keeping for mares' who stayed the season, providing multiple chances to get the mare in foal. If a mare owner did not want to send their mare for the entire season, most breeders offered a cheaper rate per mating, which was described as a 'single leap'. Like other breeders, Irish bred horses alongside mules and simultaneously offered a stallion to cover mares alongside his jack. Any mare owners who did not want to fork out $4 for the season could pay nothing for the covering as long as they agreed to let Irish buy back the mule offspring for $20 one year later.[43] The policy of buying back the mules once they matured was used time and time again by New England breeders.

Irish was not alone in diversifying his equine breeding to include mules. Following the Revolutionary War, West Indian planters were hopeful that the United States could be a reliable source for mules. Given New England's long history of supplying horses to the West Indies, it was not too much of a jump to expect that horse breeders would continue to diversify and breed more mules. Prior to the

Revolution, New England had long been frustrated by England's effort to regulate its horse trade to the French and Dutch colonies in the West Indies. Thus, with the formation of the United States, merchants were keen to resume, reinvigorate and create new trade networks in the West Indies. Simultaneously, New Englanders had more access to jacks to start breeding programmes due to the sourcing of new Cape Verdean jacks. Finally, the benefits of mule labour became more widely acknowledged within the United States as George Washington pioneered breeding mules for draught work in the late 1780s.[44] As mule-breeding increased, debate about taxing the lucrative export commodity swirled in the newly formed nation.

Profits and markets

By the time leaders gathered in Philadelphia at the Constitutional Convention in 1787, New England was abuzz with discussion about the newly proposed tax on mules. An anonymous British traveller 'of distinction' got the lowdown on the mule tax as he spent the day getting drunk on Madeira in a New England public house. Amid his drinking buddies was a 'shrewd speculating farmer', who observed 'very gravely' that nobody in the state, except a 'publick officer', could make money because of the 'exorbitant taxes'. According to the farmer, the legislature was determined to 'cramp and lessen every branch of business' by laying 'a tax on jack-asses and mules'. Another local chimed up that his fortunes had changed when he bought a jackass for £75 six years earlier. Staggeringly, he reported that the jack then covered 'between two and three hundred mares every year since, at two dollars the season, or at four if I ventured'. Covering the mares was not even a quarter of his profits, and the real money was in his scheme of buying back the mules for £5 at four months old. He kept the mules 'at a small expense' until they were one year old, before selling them for export to the West Indies at $40 to $50 per head. He further calculated that his jack had cleared him £150 'hard money, every year since I owned him'. His scheme 'would have been something clever in a few more [years] if our assembly could have been easy without taxing' jacks. The British visitor did some digging and 'found on inquiry that the farmer had not the least exaggerated the profits arising from his jack-ass and mules'. The anonymous British traveller was so astounded by this that he promptly wrote to inform his friend in Europe, and the subsequent letter was published in east coast newspapers in the spring of 1787.[45]

As the alcohol flowed, the British visitor got to the heart of why some equine breeders were not 'adventurous enough' to embrace mule-breeding, which was the 'most lucrative' branch of husbandry. In addition to the new tax, some breeders were attached to their ancestors' traditions of breeding horses. The British visitor reminded his companions about the 'immense profits other countries' reaped from breeding mules. But, he acknowledged that exporting mules was a complicated business as there were 'high embargoes' laid on them everywhere to prevent their exportation. The British visitor was clear that if New Englanders 'vigorously attended' to mule-breeding, in a few years, they would make enough money to discharge the foreign debt, 'of which they so loudly complain'. He believed that if New Englanders put their mind to it, they 'could raise more mules than are wanted in the West India islands ... [or] in all South America'.[46] Others agreed, and another anonymous gentleman informed his friends in Connecticut that mules were the 'best exports' to the West Indies as cargo of mules of 'good size and age, would sell at thirteen joes per mule'.[47] According to the gentleman, there were two key reasons why the US mule trade was so attractive to West Indian planters in the 1780s. Firstly, West Indian planters had read the 'pompous account' about the 'extraordinary Jacks' that George Washington had acquired. The two jacks, Royal Gift and Knight of Malta, were sent from the King of Spain and Marquis de la Fayette respectively.[48] By all accounts, Washington's jacks were an 'extraordinary ... size'; thus, West Indian planters hoped that any mules that were exported from the US 'would exceed for sizes those ship'd from any other part of the world'.[49] Secondly, planters knew that several Rhode Island vessels had recently taken a large number of 'wild Jacks' from the Cape Verde Islands, with a view to breed mules for exportation.[50]

According to the former Connecticut resident, the Cape Verdean jacks ran wild on the mountains and were rounded up by 'the Negroes' who would 'hem them in between the ledges of rocks and mountains', then slit their noses, 'each one with his mark', tie them together with bark and drive them to their employer, to be sold by the score. However, the former Connecticut resident was not impressed with Rhode Island's efforts to use the captured wild jacks to propagate mules for exportation. He hoped that his friends in Connecticut would not make the same mistake in breeding a 'very contemptable breed of mules' from the wild jacks. According to the gentleman, Rhode Islanders intended their mules 'for a foreign market', which would 'ruin the price of those mongrel animals' and that in a few years, the markets would be glutted. He hoped that his friends in Connecticut would not take part in this 'consummate villainy' and propagate mules from a 'miserable race of animals for sires'. There was clear interstate rivalry at play, and the former Connecticut resident's distaste for Rhode Islanders went further and he explained the 'burlesques which resound from one end of the continent to the other against our sister State (Rhode Island)'. The gentlemen reminded readers how Rhode Island was known as 'Rogues Island', with 'leaden headed legislators' and 'leather apron worthies'.[51]

In addition to interstate rivalry, concerns about the 'quality' of the mules were often prejudiced with a racial bias. Historians must grapple with making what Marjorie Spiegel has termed the 'dreaded comparison'.[52] These are uncomfortable truths to confront given the growing 'animal turn' in history.[53] As David Lambert has observed, 'if the animal turn has been controversial in other contexts, then it is particularly so in (former) enslaved societies. Even to mention animal domestication in the same breath as human slavery could be seen as disrespectful, offensive or simply irrelevant'.[54] Planters used the same language to describe their human and animal property, evaluated the different forms of human and animal labour in the same breath and saw both as tradable commodities. New England mule experts believed that the 'different races of the ass' had distinct properties. The Connecticut gentleman was not alone in lambasting African jacks, and other accounts described how African jacks, particularly those from Senegal and the Cape de Verde Islands, were a '*diminutive* domestic race'.[55]

Most agreed that Spain bred a 'superior race of mules to the present period'. In addition to Spain, which dominated mule-breeding, mules were common in France and Portugal. Contemporary reports also noted that 'in Barbary … the trusty mule has no rival in the horse; he requires no pen to speak in his praise, for his character has long been established'.[56] Mules were not common in Britain, which partly explains New England's reluctance to embrace them for their own agricultural labour. Published in 1737, John Chamberlayne's *Magnæ Britanniæ Notitia* described how 'Mules and asses, so generally made use of in France, Italy and Spain, are utterly despised in England'.[57] While Catholic prelates transported a few mules to England prior to the Reformation, they were attacked during the reign of Elizabeth I. For example, in Devon, some mules from French jacks 'were knocked on the head' and viewed 'as monsters'. Some mules were bred in the New Forest, Cornwall and Leicestershire, with limited success. In the eighteenth century, the Duke of Cumberland had fifty mules 'presented to him by the Empress Queen', but mule-breeding did not widely catch on. One of the key advocates of breeding quality mules in New England was Samuel Wyllys Pomeroy, of Brighton, Massachusetts. Unlike many breeders around New England, Pomeroy was interested in breeding quality mules and keeping them in New England. Pomeroy's time in the West Indies convinced him that mules could work longer and 'endure labour in a temperature of heat that would be destructive to the horse'. Pomeroy knew that some New Englanders were reluctant to breed mules due to an almost 'superstitious attachment to the horse'.[58]

In a piece published in *Farmer's Monthly Visitor*, an anonymous 'muleteer' agreed with Pomeroy that fashion was 'a tyrant' with New Englanders' animal labour preferences. The writer exhorted New Englanders to dismiss their 'pride, habits, prejudices' about mules, acknowledging that while mules were 'sleepy looking, long-eared, slope-tailed' animals, they were superior workers. According to the muleteer, mules lived longer than horses and could work 'more than three times as long as the horse'. Mules were also cheaper to raise and were fit for service much earlier. Even small mules could manage 'heavy loads as an equal number of horses'.[59] Mules were renowned for their sure-footedness, which meant that they could travel to acclivities where horses could not. In 1734 in the Dutch colony of Essequibo, Hermanus Geleskerke knew full well that mules were a 'considerable advantage to this colony', and even though mules were expensive at $60 per head, 'one of those animals is more useful than four horses'.[60] Mules were more versatile than horses and they performed a variety of tasks in the West Indies, from crushing sugar cane in the mills to transporting goods from the field to the market. While planters used a range of animals for draught work, horses were markers of status and remained the choice animal for riding and carriages.[61]

Diversifying breeding

Despite of all the arguments in favour of mules, most New England farmers were reluctant to use mules for their own agricultural labour, and oxen were New England's choice draught animal. Consequently, New England breeders were only interested in the jack's capacity to propagate a mule for export, and there was little regulation on the type of mares they put to the jack. Focusing on profit, some breeders put their jacks to mares that were worth 'not half that value' and of 'qualities so inferior'.[62] Once exported to the West Indies, the mules still fetched '20 to 30 guineas'.[63] Towards the end of the eighteenth century, New Englanders were able to increase and improve their breeding stock. In addition to Cape Verdean jacks, other jacks arrived from St Michael's in the Azores. While the exportation of jacks from Spain was still strictly prohibited, a few were smuggled from the Spanish part of Hispaniola into Cape Francois. The value of Maltese jacks at this time was cemented when George Washington received the Knight of Malta, while other jacks entered the US onboard the *Constitution* or via the navy through Minorca and Majorca.

By the end of the eighteenth century, some New England breeders had acquired jacks that were 'high grades' and a 'small number of good sized mules were bred'.[64] In 1787, Mark Prindle, from Harwinton, Connecticut, had 'just imported from Africa ... with much trouble and expence' a 'neat and elegant' jack, named Jackverdille. Prindle offered the following rates: $1 the single leap, $2 for the season or 'gratis, if at the time of covering the customer will engage the Mule-Colt, at four months old, to the subscriber, who will ... give ... the generous sum of Four Pounds'. Like many other equine breeders around New England, Prindle was 'fully convinced' of the 'advantage arising from the business of raising mules, [rather] than that of horses'.[65] Increasingly, New England breeders bragged about the pedigree and size of their imported jacks. In June 1787, Daniel Goddard Jr 'exerted himself' to procure valuable jackasses.

Goddard, who was based in Shrewsbury, Massachusetts, offered two of his jacks for sale in June 1787 to people within the state. While it might seem like Goddard simply wanted to make money by selling the jacks, he assured potential buyers that he had different motives: he offered them for sale 'to those who wish to second his efforts in promoting the publick good'. To mitigate the scarcity of cash, he was willing to take payment in shipping horses, beef and pork. He reiterated that the business of propagating mules 'is known to be so profitable, that it needs no comment'.[66] Others, including Frederick Bull, had the same idea. In 1787, Bull offered seven jacks for sale in Hartford, Connecticut that were 'of very largest and best breed that has been imported'. Bull offered his jacks for sale in between June and August, which was the end of the breeding season; thus, he reassured potential buyers that even if they did not use the jacks this season, they would easily prove their worth the following season. Bull's jacks were 'of the true Malta breed', and he was willing to offer 'a very low rate considering the value of those animals in this country' in exchange for shipping horses.[67]

Equine breeders around New England used the same techniques of diversifying their equine breeding by offering stallions and jacks at stud at the same time, but with very different terms to reflect the different markets. James Eldredge's practices reflect this trend. Eldredge advertised the services of 'a famous imported jack, perhaps the largest in the State' in Pomfret, Connecticut in 1786. Like many other breeders, Eldredge bought the mules back at four months old and varied his payment based on size, offering between $12 and $15, while not charging for mares who failed to get in foal. Eldredge kept an interest in horse-breeding alongside his mule-raising efforts, offering a stallion, Royal American, alongside the jack. Owners who wanted to breed their mares with Royal American paid $2 for the season (with good keeping) and $1 for the single leap. Royal American was a pacer who was fifteen hands high, 'as beautiful a horse as is in the State ... exceeding handsomely mark'd'.[68]

Other equine breeders used the same practices, and a few miles south in Preston, Connecticut, Nathan Ayres thought that he had the finest stallion in the state. At the same time that Eldredge advertised his stallion and jack, Ayres did the same thing. Ayres offered the 'famous horse' Macaroni for twelve shillings for the season 'if paid in hand' or eighteen shillings 'if charged, to be paid at Christmas'. Macaroni was a fine dapple grey, fifteen and a half hands high, five years old and 'for courage, activity and figure, exceeded by none'. The advert waxed lyrical about his fine pedigree. At the same time, Ayres offered the services of his 'famous Jack'. However, the terms were very different to those offered for Macaroni. Rather than paying to put the mare with the stallion, putting a mare to the jack was 'free of any expense'. Moreover, Ayres would pay the mare's owners for the privilege. Once the mules were four months old, Ayers would pay the owner $15 for the 'largest kind' of mules and $14 for 'smaller size'. Ayers would not charge owners anything for any mare 'not proving with foal'.[69] Samuel Whitman, of Hartford, Connecticut, also used the same technique of offering a stallion and jack for stud at the same time. In May 1787, he offered the 'fine bay', fifteen-hand-high stallion Bajazett for nine shillings for a single leap or $3 for the season. Alongside Bajazett, Whitman also offered 'a fine Jack', Sanco, with the provision that he would contract any mule offspring.[70]

Others, including Abel Clark, also bred horses and mules. Clark, who was based in Windham, Connecticut, offered the services of Narragansett Pacing, English thoroughbred, and shipping stallions, in addition to jacks in the 1790s.[71] Aside from his stallions, Clark boasted that one of his jacks was 'so well known' it was almost 'needless to say anything in his favour'. However, as the jack had only been in Windham for one season, Clark decided that it was best to post in the *Windham Herald* to ensure that everyone knew that the jack was 'without exception the likeliest, most vigorous and surest Jack that is kept in the state of Connecticut'. The jack was eleven hands and two inches high, and 'in proportion'. Clark was so certain that his mules were the 'largest and likeliest in the state' that he invited doubters to come and visit the mules to see that he had 'not in the least exaggerated' their size. Like many breeders, he wanted to buy the mules back at four months and offered £10 4s for large mules and £4 10s for smaller ones, with 'the jacking in the bargain' for both. The jack was so 'remarkably sure for foals', that any mares that lost their foals could be put to the jack for free next season.[72] After buying the mules back at four months, most breeders kept the mules in herds until they were ready to export. Between the age of four months and two years, many mules were left out in pasture with little human contact beyond basic attendance. Often, the mules had precarious shelter in winter, as breeders wanted to keep costs down prior to shipping.

There was evidently a ready market for mules of any kind for exportation, and merchants were always on the lookout for mules that were old enough to export. For example, in Hartford, Connecticut, John Chenevard wanted a 'number of good mules' that were two years old and 'fit for shipping' immediately in January 1785.[73] Chenevard was not alone, and in 1793 in Middletown, Connecticut, Daniel Henshaw wanted to purchase a number of likely shipping horses, cattle and mules that were suitable for 'an English market' in the West Indies.[74] A few years later in the same town, Lemuel Storrs wanted both shipping horses and mules. He was happy to make immediate payment in cash or produce.[75] John Fanning, master of the brig *Union*, shipped both horses and mules to Barbados from Norwich, Connecticut in 1794.[76] John Caussines, who was based in Warren, Rhode Island, also did a brisk trade with the West Indies in the 1790s. Caussines offered coffee, sugar, molasses and raw hides 'exceeding low' for cash or in exchange for good shipping horses and mules.[77] In 1797, Benjamin Williams, who operated out of Middletown, Connecticut, offered Jamaica and Tortola rum and rock salt for sale, while wanting to buy both mules and horses to ship. In New Haven in 1798, Shipman and Denison, were willing to pay in 'good rum' for 'a few likely saddle horses' and 'twenty good mules'.[78] In Hartford, Connecticut in 1799, Charles Morgan traded in shipping horses and mules.[79] One contemporary evaluation of the shipments from New London, Connecticut in 1797 concluded that 'shipments of alive stock from this port form by no means an inconsiderable article in the exports of the United States'. The report estimated that 385 horses and 245 mules were annually shipped from Deshon's Wharf alone.[80]

Not all of the animals who left New England made it to the West Indies. Crossing the Atlantic with any cargo was a challenge, but it was especially difficult with live animals. Equines crossed the Atlantic on deck in a temporary stable, with an eight-foot roof awning, on top of which food and water were stored. The animals were packed tightly and tied in parallel rows, with their heads towards each other, standing for the duration of the voyage. Contemporary observers described how this was 'tedious to the poor brutes, and ... they suffer a great deal'.[81] Equines, like humans, needed to get their 'sea legs', and, unsurprisingly, many animals got sick.[82] Travelling on deck with only a temporary awning for protection meant that when bad weather hit, the animals were often thrown overboard and drowned.[83] In order to protect their interests, merchants insured their equine cargo.[84] In addition to animal sickness and bad weather, pirates and privateers also interrupted the trade.[85] Exporting mules from New England to the West Indies was a risky business, but a profitable one.

As the nineteenth century progressed, other US states, especially Ohio, Kentucky and Tennessee, began to overshadow New England's mule-breeding efforts.[86] By 1844, the *New England Farmer & Horticultural Register* reported that most of the mules that were exported from New Haven, Connecticut were actually brought down 'in large droves from Canada' or 'driven from the West, even as far as from Ohio and Kentucky'.[87] In the south, especially on the sugar plantations of Louisiana, mules had long held prime place as key labourers, and they were increasingly bred and utilised in Pennsylvania, Maryland and Virginia.[88] In New England, mules (just like draught horses) were bred primarily for exportation to the West Indies, and they never caught on as the preferred form of labour within the region. New England's mule-breeding efforts never seriously challenged its main equine export in horses, but the very fact that New Englanders tried to diversify their equine exports is important. The lengths that New Englanders went to get jacks to start a breeding programme demonstrates how wider Atlantic markets drove New England's economy, both before and after independence. If planters in the sugar colonies were willing to pay good money for mules, the ever-enterprising merchants in New Englanders would try to supply them. In the midst of a complex and interconnected Atlantic world, equine breeders in New England, Atlantic merchants and West Indian sugar planters were all connected by their roles in mule-breeding, shipping and labouring for their own particular commercial efforts. The mule-breeding and export business demonstrates the friction between imperial directives and the innovation and autonomy of agents in their own commercial plans. Building upon the animal turn in history, this case study of mules reveals the importance of non-human animal labour in powering plantations and driving markets. The competition for equine labour within and across imperial projects and dominions underscores how non-human animals were central agents in European overseas empires.

Notes

1. Joes were Portuguese coins, named after the Portuguese King, Joaõ V.
2. The piece first appeared in the *New-York Packet* on 20 April 1787 and then in the following publications: *Independent Journal, Independent Gazetteer, New Haven Gazette, Pennsylvania Packet, Providence Gazette, American Mercury, Weekly Monitor, Middlesex Gazette, Massachusetts Gazette, Connecticut Journal, New Hampshire Spy, Newport Herald, Vermont Gazette, Columbian Herald* and *Salem Mercury*.
3. *Christian's, Scholar's, & Farmer's Magazine*, December 1789–January 1790.
4. Samuel Wyllys Pomeroy, 'A dissertation on the mule', in *New England Farmer*, 16 September 1825.
5. 'Extract from a letter from a British traveller of distinction in this country to his friend in Europe', first published in *Salem Mercury*, 22 May 1787, and subsequently in *American Mercury, Continental Journal, Norwich Packet, New York Packet, American Herald, Providence Gazette* and *Connecticut Gazette*.
6. Pomeroy, 'A dissertation on the mule'.
7. For environmental problems, see François Brizay in Chapter 2 of this volume.
8. Verene A. Shepherd, *Livestock, Sugar and Slavery: Contested Terrain in Colonial Jamaica* (Kingston: Ian Randle Publishers, 2009), 65.
9. *Ibid.*, 65–9, 72–3.
10. The cross-breeding of a female ass and a male horse produced a hinny and was rare in the eighteenth century: *Christian's, Scholar's, & Farmer's Magazine*, December 1789–January 1790; Pomeroy, 'A dissertation on the mule'.
11. For more on New England's horse-breeding and export trade, see Charlotte Carrington-Farmer, 'Trading horses in the eighteenth century: Rhode Island and the Atlantic World', in Kristen Guest and Monica Mattfeld (eds), *Equestrian Cultures: Horses, Human Society,*

and the Discourse of Modernity (Chicago: University of Chicago Press, 2019), 92–109.
12 Samuel Martin, An Essay on Plantership, 7th ed. (London, 1785), 1.
13 William Bayard Papers, 1765–75, Connecticut Historical Society, Hartford, CT.
14 Journals of the House of Commons (London: House of Commons, 1730, reprinted 1803), 21, 685–6; John Camberlayne, Magnæ Britanniæ Notitia (London, 1737), 39.
15 Anon., The British Empire in America, Consider'd ... from a Gentleman of Barbadoes, to His Friend in London (London, 1732), 19; Robert Robertson, A Supplement to the Detection of the State and Situation of the Present Sugar Planters of Barbadoes and the Leeward-Islands (London, 1733), 20–1; William Cleland, The Present State of the Sugar Plantations Consider'd; but More Especially That of the Island of Barbadoes (London, 1714), 26.
16 Anon., British Empire in America, 20–8.
17 Robert Robertson, A Detection of the State and Situation of the Present Sugar Planters (London, 1732), 41–5.
18 Robertson, A Supplement, 24–5, 51.
19 David Macpherson, Annals of Commerce, Manufactures, Fisheries, and Navigation, 4 vols. (London, 1805), 3: 49.
20 Nicholas Brown Papers, John Carter Brown Library, Providence, RI. Manuscript – BFBR B. 357, ML 1764–67; Providence Gazette, 29 January 1763.
21 Thomas Bannister, A Letter to the Right Honourable the Lords Commissioners of Trade & Plantations (London, 1715), 12.
22 Anon., The British Empire in America, 12.
23 Providence Gazette, 20 October 1764; Macpherson, Annals of Commerce, 175.
24 'Debate in the Commons on the Sugar Colony Bill February 23, 1732', in Cobbett's Parliamentary History of England from the Norman Conquest in 1066, to the Year 1803, 36 vols. (London, 1811), 3: 995–7.
25 Wim Klooster, 'Curaçao as a transit center to the Spanish Main and French West Indies', in Gert Oostindie and Jessica V. Roitman (eds.), Dutch Atlantic Connections, 1680–1800: Linking Empires, Bridging Borders (Leiden and Boston: Brill, 2014), 30–2.
26 Linda Rupert, Creolization and Contraband: Curaçao in the Early Modern Atlantic World (Athens: The University of Georgia Press, 2012), 170–3.
27 Alexander von Humboldt, Personal Narrative of Travels to the Equinoctial Region of America, 3 vols. (London: George Bell and Sons, 1899), 2: 46.

28 'H. Gelskerke to the West India Company, 4 November 1734', in *Extracts from Dutch Archives* (Washington: Government Printing Office, 1879), no. 125, 268–9, and no. 128, 273–4.
29 In 1748, Ignance Courthial went 'up the Orinoco' to get 'some hundred cattle and mules to import for trade'. 'Storm van's Gravesande to the West India Company, December 2 1748', in *Extracts from Dutch Archives*, no. 167, 321–3.
30 Juan Giusti-Cordero, 'Beyond sugar revolutions: Rethinking the Spanish Caribbean in the seventeenth and eighteenth centuries', in George Baca, Aisha Khan and Stephan Palmié (eds.), *Empirical Futures: Anthropologists and Historians Engage the Work of Sidney W. Mintz* (Chapel Hill: University of North Carolina Press, 2009), 58–83 at 68.
31 Shepherd, *Livestock, Sugar and Slavery*, xxxiii, 65; Philip D. Morgan, 'Slaves and livestock in eighteenth-century Jamaica: Vineyard Pen, 1750–1751', *WMQ* 52, no. 1 (1995), 47–76.
32 Yu Wu, 'Jamaican Trade: 1688–1769: A Quantitative Study' (Ph.D. diss., Johns Hopkins University, 1995), 286; Shepherd, *Livestock, Sugar and Slavery*, 65.
33 Edward Long, History of Jamaica (London, 1774), 1: 412; Shepherd, *Livestock, Sugar and Slavery*, 67.
34 Elizabeth Sutton, *'Bittersweet: Sugar, Slavery, and Science in Dutch Suriname', Midwestern Arcadia: Essays in Honor of Alison Kettering* (2015), 143–53, https://apps.carleton.edu/kettering/sutton/#_edn26.
35 Samuel Maverick, 'A briefe description of New England' (1660), in *Proceedings of the Massachusetts Historical Society* (Boston: John Wilson and Son, 1885), 2nd ser., 1: 247.
36 For more information on the Narragansett Pacer, see Charlotte Carrington-Farmer, 'The rise and fall of the Narragansett Pacer', *Rhode Island History* 76, no. 1 (2018), 1–38.
37 Carrington-Farmer, 'Trading horses in the eighteenth century', 92–109.
38 'William Mackinen to Abraham Redwood' (4 October 1753), Letters Concerning the Plantation in Antigua, Vault A, Newport Historical Society, Newport, RI, 3884, Box 36, Folder B.
39 For more on Anglo-Moroccan relations, James Brown, *Crossing the Strait: Morocco, Gibraltar and Great Britain in the 18th and 19th Centuries* (Leiden: Brill, 2012).
40 *Boston Chronicle*, 19 September 1768.
41 *Boston Weekly News-Letter*, 13 April 1769.
42 The advert made no mention of Ottoman's colour, but he was likely what contemporaries called a 'large white'. Muslims rarely employed

the big dark jacks of Europe and China, whereas some European jacks were like the Islamic ones, notably in Andalusia and Tuscany. *Newport Mercury*, 9 May, 16 May, 23 May 1774.
43 Ibid.
44 Ron Chernow, *Washington: A Life* (New York: Penguin, 2010); Alexis Coe, 'George Washington saw a future for America: mules', *Smithsonian Magazine*, February 2020, www.smithsonianmag.com/history/george-washington-saw-future-america-mules-180974182/.
45 'Extract from a letter from a British traveller'.
46 Ibid.
47 'An Extract of a Letter from a Gentleman from this State now in the West Indies to his friend, dated June 1787', published in *Norwich Packet*, 30 August 1787, and subsequently in *American Mercury*, *Weekly Monitor*, *Daily Advertiser*, *Salem Mercury*, *New Jersey Journal* and *Pennsylvania Packet*.
48 Pomeroy, 'A dissertation on the mule'.
49 Coe, 'George Washington'.
50 'An Extract of a Letter from a Gentleman'.
51 Ibid.
52 Marjorie Spiegel, *The Dreaded Comparison: Human and Animal Slavery* (New York: Mirror Books, 1996).
53 Dan Vandersommers, 'The "animal turn" in history', *Perspectives on History* (November 2016), www.historians.org/publications-and-directories/perspectives-on-history/november-2016/the-animal-turn-in-history.
54 David Lambert, 'Runaways and strays: Rethinking (non)human agency in Caribbean slave societies', in Sharon Wilcox and Stephanie Rutherford (eds.), *Historical Animal Geographies* (New York: Routledge, 2018), 185–98.
55 Pomeroy, 'A dissertation on the mule'.
56 *Farmer's Monthly Visitor*, 31 October 1843.
57 John Camberlayne, *Magnæ Britanniæ Notitia* (London, 1737), 32.
58 Pomeroy, 'A dissertation on the mule'.
59 *Farmer's Monthly Visitor*, 31 October 1843.
60 'H. Gelskerke to the West India Company, 4 November 1734', in *Extracts from Dutch Archives*, no. 125, 268–9.
61 David Lambert, 'Master–horse–slave: Mobility, race and power in the British West Indies, c. 1780–1838', *Slavery & Abolition* 36, no. 4 (2015), 618–41; J.B. Moreton, *West India Customs and Manners* (London, 1793), 97; Hector McNeil, *Observations on the Treatment of the Negros* (London, 1788), v.
62 Pomeroy, 'A dissertation on the mule'.

222   *Local adaptations and developments*

63 *Christian's, Scholar's, & Farmer's Magazine*, December 1789–January 1790.
64 Pomeroy, 'A dissertation on the mule'.
65 *Weekly Monitor*, 14 May, 21 May, 28 May, 4 June 1787.
66 *Worcester Magazine*, 7 June 1787.
67 *Connecticut Courant*, 25 June, 20 August 1787.
68 Equines are measured in 'hands high' from the hoof to the withers, with every hand being four inches, *Connecticut Gazette*, 12 May, 19 May, 26 May, 2 June 1786.
69 *Connecticut Gazette*, 19 May, 26 May, 2 June 1786.
70 *Connecticut Courant*, 21 May, 28 May 1787.
71 *Windham Herald*, 30 April, 3 May 1791; 3 May 1794.
72 *Ibid.*, 30 April 1791; 9 June 1792.
73 *Connecticut Courant*, 18 January 1785.
74 *Middlesex Gazette* (Middletown, CT), 12 January, 2 February, 9 February, 16 March 1793.
75 *Connecticut Courant*, 13 April 1795.
76 *Weekly Register*, 11 November 1794.
77 *Herald of the United States*, 19 January, 26 January, 2 February 1793.
78 *Connecticut Journal*, 5 September 1798.
79 *American Mercury*, 28 March, 4 April 1799.
80 *The Bee*, 6 September 1797.
81 *New England Farmer, & Horticultural Register*, 10 January 1844.
82 See Captain Samuel Capron's voyage on the sloop, *Prudence*, from Stonington, CT to Suriname for animal illness onboard when travelling, Mystic Seaport Archives, Mystic, CT, Log 692.
83 *Providence Gazette*, 10 March 1792.
84 Greg H. Williams, *The French Assault on American Shipping, 1793–1813: A History and Comprehensive Record of Merchant Marine Losses* (Jefferson: McFarland & Company, Inc., 2009), 375.
85 For pirates and privateers interrupting the equine trade, Mystic Seaport Archives, log 386; *Boston News-Letter*, 19 March 1716; *Boston Evening Post*, 26 September 1757; *The Bee*, 24 April 1799.
86 *Cultivator: A Monthly Publication; Devoted to Agriculture*, 1: 5 (May 1844), 149.
87 *New England Farmer, & Horticultural Register*, 10 January 1844.
88 *Farmer's Monthly Visitor*, 31 October 1843.

Epilogue: Perspectives on the mechanisms and impacts of overseas colonisation in the early modern era – then and now

Bertrand Van Ruymbeke

In the 1780s, l'abbé Guillaume-Thomas Raynal was at the height of his editorial glory and fame as a historian and philosophe. The work of his life, *Histoire philosophique et politique des établissements et du commerce des Européens dans les deux Indes* (*The Philosophical and Political History of the Settlements and Trade of the Europeans in the Two Indies*), hereafter *Histoire des Deux Indes*, object of François Brizay's contribution (Chapter 2), was going through its third edition, clearly the most radical in its overall, even if at times nuanced, condemnation of colonisation.[1] Although signed solely by Raynal, *Histoire des deux Indes* was a multi-authored book. Raynal hired and paid a series of experts and philosophers to contribute to it, among whom Diderot stands out for the profoundness and quality of his contributions, his incisive style, his radical thoughts and the role he played in restructuring the decisive, influential and conclusive 1780 third edition. Raynal also borrowed from previous authors and had correspondents in colonial administrations as well as in the colonies – and not only of France – who provided him with precious information, memoirs and statistics. *Histoire des deux Indes* is undoubtedly a complex work in its architecture, its message and its reading.[2] The book was meant to be an ambitious survey of the worldwide expansion and trade of Europeans and of its consequences for humankind.

With the condemnation and public burning of *Histoire des deux Indes* in 1781, Raynal had to go into exile. A few months earlier, however, on 29 August 1780, Raynal was feted by the *Académie des sciences, belles-lettres et arts* in Lyon; the large crowd present that day not only sought 'to have his writings [but] even pieces of his clothes', as a witness described.[3] Raynal was at the *Académie* to finance two contests, one on the manufactures of Lyon for 600 *livres* and another on the consequences of the discovery of the 'New World' for 1,200 *livres*, or twice as much. Raynal's presence at the *Académie*, and in the city of Lyon as he was received in the town hall, was an opportunity to draw much attention and to strengthen the influence of the city locally and extend it nationally, possibly to Europe and beyond.

Prize-winning contests (*concours*) became a central part of French, and to some extent European, academic culture in the second half of the eighteenth century. In France, they were immensely popular. While the thirty-odd Académies and various learned societies offered forty-eight contests in the 1700–09 decade, the number reached 618 in the 1780s, 175 for Paris alone. More than two thousand contests were held over the long eighteenth century from 1670 to 1790. One estimate places the number of contestants at fifteen thousand from 1670 to 1790.[4] This was quite a contest frenzy. Whereas under Louis XIV *concours* served essentially to honour the Sun King, topics increasingly diversified throughout the eighteenth century to address a variety of social, medical, scientific, agricultural, moral, philosophical, geographic and historical issues exclusive of continuously popular poetry and eloquence competitions. Topics ranged from the severity of laws to the role of the historian, the empire of fashion, the passion of gambling, the impact of luxury, public education, freedom, inoculation, overseas colonisation, the traffic in enslaved people and enslavement, urbanism, poor relief, aerostatics and electricity, as well as a myriad of regional issues. Studying the evolution of topics over time, identifying the sponsors who financed these prizes and, most importantly, analysing the memoirs themselves give the historian a precious angle on what can be called mainstream Enlightenment culture. It reveals much on the diffusion of ideas and it allows us to take the pulse of what the elite read, wrote and thought on a vast range of issues. For even if the *Académies* could undoubtedly lead the way in terms of cultural and societal reflection, contests were in essence a mirror of contemporaneous preoccupations and reflected time-specific *mouvements d'idées* that, in turn, they stimulated.

A well-publicised contest that drew many memoirs from France and Europe was extremely beneficial to an *Académie* for its reputation and clout. The reverse is also true for the contest patron, particularly so in the case of Raynal, who sponsored thirty-three *concours* on a variety of topics in Lyon, Marseille, Paris and Berlin from 1781 to 1793.[5] This was even more so true in the case of the Lyon contest on the discovery of the Americas as its success maintained the promotion of his *Histoire des deux Indes*, as contestants felt the obligation to mention it or simply used it as their main source, thereby spreading its content. Raynal could also borrow ideas from memoirs submitted to the *Académie* or essays published on the occasion of the *concours* without their authors wishing to formerly compete. He therefore engaged in a dialogue with the learned public and the best thinkers of the day meant to eventually nourish a future edition of his *Histoire des deux Indes*. Raynal consequently took an active part in promoting the contest by sending the announcement to his correspondents and by publishing it in his 1781 *Révolution de l'Amérique*, extracted from *Histoire des deux Indes* and published as a separate book.[6]

The questions proposed by the Lyon *Académie* were: 'Has the discovery of America been useful or harmful to humankind? If good resulted from it what are the means to preserve and increase it? If it caused ills how can they be remedied?'[7] With fifty submissions, over five times the average number, the contest met with enormous success, which mirrored that of *Histoire des deux Indes*. However, unsatisfied with the quality of the memoirs, the Lyon *académiciens*, with Raynal's approval, renewed the contest until 1789 and eventually decided against awarding the prize. Therefore, the contest unexpectedly lasted a decade. Authors who addressed their memoirs to the *Académie*, who belonged to the mercantile, judicial, medical and clerical elite, were relatively unknown for the most part, but the contest benefited from widespread publicity through the press and the *académiciens*' own epistolary networks, not only in Europe but as far away as Philadelphia and Boston. As it perfectly fitted into what Italian historian Antonello Gerbi once called 'the dispute of the New World', namely, a collective transatlantic eighteenth-century reflection on the meaning and essence of America and the consequences of its colonisation by Western Europeans, the contest drew into the discussion the best transatlantic pens of the time, such as Condorcet, Belknap, Chastellux, Von Gentz, Crèvecoeur, Brissot, the Abbé Genty, Meude-Monpas and Jefferson, whether or not they competed.[8]

Raynal himself had posed and answered the question in conclusion of the 1780 edition of *Histoire des deux Indes* but restricting the consequences of the colonisation of the Americas to Europe. The very last section of book XIX (Volume 4) is thus titled: 'Reflections on the good and the evil that the discovery of the New World has brought upon Europe'.[9] It obviously makes a notable difference as the Lyon contest includes Africa and, in an ambitious and universal approach, invited the contestants to address the consequences of the colonisation of the Americas on humankind. In fact, probably because no memoirs were crowned by the Lyon *académiciens* and possibly because, after all, Europeans were primarily interested in themselves, the contest was picked up by the *Académie Française* in Paris in 1791 as 'What has been the influence of the discovery of America on the mores, politics and commerce of Europe?'[10] A much narrower scope. Under Raynal's pen, the New World is to be understood generically as the two Indies – East and West – (*'l'Amérique et l'Inde'*). His reflections underscored the ills that European colonisation caused, what he called 'calamities without compensation'. In other words, the disastrous consequences of colonisation – slavery standing out as the worst – did not bring anything to Europeans that could make them acceptable, even as necessary evil.

By spanning the 1780s, the Lyon contest allows historians to study the contemporaneous perception of the New World and of three centuries of overseas colonisation by European elites over an eventful decade, and how that image quickly and radically changed in light of the American Revolution and the birth of the United States. The memoirs submitted to the *Académie* or simply published offered an ample reflection on the colonisation of the Americas, 'the most interesting question ever submitted to the tribunal of Reason and Philosophy', as one author stated. The topic invited authors to reflect not only on the negative and positive consequences of European expansion since 1492 on humankind ('to embrace the whole universe', as the *académiciens* put it) but also on ways to preserve its advantages and remedy its ills. This was quite a difficult question, 'a topic that multiplies difficulties', as one contestant wrote, and unsurprisingly, most authors limited their answers to the first part of the subject.[11] As the *académiciens* noted in their 1790 final report, 'our question contained three elements well distinct although intimately woven into one another'. In other words, one had to reflect on the pros and cons of colonisation and also suggest how to perpetuate its good consequences and remedy its disastrous effects. 'After about three centuries of insensitivity, [when Europe] started to feel embarrassed of a conquest long celebrated with excess', the time seemed ripe for such a global reflection.[12]

The majority of contestants drew a dark portrait of colonisation and underscored the catastrophic consequences of European expansion, with a strong emphasis on Spain, on the three continents of Europe, Africa and America. 'Outraged by the excesses that have stained the most beautiful discovery made by Europeans', explained the *académiciens*, 'our orators for the most part decided that it had been more fatal than useful'.[13] As one of the authors summarised it:

> It is doubtless beautiful to see the European soar beyond the Pillars of Hercules, tame that ocean that we believed intractable, to unify two hemispheres separated by an oceanic immensity, to acquire and spread throughout the world the productions of a new world and double one's resources and pleasures. Yet how bitter those pleasures are when we think how high their prices were.[14]

Clearly, wrote another, it is 'unquestionable that the discovery of America is the worst tragedy that affected the other three parts of the world'.[15] Arguments against colonisation that are presented in the memoirs are the violence of a conquest perceived as illegitimate; the destruction of Indigenous peoples; the traffic in enslaved people and enslavement; privateering; the sudden inflow of precious metals and the development of luxury 'that has offered [in Europe] the distressing spectacle of the most excessive wealth next to the most hideous poverty' and imposed 'the reign of money'; the financial cost of expansion; the increased number of 'ruinous wars' due to colonial and imperial rivalries; the negative consequences of emigration on European societies; and the introduction of syphilis to Europe. Slavery, 'the right of life and death on your fellow man', and the slave trade, 'this commerce most shameful to humanity ... born out of the depopulation of America and European cupidity', are highlighted as the worst consequences of the colonisation of the Americas. As another author denounced: 'I do not know if coffee and sugar are necessary to Europe's happiness but I know well that those two plants have brought unhappiness to two parts of the world. America was depopulated to have land to plant them and Africa is being depopulated to have a people to grow them'.[16]

A few authors suggested remedies to the ills brought about by the colonisation of the Americas, namely, to abolish the slave trade and gradually free the enslaved over several generations (the 1780 Pennsylvania gradual abolition act being mentioned as a case in point) and have them marry settlers; turn Natives into citizens-farmers (to have them abandon 'the bow and arrows for the spade and the plough') while giving them more autonomy; break the metropole's commercial monopoly on colonial trade; give economic autonomy to the colonies, and for the most radical among them, even outright independence, while maintaining some sort of commercial partnership with their former metropoles. Apart from the abolition of the slave trade and the gradual emancipation of the enslaved, which seemed attainable in the 1780s, all the other suggestions made by writers largely unfamiliar with America sound a bit chimerical. It is striking, though, that the memorialists saw the commercial restrictions imposed on the colonies by metropoles through the French monopoly (*Exclusif*) or the English Navigation Acts as no longer beneficial to either one, and that they were confident that they were no longer needed. Rightly so, if we consider that the United States maintained a fruitful trade with Great Britain after independence, showing that transatlantic commerce could flourish beyond political dependence. At any rate, as another contestant undoubtedly influenced by the American Revolution stated, 'sooner or later, [European nations] will have to renounce colonies. Are we not already seeing [that] northern America, whose strength grows to the point of setting the tone for the other parts of the Americas, will one day be the queen of the universe as the other three parts of the world have in turn been?'[17] Conversely, the benefits of colonisation were very few according to the contestants, who briefly listed them: progress in geography, navigation, astronomy, natural history and pharmacopoeia, as well as the introduction of the potato to Europe, considered as a most useful means to prevent famines.

The newly founded American Republic, and before the adoption of the Federal Constitution in 1788, *les républiques américaines*, as the United States were then perceived in France as thirteen autonomous republics, entered the scene only in the last memoirs when the contest was renewed in 1785 and 1787. But it played a fundamental role as it offered hope to redeem the disastrous effects of the colonisation of the Americas, and even to some authors a way to remedy them. In spite of the 'unheard-of cruelty of the Europeans', the Lyon *académiciens* emphasised in their report that 'the discovery of America' allowed for the momentous expansion of civilisation and freedom, a sentiment echoed in one of the memoirs: 'You nascent Republic, carved out of one of the extremities of the new continent, and whose liberation, the price of your virtues, your enlightened ideas, your courage, seem proper to fasten the progress of America's prosperity, you in which humankind hope more today, do not deceive our expectations! Everything favors your success'.[18] The United States, 'this vast expanse where liberty seems to have established its empire', as one of the competitors, the banker and *littérateur* Joseph Mandrillon wrote, are the embodiment and herald of the benefits of the 'discovery' and colonisation of the Americas. Undoubtedly, Mandrillon added, 'it will be the independent colonies that will have the glory to civilize the rest of the Americas'.[19] The *académiciens* underlined that to fully and accurately answer the question, 'it was principally the present generation and those who are eager to replace it' and not past centuries that had to be considered. In the 1780s, the United States therefore raised momentous hope in Europe. There, 'freedom's banner unfolded for the entire universe,' concluded the Lyon *académiciens*, adding that 'with freedom's irresistible bait, English America will attract many immigrants from Europe, who will consolidate its population already so fruitful'.[20]

Raynal's reflections and the Lyon contest beautifully echo the global scope and content of this volume. The authors address, with a most justified emphasis on private colonisers, many aspects of overseas European colonisation, such as migration and settlement, slavery, trade, imperial rivalries and wars, Indigenous land dispossession, the role of merchant companies as well as individuals as main colonising actors or agents versus rather weak or inefficient, perhaps little concerned, early modern states. In a comparative English and French approach, essays in Part I (Chapters 1, 2 and 3) show the crucial importance of trading and colonisation companies in European expansion and their complex relations to states and nations which played to their advantage, at least before the end of the eighteenth century. Contributions in Part II (Chapters 4, 5 and 6) focus on the concrete realities of colonisation through a close study of migrations and slavery – a central institution in overseas territories in the West and East Indies – showing the absolute need for a massive labour force, free and unfree, as well as highlighting the failure of states to control its flows. Essays in Part III (Chapters 7, 8 and 9) pursue this close-up study further, to show how settlers – present in massive numbers in the case of British North America – were a key element in not only embodying actual colonisation but also in designing the shape and strength of the empire they largely contributed to building, sometimes with slow or limited success, as in the case of the Cape of Good Hope. They developed intercolonial trade, as in the case of mules and horses between New England and the Caribbean, whether legal or illegal, to supplement commerce with the metropole, which, at least in the case of Spain and France, did not satisfy their needs. Whereas Raynal stated in 1780 that 'there will not be a moment when [this] question has as much strength', 250 years later seems also an opportune moment to examine the inner workings of expansion and colonisation, the dominant paradigms that shaped the various European overseas empires, and emphasise the roles played by their various agents.

Notes

1 Guillaume-Thomas Raynal, *Histoire philosophique et politique des établissements et du commerce des Européens dans les deux Indes* (Geneva, 1780).
2 Hans-Jürgen Lüsebrink and Anthony Strugnell (eds.), *Lectures de Raynal: L'Histoire des deux Indes: Réécriture et Polygraphie* (Oxford: Voltaire Foundation, 1995); Gilles Bancarel (ed.), *Raynal et ses réseaux* (Paris: Champion, 2011).
3 Paul Feula, 'Les relations lyonnaises de l'Abbé Raynal', *Mémoires de l'Académie des sciences, belles-lettres et arts de Lyon*, 4th ser., 14 (2015), 142–51 at 143.
4 Daniel Roche, *Le Siècle des Lumières en Province. Académies et Académiciens Provinciaux, 1680–1789*, 2 vols. (Paris: Éditions de l'École des Hautes Études en Sciences Sociales, 1989 [1978]), 1: 325–6; Jeremy Caradonna, *The Enlightenment in Practice: Academic Prize Contests and Intellectual Culture in France, 1670–1794* (Princeton: Princeton University Press, 2012), 90.

5 Gilles Bancarel, *Raynal ou le devoir de vérité* (Paris: Champion, 2004), 'Tableau récapitulatif des prix fondés par l'abbé Raynal', 482–6.
6 Guillaume-Thomas Raynal, *Révolution de l'Amérique* (1781), 'Avertissement de l'Académie des Sciences, Belles-Lettres et Arts de Lyon', ix–xii.
7 '*La découverte de l'Amérique a-t-elle été utile ou nuisible au genre humain? S'il en est résulté des biens, quels sont les moyens de les conserver et de les accroître? Si elle a produit des maux quels sont les moyens d'y remédier?*'. 'Registres des procès verbaux des séances de l'Académie de Lyon', Ms. 266, 'Nouveaux sujets pour l'année 1782' (5 September 1780), Archives de l'Académie des Sciences, Belles-Lettres et Arts de Lyon.
8 Antonello Gerbi, *The Dispute of the New World: The History of a Polemic, 1750–1900*, trans. Jeremy Moyle (Pittsburgh: University of Pittsburgh Press, 1973). See also Henry Steele Commager and Elmo Giordanetti (eds.), *Was America a Mistake? An Eighteenth-Century Controversy* (New York: Harper & Row Publishers, 1967). Examples of essays published directly or indirectly on the occasion of the Lyon contest are Condorcet, *De l'Influence de la Révolution d'Amérique sur l'Europe* (1786); Jeremy Belknap, *Has the Discovery of America Been Useful or Hurtful to Mankind?* (1784); François-Jean de Chastellux, *Discours sur les Avantages ou les Désavantages qui résultent pour l'Europe de la Découverte de l'Amérique* (1787); Friedrich von Gentz, *On the Influence of the Discovery of America on the Prosperity and Culture of the Human Race* (1795); St. John de Crèvecoeur, *Lettres d'un Cultivateur Américain* (1784) (English edition, 1782); Etienne Clavière and Jacques-Pierre Brissot, *De la France et des États-Unis ou de l'Importance de la Révolution de l'Amérique pour le bonheur de la France* (1787); Abbé Genty, *L'Influence de la Découverte de l'Amérique sur le Bonheur du Genre Humain* (1788); J.J.O. de Meude-Monpas, *Les Richesses ont Toujours Causé nos Malheurs* (1788); and Thomas Jefferson, *Notes on the State of Virginia* (1785).
9 Guillaume-Thomas Raynal, *Histoire des deux Indes* (Geneva, 1780), '*Réflexions sur le bien et sur le mal que la découverte du Nouveau-Monde a fait à l'Europe*', 701–6.
10 '*Quelle a été l'influence de la découverte de l'Amérique sur les mœurs, la politique et le commerce de l'Europe?*', Marie-Claire Chatelain, 'De l'Académie lyonnaise à la française', in Yann Sordet (ed.), *Raynal. Un Regard vers l'Amérique* (Paris: Bibliothèque Mazarine/Éditions des Cendres, 2013), 156.

11 Memoir #4 (10 March 1789), fo. 84, Archives de l'Académie des Sciences, Belles-Lettres et Arts de Lyon.
12 'Coup d'œil sur les quatre concours qui ont eu lieu en l'Académie des Sciences, Belles-Lettres et Arts de Lyon, pour le prix offert par M. l'Abbé Raynal sur la découverte de l'Amérique' (20 April 1790), in Hans-Jürgen Lüsebrink and Alexandre Mussard, *Avantages et Désavantages de la Découverte de l'Amérique. Chastellux, Raynal et le Concours de Lyon* (Saint-Etienne: Publications de l'Université de Saint-Etienne, 1994), 128, 133.
13 *Ibid.*, 133.
14 Memoir #7 (30 March 1789), fos. 185–97, Archives de l'Académie des Sciences, Belles-Lettres et Arts de Lyon.
15 Memoir #2 (23 April 1788), fo. 106, Archives de l'Académie des Sciences, Belles-Lettres et Arts de Lyon.
16 Henri Méchoulan, 'La découverte de l'Amérique a-t-elle été utile ou nuisible au genre humain. Réflexions sur le concours de Lyon 1783–1789', *Cuadernos Salmantinos de Filosofía*, 1988, 130, 134; Lüsebring and Mussard, *Avantages et Désavantages de la Découverte de l'Amérique*, 100–1.
17 Memoir #2 (23 April 1788), fo. 107, Archives de l'Académie des Sciences, Belles-Lettres et Arts de Lyon.
18 'Coup d'œil sur les quatre concours', 137.
19 Joseph Mandrillon, *Recherches Philosophiques sur la Découverte de l'Amérique ou Discours sur cette question proposée par l'Académies des Sciences, Belles-Lettres et Arts de Lyon: La découverte de l'Amérique a-t-elle été utile ou nuisible au genre-humain? S'il en est résulté des biens, quels sont les moyens de les conserver & de les accroître? Si elle a produit des maux, quels sont les moyens d'y remédier?* (Amsterdam, 1784), 19.
20 'Coup d'œil sur les quatre concours', 143.

Select bibliography

Acosta Rodríguez, Antonio et al. (eds.), *La Casa de la Contratación y la Navegación entre España y las Indias* (Sevilla: Universidad de Sevilla, CSIC, Fundación El Monte, 2003).
Aje, Lawrence, Anne-Claire Faucquez and Elodie Peyrol-Kleiber (eds.), 'Servitudes et libertés dans les Amériques avant l'abolition de l'esclavage', *Les cahiers du MIMMOC* [online], 19 (2018), http://journals.openedition.org/mimmoc/3077.
Alimento, Antonella and Gianluigi Goggi (eds.), *Autour de l'abbé Raynal: genèse et enjeux politiques de l'Histoire des deux Indes* (Ferney-Voltaire: Centre international d'étude du XVIIIe siècle, 2018).
Alimento, Antonella and Koen Stapelbroek, 'Trade and treaties: Balancing the interstate system', in A. Alimento and K. Stapelbroek (eds.), *The Politics of Commercial Treaties in the Eighteenth Century: Balance of Power, Balance of Trade* (New York: Palgrave Macmillan, 2017), 1–75.
Almorza Hidalgo, Amelia, *'No se hace pueblo sin ellas'. Mujeres españolas en el Virreinato de Perú: emigración y movilidad social (siglos XVI–XVII)* (Madrid: CSIC, Universidad de Sevilla, Diputación de Sevilla, 2018).
Altenbernd, Erik and Alex Trimble Young, 'Introduction: The significance of the frontier in an age of transnational history', *Settler Colonial Studies* 4, no. 2 (2014), 127–50.
Altman, Ida and James Horn (eds.), *'To Make America': European Emigration in the Early Modern Period* (Berkeley: University of California Press, 1991).
Anderson, Chad, 'Rediscovering Native America: Settlements, maps, and empires in the eastern woodlands', *Early American Studies* 14, no. 3 (2016), 478–505.
Anderson, Virginia DeJohn, *Creatures of Empire: How Domestic Animals Transformed Early America* (Oxford: Oxford University Press, 2004).
Anderson, Virginia DeJohn, 'New England in the seventeenth century', in Nicholas P. Canny (ed.), *The Origins of Empire* (Oxford: Oxford University Press, 1998), 193–217.

Andreo García, Juan and Lucía Provencio Garrigós, 'Pasajeros a América: aportación al estudio de la emigración del reino de Murcia durante el S. XVI', *Anales de Historia Contemporánea* 8 (1991), 97–130.

Anes Álvarez, Andreas, *La Emigración de Asturianos a América* (Colombres: Fundación Archivo de Indianos, 1993).

Anore Horton, M., *New Perspectives on Women and Migration in Colonial Latin America* (Princeton: Princeton University Press, 2001).

Antunes, Catia and Amelia Polonia (eds.), *Beyond Empires: Global, Self-Organizing, Cross-Imperial Networks, 1500–1800* (Leiden: Brill, 2016).

Antunes, Catia and Filipa Ribeiro da Silva, 'Amsterdam merchants in the slave trade and African commerce, 1580s–1670s', *Tijdschirft voor Economisch en Sociale Geschiedenis* 9, no. 4 (2012), 3–30.

Armitage, David, 'The Cromwellian protectorate and the languages of empire', *Historical Journal* 59, no. 3 (1992), 531–55.

Armitage, David and Michael J. Braddick (eds.), *The British Atlantic World, 1500–1800* (Basingstoke: Palgrave Macmillan, 2002).

Asaka, Ikuko, *Tropical Freedom: Climate, Settler Colonialism, and Black Exclusion in the Age of Emancipation* (Durham: Duke University Press, 2017).

Azcona Pastor, José Manuel (ed.), *Identidad y Estructura de la Emigración vasca y navarra hacia Iberoamérica Siglos (XVI–XXI): Redes Sociales y Desarrollo Socioeconómico* (Cizur Minor: Thomson Reuters Aranzadi, 2015).

Badorrey Martín, Beatriz, 'La Audiencia de México y el Gobierno de Nueva España a través de las instrucciones y memorias de los virreyes (Siglos XVI y XVII)', *Anuario de historia del derecho español* 88–9 (2018–19), 45–75.

Bailey, Mark, 'Historiographical essay: The commercialisation of the English economy, 1086–1500', *Journal of Medieval History* 24, no. 3 (1998), 297–311.

Bancarel, Gilles, *Raynal ou le devoir de vérité* (Paris: Honoré Champion, 2004).

Bancarel, Gilles and Gianluigi Goggi (eds.), *Raynal, de la polémique à l'histoire* (Oxford: The Voltaire Foundation, 2000).

Bangs, Jeremy Dupertuis, *Pilgrim Edward Winslow: New England's First International Diplomat* (Boston: New England Historic Genealogical Society, 2004).

Barcia, Manuel, 'Into the future: A historiographical overview of Atlantic history in the twenty first century', *Atlantic Studies* 19, no. 2 (2021), 1–19, https://doi.org/10.1080/14788810.2021.1948284.

Bayly, Christopher A., *The Birth of the Modern World, 1780–1914* (Oxford: Oxford University Press, 2005).

Belich, James, *Replenishing the Earth: The Settler Revolution and the Rise of the Anglo-World, 1783–1939* (Oxford: Oxford University Press, 2009).

Belissa, Marc, *Repenser l'Ordre Européen (1795–1802). De la Société des Rois aux Droits de Nations* (Paris: Kimé, 2006).

Belknap, Jeremy, 'Observations upon the question, has the discovery of America been useful or hurtful to mankind?', *Boston Magazine* (1 May 1784), 280–6.

Ben-Ur, Aviva, 'Purim in the public eye: Leisure, violence, and cultural convergence in the Dutch Atlantic', *Jewish Social Studies* 20, no. 1 (2013), 32–76.

Berg, Maxine, Felicia Gottmann, Hanna Hodacs and Chris Nierstrasz (eds.), *Goods from the East, 1600–1800: Trading Eurasia* (London: Palgrave Macmillan, 2015).

Beyers, Coenraad, *Die Kaapse Patriotte* (Pretoria: Van Schaik, 1967).

Bickers, Robert, 'Introduction: Britain and Britons over the seas', in Robert Bickers (ed.), *Settlers and Expatriates* (Oxford: Oxford University Press, 2010), 1–17.

Birchall, Matthew, 'History, sovereignty, and capital: Company colonization in Australia and New Zealand', *Journal of Global History* 16, no. 1 (2021), 141–57, doi:10.1017/S1740022820000133.

Blackhawk, Maggie, 'Federal Indian law as paradigm within public law', *Harvard Law Review* 132, no. 7 (2019), 1787–877.

Bohls, Elizabeth A., 'The gentleman planter and the metropole: Long's history of Jamaica', in Gerald Maclean et al. (eds.), *The Country and the City Revisited: England and the Politics of Culture, 1550–1850* (Cambridge: Cambridge University Press, 1999), 180–96.

Bosma, Ulbe, and Remco Raben, *De oude Indische wereld 1500–1920. De geschiedenis van Indische Nederlanders* (Amsterdam: Bakker, 2003).

Bougainville, Louis Antoine de, *Voyage autour du monde, par la frégate la Boudeuse et la flûte l'Etoile* ([1771] Paris: La Découverte/Poche, 1997).

Boxer, Charles Ralph, *The Dutch Seaborne Empire, 1600–1800* (London: Hutchinson, 1965).

Boxer, Charles Ralph, *The Dutch in Brazil, 1624–1654* (Oxford: Clarendon Press, 1957).

Bradshaw, Brendan and Peter Roberts, 'Introduction', in Brendan Bradshaw and Peter Roberts (eds.), *British Consciousness and Identity: The Making of Britain, 1533–1707* (Cambridge: Cambridge University Press, 2000).

Brandon, Pepijn, 'Between the plantation and the port: Racialization and social control in eighteenth-century Paramaribo', *International Review of Social History* 64, no. S27 (2019), 95–124.

Brandon, Pepijn, Niklas Frykman and Pernille Røge, 'Free and unfree labor in Atlantic and Indian Ocean port cities (seventeenth–nineteenth centuries)', *International Review of Social History* 64, no. S27 (2019), 1–18.

Brink, Yvonne, *They Came to Stay: Discovering Meaning in the 18th Century Cape Country Dwelling* (Stellenbosch: SUN Press, 2008).

Brown, Elizabeth A.R., 'The tyranny of a construct: Feudalism and historians of Medieval Europe', *American Historical Review* 79, no. 4 (1974), 1063–88.

Brown, James, *Crossing the Strait: Morocco, Gibraltar and Great Britain in the 18th and 19th Centuries* (Leiden: Brill, 2012).

Brown, Stephen R., *Merchant Kings: When Companies Ruled the World, 1600–1900* (New York: Thomas Dunne Books, 2009).

Burbank, Jane and Frederick Cooper, *Empires in World History: Power and the Politics of Difference* (Princeton: Princeton University Press, 2010).

Burgess, Glenn P., 'From the common law mind to the *Discovery of Islands*: J.G.A. Pocock's journey', *History of Political Thought* 29, no. 3 (2008), 543–61.

Burnard, Trevor, 'The historiography of Jamaica in the time of James Knight', in Jack P. Greene (ed.), *The Natural, Moral, and Political History of Jamaica ... by J[ames] K[night]* (Charlottesville: University of Virginia Press, 2021).

Burnard, Trevor, *The Atlantic in World History, 1492–1830* (London: Bloomsbury, 2020).

Burnard, Trevor, 'Empire matters? The historiography of imperialism in early America, 1491–1830', *History of European Ideas* 33, no. 1 (2007), 87–107.

Burnard, Trevor, 'Prodigious riches: The wealth of Jamaica before the American Revolution', *Economic History Review* 54, no. 3 (2001), 506–24.

Burnard, Trevor, 'A failed settler society: Marriage and demographic failure in early Jamaica', *Journal of Social History* 28, no. 1 (1994), 63–82.

Burnard, Trevor and John Garrigus, *The Plantation Machine: Atlantic Capitalism in French Saint-Domingue and British Jamaica* (Philadelphia: University of Pennsylvania Press, 2018).

Cañizares-Esguerra, Jorge, and Benjamin Breen, 'Hybrid Atlantic: Future directions for the history of the Atlantic World', *History Compass* 11, no. 8 (2013), 597–609.

Canny, Nicholas (ed.), *Europeans on the Move: Studies in European Migration, 1500–1800* (Oxford: Clarendon Press, 1994).

Carrington-Farmer, Charlotte, 'Trading horses in the eighteenth century: Rhode Island and the Atlantic World', in Kristen Guest and Monica

Mattfeld (eds.), *Equestrian Cultures: Horses, Human Society, and the Discourse of Modernity* (Chicago: University of Chicago Press, 2019), 92–109.

Carrington-Farmer, Charlotte, 'The rise and fall of the Narragansett Pacer', *Rhode Island History* 76, no. 1 (2018), 1–38.

Chaunu, David and Séverin Duc (eds.), *La domination comme expérience européenne et américaine à l'époque moderne* (Brussels: Peter Lang, 2019).

Chernow, Ron, *Washington: A Life* (New York: Penguin, 2010).

Clark, Ian, *Globalization and Fragmentation* (Oxford: Oxford University Press, 1997).

Clément, Alain, 'Du bon et du mauvais usage des colonies: politique coloniale et pensée économique française au XVIIIe siècle', *Cahiers d'économie politique* 56, no. 1 (2009), 101–27.

Clulow, Adam and Tristan Mostert (eds.), *The Dutch and English East India Companies: Diplomacy, Trade and Violence in Early Modern Asia* (Amsterdam: Amsterdam University Press, 2018).

Clutton-Brock, Julia, *Horse Power: A History of the Horse and the Donkey in Human Societies* (London: Natural History Museum Publications, 1992).

Coe, Alexis, 'George Washington saw a future for America: mules', *Smithsonian Magazine* (February 2020).

Coleman, Donald C., 'Politics and economics in the age of Anne: The case of the Anglo-French trade treaty of 1713', in D.C. Coleman and A.H. John (eds.), *Trade, Government and Economy in Pre-Industrial England* (London: Weidenfeld and Nicolson, 1976), 187–213.

Cooper, Frederick and Ann Laura Stoler (eds.), *Tensions of Empire: Colonial Cultures in a Bourgeois World* (Berkeley: University of California Press, 1997).

Cox, Alicia, 'Settler colonialism', in *Oxford Bibliographies Online: Literary and Critical Theory* (2017), www.oxfordbibliographies.com.

Crouzet, François, *De la supériorité de l'Angleterre sur la France. L'économique et l'imaginaire. XVIIe-XXe siècle* (Paris: Perrin, 1985).

Davis, Natalie Zemon, 'Judges, masters, diviners: Slaves' experience of criminal justice in colonial Suriname', *Law and History Review* 29, no. 4 (2011), 925–84.

Delahaye, Agnès, 'Jeremy Belknap's history of New Hampshire in context: Settler colonialism and the historiography of New England', *Journal of Early American History* 8, no. 1 (2018), 60–91.

Depkat, Volker and Susanne Lachenicht, 'Rückkehr des nationalismus?', https://geschichtedergegenwart.de.

Depkat, Volker and Susanne Lachenicht, 'Nations, nationalism, and transnationalism revisited', in *Yearbook of Transnational History*, Vol. 5 (Fairleigh Dickinson University Press, 2022).

Derby, Lauren, 'Bringing the animals back in: Writing quadrupeds into the environmental history of Latin America and the Caribbean', *History Compass* 9, no 8 (2011), 602–21.

Dewar, Helen, 'Government by trading company? The corporate legal status of the Company of New France and colonial governance', *Nuevo Mundo Mundos Nuevos* (2018), http://journals.openedition.org/nuevomundo/72105.

Diop, Davis, 'Raynal, les colonies, la Révolution française et l'esclavage', *Outre-Mers, revue d'Histoire* 103, no. 386–7 (2015), 218–21.

Domínguez Ortiz, Antonio, *Los Judeoconversos en España y América* (Madrid: Istmo, 1971).

Domínguez Ortiz, Antonio and Bernard Vincent, *Historia de los Moriscos. Vida y Tragedia de una Minoría* (Madrid: Alianza, 1978).

Dubow, Saul, 'How British was the British world? The case of South Africa', *Journal of Imperial and Commonwealth History* 37, no. 1 (2009), 1–27.

Duchet, Michèle, *Diderot et l'Histoire des deux Indes ou l'écriture fragmentaire* (Paris: Nizet, 1978).

Duin, Pieter van and Robert Ross, *The Economy of the Cape Colony in the Eighteenth Century* (Leiden: Centre for the History of European Expansion, 1987).

Dulac, Georges, 'Les gens de lettres, le banquier et l'opinion: Diderot et la polémique sur la Compagnie des Indes', *Dix-huitième Siècle* 26 (1994), 177–99.

Dulany, Daniel, 'The right of the inhabitants of Maryland to the benefit of the English laws (1728)', in Jack P. Greene and Craig B. Yirush (eds.), *Exploring the Bounds of Liberty: Political Writings of Colonial British America from the Glorious Revolution to the American Revolution*, 3 vols. (Indianapolis: Liberty Fund, 2018), 1: 649–76.

Dunn, Richard S., James Savage and Laetitia Yeandle (eds.), *The Journal of John Winthrop, 1630–1649* (Cambridge, MA: Harvard University Press, 1996).

Eiras Roel, Antonio (ed.), *La Emigración Española a Ultramar, 1492–1914* (Madrid: Ediciones Tabapress, 1991).

Eiras Roel, Antonio, 'Sobre las motivaciones de la emigración Gallega a América y otros aspectos. un enfoque comparative', *Revista da Comisión Galega do Quinto Centenario* 2 (1989), 57–72.

Elliott, J.H., *Empires of the Atlantic World: Britain and Spain in America, 1492–1830* (New Haven: Yale University Press, 2006).

Ellis, Elizabeth, 'The Natchez War revisited: Violence, multinational settlements, and Indigenous diplomacy in the Lower Mississippi Valley', *WMQ* 77, no. 3 (2020), 441–72.

Elton, Geoffrey R., *The Tudor Revolution in Government: Administrative Changes in the Reign of Henry VIII* (Cambridge: Cambridge University Press, 1953).

Emmer, Pieter, *The Dutch Slave Trade, 1500–1800* (New York: Berghahn Books, 2006).

Emmer, Pieter, *The Dutch in the Atlantic Economy, 1580–1880: Trade, Slavery and Emancipation* (Aldershot: Variorum, 1998).

Emmer, Pieter and Magnus Mörner, *European Expansion and Migration: Essays on the Intercontinental Migration from Africa, Asia, and Europe* (New York: Berg, 1992).

Ewen, Misha, *The Virginia Venture: American Colonization and English Society, 1580–1660* (Philadelphia: University of Pennsylvania Press, 2022).

Fairchilds, Cissie, 'The production and marketing of populuxe goods in eighteenth-century Paris', in J. Brewer and R. Porter (eds.), *Consumption and the World of Goods* (London, New York: Routledge, 1993), 228–48.

Farnell, J.E., 'The Navigation Act of 1651, the First Dutch War, and the London merchant community', *Economic History Review* 16, no 3 (1964), 439–54.

Farrington, Anthony, 'Bengkulu: An Anglo-Chinese partnership', in H.V. Bowen (ed.), *The Worlds of the East India Company* (Woodbridge: Boydell & Brewer, 2002), 111–17.

Fatah-Black, Karwan, 'The usurpation of legal roles by Suriname's governing council, 1669–1816', *Comparative Legal History* 5, no. 2 (2017), 243–61.

Feinberg, Harvey M., *Africans and Europeans in West Africa: Elminans and Dutchmen on the Gold Coast during the Eighteenth Century* (Philadelphia: American Philosophical Society, 1989).

Fernández López, Fransisco, *La Casa de la Contratación. Una Oficina de Expedición Documental para el Gobierno de las Indias (1503–1717)* (Sevilla/Zamora: Editorial Universidad de Sevilla/El Colegio de Michoacán, 2018).

Fick, Carolyn E., *The Making of Haiti: The Saint Domingue Revolution from Below* (Knoxville: University of Tennessee Press, 1990).

Fogleman, Aaron Spencer, 'From slaves, convicts, and servants to free passengers: The transformation of immigration in the era of the American Revolution', *Journal of American History* 85, no. 1 (1998), 43–76.

Fortin, Jeffrey A. and Mark Meuwese (eds.), *Atlantic Biographies: Individuals and Peoples in the Atlantic World* (Leiden: Brill, 2014).

Fouché, Léo (ed.), *The Diary of Adam Tas* (Cape Town: VRS, 1970).
Freeman, Mark, Robin Pearson and James Taylor, *Shareholder Democracies? Corporate Governance in Britain and Ireland Before 1850* (Chicago: University of Chicago Press, 2012).
Freist, Dagmar and Susanne Lachenicht (eds.), *Connecting Worlds and People: Early Modern Diasporas* (London: Routledge, 2016).
Freund, William, 'The Cape under the transitional governments', in Richard Elphick and Hermann Giliomee (eds.), *The Shaping of South African Society* (Middletown: Wesleyan University Press, 1989), 324–57.
Gaastra, Femme, *The Dutch East India Company: Expansion and Decline* (Zutphen: Walburg Pers, 2003).
Gaastra, Femme, *De geschiedenis van de VOC*, 10th ed. (Zutphen: Walburg Pers, 2002).
Gainot, Bernard, *L'empire colonial français de Richelieu à Napoléon (1630–1810)* (Paris: A. Colin, 2015).
Galeana, Patricia (ed.), *Historia Comparada de las Migraciones en las Américas* (Mexico: UNAM, 2014).
García-Baquero González, Antonio, 'Los extranjeros en el tráfico con Indias: entre el rechazo legal y la tolerancia functional', in M.B. Villar García and P. Pezzi Cristóbal (eds.), *Los Extranjeros en la España Moderna*, 2 vols. (Málaga: Universidad de Málaga, 2003), 1: 73–99.
García-Baquero González, Antonio, *La Carrera de Indias. Histoire du Commerce Hispano-Américain (XVIe–XVIIIe Siècles)* (Paris: Desjonquères, 1997).
Garcia-Chapleau, Marylin, *Le Refuge huguenot du cap de Bonne-Espérance. Genèse, assimilation, héritage* (Paris: Honoré Champion, 2016).
Gerritsen, Anne and Giorgio Riello (eds.), *The Global Lives of Things: The Material Culture of Connections in the Early Modern World* (Abingdon: Routledge, 2016).
Gervais, Pierre, 'Neither imperial, nor Atlantic: A merchant perspective on international trade in the eighteenth century', *History of European Ideas* 34, no. 4 (2008), 465–73.
Gervais, Pierre, Yannick Lemarchand and Dominique Margairaz (eds.), *Merchants and Profit in the Age of Commerce, 1680–1830* (London: Pickering & Chatto, 2014).
Giliomee, Hermann, *The Afrikaners: Biography of a People* (Cape Town: Tafelberg, 2006).
Giliomee, Hermann, 'The Eastern Frontier 1770–1812', in Richard Elphick and Hermann Giliomee (eds.), *The Shaping of South African Society* (Middletown: Wesleyan University Press, 1989), 421–72.
Giusti-Cordero, Juan, 'Beyond sugar revolutions: Rethinking the Spanish Caribbean in the seventeenth and eighteenth centuries', in George Baca,

Aisha Khan and Stephan Palmié (eds.), *Empirical Futures: Anthropologists and Historians Engage the Work of Sidney W. Mintz* (Chapel Hill: University of North Carolina Press, 2009), 58–83.

Gottmann, Felicia, *Global Trade, Smuggling, and the Making of Economic Liberalism: Asian Textiles in France 1680–1760* (New York: Palgrave Macmillan, 2016).

Gottmann, Felicia and Philip Stern (eds.), 'Introduction: Crossing companies', *Journal of World History* 31, no. 3 (2020), 477–88.

Gould, Eliga and Rosemarie Zagarri, 'Situating the United States in vast early America: Introduction', *WMQ* 78, no. 2 (2021), 189–200.

Greene, Jack P., 'Transatlantic colonization and the redefinition of empire in the early modern era: The British–American experience', in Christine Daniels and Michael V. Kennedy (eds.), *Negotiated Empires: Centers and Peripheries in the Americas, 1500–1820* (New York: Routledge, 2002), 267–82.

Greenwald, Erin M., *Marc-Antoine Caillot and the Company of the Indies in Louisiana: Trade in the French Atlantic World* (Baton Rouge: Louisiana State University Press, 2016).

Greer, Allan, 'Settler colonialism and empire in early America', *WMQ* 76, no. 3 (2019), 383–90.

Grégoire, Vincent, *Théories de l'Etat et problèmes coloniaux (XVIe–XVIIIe siècles)* (Paris: Honoré Champion, 2017).

Gunder Frank, André, *ReOrient: Global Economy in the Asian Age* (Berkeley: University of California Press, 1998).

Hall, Catherine and Sonya Rose (eds.), *At Home with the Empire: Metropolitan Culture and the Imperial World* (Cambridge: Cambridge University Press, 2006).

Hall, Stuart, 'The question of cultural identity', in T. McGrew, S. Hall and D. Held (eds.), *Modernity and Its Futures* (Cambridge: Polity Press, 1992), 273–326.

Hämäläinen, Pekka, *Lakota America: A New History of Indigenous Power* (New Haven: Yale University Press, 2019).

Harris, Ron, *Going the Distance: Eurasian Trade and the Rise of the Business Corporation, 1400–1700* (Princeton: Princeton University Press, 2020).

Haudrère, Philippe, *Les Compagnies des Indes orientales. Trois siècles de rencontre entre Orientaux et Occidentaux (1600–1858)* (Paris: Éditions Desjonquères, 2006).

Havard, Gilles and Cécile Vidal, *Histoire de l'Amérique française* (Paris: Flammarion, 2003).

Helgerson, Richard, *Forms of Nationhood: The Elizabethan Writing of England* (Chicago: University of Chicago Press, 1992).

Hernández Franco, Juan, *Cultura y Limpieza de Sangre en la España Moderna*. *Puritate Sanguinis* (Murcia: Universidad de Murcia, 1996).

Heywood, Linda and John Thornton, *Central Africans, Atlantic Creoles and the Foundation of the Americas, 1585–1660* (Cambridge: Cambridge University Press, 2007).

Hirschi, Caspar, *Wettkampf der Nationen. Konstruktionen einer deutschen Ehrgemeinschaft an der Wende vom Mittelalter zur Neuzeit* (Göttingen: Wallstein, 2005).

Hixson, Walter, *American Settler Colonialism: A History* (New York: Palgrave MacMillan, 2013).

Hofstra, Warren, '"The extention of his majesties dominions": The Virginia backcountry and the reconfiguration of imperial frontiers', *Journal of American History* 84, no. 4 (1998), 1281–312.

Holtz, Grégoire, 'The model of the VOC in early seventeenth-century France', in Siegfried Huigen, Jan L. de Jong and Elmer Kolfin (eds.), *The Dutch Trading Companies as Knowledge Networks* (Leiden: Brill, 2010), 319–35.

Hont, Istvan, *Jealousy of Trade: International Competition and the Nation-State in Historical Perspective* (Cambridge, MA: Harvard University Press, 2010).

Hoxie, Frederick E., 'Retrieving the Red Continent: Settler colonialism and the history of American Indians in the US', *Ethnic and Racial Studies* 31, no. 6 (2008), 1153–67.

Hugon, Alain, *La Grande Migration. De l'Espagne à l'Amérique, 1492–1700* (Paris: Vendémiaire, 2019).

Hume, David, 'Of the balance of power', in E. Miller (ed.), *Essays Moral, Political, and Literary* (Indianapolis: Liberty Fund, 1975), 332–41.

Ignatieff, Michael, *Blood and Belonging* (London: Vintage, 1994).

Israel, Jonathan I., *Dutch Primacy in World Trade, 1585–1740* (Oxford: Clarendon Press, 1989).

Ittersum, Martine J. van, 'Debating natural law in the Banda Islands: A case study in Anglo-Dutch imperial competition in the East Indies, 1609–1621', *History of European Ideas* 42, no. 4 (2016), 459–501.

Ittersum, Martine J. van, *Profit and Principle: Hugo Grotius: Natural Rights, Theories and the Rise of Dutch Power in the East Indies, 1595–1615* (Leiden: Brill, 2006).

Ives, Pedro A., Pepa Vega and Jesús Oyamburu (eds.), *Historia General de la Emigración Española a Iberoamérica* (Madrid: Historia 16, 1992).

Jacq-Hergoualc'h, Michel, 'La France et le Siam de 1685 à 1688. Histoire d'un échec', *Revue française d'histoire d'outre-mer* 84, no. 317 (1997), 71–91.

Jacobs, Jaap, *The Colony of New Netherland: A Dutch Settlement in Seventeenth-Century America* (Ithaca: Cornell University Press, 2009).

Jacobs, Jaap, *Koopman in Azië: de handel van de Nederlandse Oost-Indische Compagnie in de 18de eeuw* (Zutphen: Walburg Pers, 2000).

Jessenne, Jean-Pierre, Renaud Morieux and Pascal Dupuy (eds.), *Le Négoce de la Paix. Les Nations et les Traités franco-britanniques, 1713–1802* (Paris: Société des études robespierristes, 2011).

Jordaan, Han, 'Free blacks and colored and the administration of justice in eighteenth-century Curaçao', *New West Indian Guide/Nieuwe West-Indische Gids* 84, no. 1–2 (2010), 63–86.

Kamen, Henry, 'La política religiosa de Felipe II', *Anuario de Historia de la Iglesia* 7 (1998), 21–33.

Kammen, Michael, *A Rope of Sand: The Colonial Agents, British Politics, and the American Revolution* (Ithaca: Cornell University Press, 1968).

Kars, Marjolein, 'Dodging rebellion: Politics and gender in the Berbice slave uprising of 1763', *American Historical Review* 121, no. 1 (2016), 39–69.

Kelley, Robin D.G., 'The rest of us: Rethinking settler and native', *American Quarterly* 69, no. 2 (2017), 267–76.

Kidd, Colin, 'Europe, what Europe?', *London Review of Books* 30 (2008).

Klooster, Wim, *The Dutch Moment: War, Trade, and Settlement in the Seventeenth-Century Atlantic World* (Ithaca: Cornell University Press, 2016).

Klooster, Wim, 'Curaçao as a transit center to the Spanish Main and French West Indies', in Gert Oostindie and Jessica V. Roitman (eds.), *Dutch Atlantic Connections, 1680–1800: Linking Empires, Bridging Borders* (Leiden: Brill, 2014), 25–51.

Klooster, Wim, *Illicit Riches: Dutch Trade in the Caribbean, 1648–1795* (Leiden: KITLV Press, 1998).

Konetzke, Richard, 'Legislación sobre immigración de extranjeros en América durante la época Colonial', *Revista Internacional de Sociología* 11–12 (1945), 269–99.

Kupperman, Karen (ed.), *America in European Consciousness, 1493–1750* (Chapel Hill: University of North Carolina Press, 1995).

Kupperman, Karen, *Providence Island: The Other Puritan Colony* (New York: Cambridge University Press, 1993).

Lachenicht, Susanne, *Europeans Engaging the Atlantic: Knowledge and Trade* (Frankfurt/Main, New York, Chicago: Campus and University of Chicago Press, 2014).

Lachenicht, Susanne, Lauric Henneton and Yann Lignereux (eds.), 'The spiritual geopolitics in the early modern world', special issue, *Itinerario* 40, no. 2 (2016), 182–353.

Lambert, David, 'Runaways and strays: Rethinking (non)human agency in Caribbean slave societies', in Sharon Wilcox and Stephanie Rutherford (eds.), *Historical Animal Geographies* (New York: Routledge, 2018), 185–98.

Lambert, David, 'Master–horse–slave: Mobility, race and power in the British West Indies, c. 1780–1838', *Slavery & Abolition* 36, no. 4 (2015), 618–41.

Lavalle, Bernard, *L'Amérique Espagnole de Colomb à Bolivar* (Paris: Belin, 1993).

Lawson, Donald, 'Towards demythologizing the "Australian Legend": Turner's frontier thesis and the Australian experience', *Journal of Social History* 13, no. 4 (1980), 577–87.

Lemire, Beverly, 'Fashioning cottons: Asian trade, domestic industry and consumer demand, 1660–1780', in D. Jenkins (ed.), *The Cambridge History of Western Textiles*, Vol. 1 (Cambridge: Cambridge University Press, 2003), 493–521.

Linebaugh, Peter, *The Many-Headed Hydra: Sailors, Slaves, Commoners, and the Hidden History of the Revolutionary Atlantic* (Boston: Beacon Press, 2000).

Loewenstein, David and Paul Stevens, 'Introduction: Milton's nationalism: Challenges and questions', in D. Loewenstein and P. Stevens (eds.), *Early Modern Nationalism and Milton's England* (Toronto: University of Toronto Press, 2008), 3–21.

Loth, Vincent C., 'Armed incidents and unpaid bills: Anglo-Dutch rivalry in the Banda Islands in the seventeenth century', *Modern Asian Studies* 29, no. 4 (1995), 13–35.

Lowenhaupt Tsing, Anna, *Friction: An Ethnography of Global Connection* (Princeton: Princeton University Press, 2005).

Lüsebrink, Hans-Jürgen and Anthony Strugnell (eds.), *L'Histoire des deux Indes: réécriture et polygraphie* (Oxford: Voltaire Foundation, 1995).

Mackenzie, Eneas, 'Incorporated companies: Merchant adventurers', in *Historical Account of Newcastle-upon-Tyne including the Borough of Gateshead* (Newcastle-upon-Tyne, 1827), 662–70.

Mancall, Peter C. (ed.), *The Atlantic World and Virginia, 1550–1624* (Chapel Hill: University of North Carolina Press, 2012).

Mancke, Elizabeth, 'Empire and state', in David Armitage and Michael J. Braddick (eds.), *The British Atlantic World, 1500–1800* (Basingstoke: Palgrave Macmillan, 2002), 193–213.

Mancke, Elizabeth and Carole Shammas (eds.), *The Creation of the British Atlantic World* (Baltimore: Johns Hopkins University Press, 2005).

Margolin, Jean-Louis and Claude Markovits, *Les Indes et l'Europe. Histoires connectées XVe–XXIe siècles* (Paris: Gallimard, 2015).

Markley, Robert, *The Far East and the English Imagination, 1600–1730* (Cambridge: Cambridge University Press, 2006).

Marsh, Ben, *Unravelled Dreams: Silk and the Atlantic World 1500–1840* (Cambridge: Cambridge University Press, 2020).

Marshall, Peter James, *Trade and Conquest: Studies on the Rise of British Dominance in India* (Aldershot: Variorum, 1993).

Marshall, Peter James, *East Indian Fortunes: The British in Bengal in the Eighteenth Century* (Oxford: Clarendon Press, 1976).

Martínez Shaw, Carlos, *La Emigración Española a América, 1492–1824* (Colombres, Asturias: Archivo de Indianos, 1994).

Martínez Shaw, Carlos and José María Olivar Melgar (eds.), *El Sistema Atlántico Español* (Siglos XVII–XIX) (Madrid: Marcial Pons, 2005).

Mathieu, Jacques, *La Nouvelle-France. Les Français en Amérique du Nord. XVIe–XVIIIe siècle* (Paris: Belin, 1991).

Matson, Cathie, *Merchants & Empire: Trading in Colonial New York* (Baltimore: Johns Hopkins University Press, 1998).

McAleer, John, 'Introduction', in H.V. Bowen, J. McAleer and R.J. Blyth (eds.), *Monsoon Traders: The Maritime World of the East India Company* (London: Scala, 2011), 1–21.

McDonald, Kevin P., *Pirates, Merchants, Settlers, and Slaves: Making an Indo-Atlantic Trade World, 1640—1730* (Oakland: University of California Press, 2011).

McDonnell, Michael A., *Masters of Empire: Great Lakes Indians and the Making of America* (New York: Hill and Wang, 2015).

McNeill, J.R. and William H. McNeill, *The Human Web: A Bird's-Eye View of World History* (New York: Norton and Company, 2003).

Medford, Edna Green E. (ed.), *The New York African Burial Ground History Final Report* (Washington: Howard University Press, 2004).

Menard, Russell R., *Sweet Negotiations: Sugar, Slavery, and Plantation Agriculture in Early Barbados* (Charlottesville: University of Virginia Press, 2006).

Ménard-Jacob, Marie, *La Première Compagnie des Indes, 1664–1704. Apprentissages, Échecs et Héritage* (Rennes: Presses Universitaires de Rennes, 2016).

Miller, Joseph C., 'Central Africa during the era of the slave trade, c. 1490s–1850s', in Linda M. Heywood (ed.), *Central Africans and Cultural Transformations* (New York: Cambridge University Press, 2002), 21–69.

Mira Caballos, Esteban, 'Los prohibidos en la emigración a América (1492–1550)', *Estudios de Historia Social y Económica de América* 12 (1995), 37–54.

Morgan, Philip D., 'Slaves and livestock in eighteenth-century Jamaica: Vineyard Pen, 1750–1751', *WMQ* 52, no. 1 (1995), 47–76.

Mörner, Magnus, *Le Métissage dans l'Histoire de l'Amérique Latine*, trans. H. Favre (Paris: Fayard, 1971).

Murrin, John, 'Beneficiaries of catastrophe: The English colonies in America', in Eric Foner (ed.), *The New American History* (Philadelphia: Temple University Press, 1997), 3–30.

Nash, Gary B., 'The concept of inevitability in European–Indian relations', in Carla G. Pestana and Sharon V. Salinger (eds.), *Inequality in Early America* (Hanover: University Press of New England, 1999), 267–91.

Nierstrasz, Chris, *Rivalry for Trade in Tea and Textiles: The English and Dutch East India Companies (1700–1800)* (New York: Palgrave Macmillan, 2015).

O'Brien, Jean M., *Firsting and Lasting: Writing Indians out of Existence in New England* (Minneapolis: University of Minnesota Press, 2010).

O'Malley, Gregory E., *Final Passages: The Intercolonial Slave Trade of British America, 1619–1807* (Chapel Hill: University of North Carolina Press, 2014).

O'Malley, Gregory E., 'Beyond the middle passage: Slave migration from the Caribbean to North America, 1619–1807', *WMQ* 66, no. 1 (2009), 125–72.

Osiander, Andreas, 'Sovereignty, international relations, and the Westphalian myth', *International Organization* 55, no. 2 (2001), 251–87.

Osterhammel, Jürgen and Niels P. Petersson, *Geschichte der Globalisierung. Dimensionen, Prozesse, Epochen* (Munich: Beck, 2003).

Ostler, Jeffrey, 'Locating settler colonialism in early American history', *WMQ* 76, no. 3 (2019), 443–50.

Ostler, Jeffrey, *Surviving Genocide: Native Nations and the United States from the American Revolution to Bleeding Kansas* (New Haven: Yale University Press, 2019).

Otte, Enrique, *Cartas Privadas de Emigrantes a Indias 1540–1616* (Mexico: Fondo de Cultura Económica, 1996).

Peires, Jeffrey B., 'The British and the Cape, 1814–1834', in Richard Elphick and Hermann Giliomee (eds.), *The Shaping of South African Society* (Middletown: Wesleyan University Press, 1989), 472–518.

Pérez Joseph, *Isabelle et Ferdinand, Rois Catholiques d'Espagne* (Paris: Librarie Arthème Fayard, 1988).

Pestana, Carla Gardina, *The English Conquest of Jamaica: Oliver Cromwell's Bid for Empire* (Cambridge, MA: Harvard University Press, 2017).

Pestana, Carla Gardina, 'English character and the fiasco of the Western Design', *Early American Studies* 3, no. 1 (2005), 1–31.

Pettigrew, William, and Edmond Smith, 'Corporate management, labour relations, and community building at the East India Company's Blackwall dockyard, 1600–1657', *Journal of Social History* 53, no. 1 (2018), 133–56.

Pettigrew, William and David Veevers (eds.), *The Corporation as a Protagonist in Global History, c. 1550–1750* (Leiden: Brill, 2018).

Pettigrew, William, David Armitage, Paul Halliday, Vicki Hsueh, Thomas Leng and Philip Stern, 'Corporate constitutionalism and the dialogue between the global and the local in seventeenth-century English history', *Itinerario* 39, no. 3 (2015), 487–525.

Piat, Denis, *Pirates and Privateers in Mauritius* (Singapore: éditions Didier Millet, 2014).

Pincus, Steve and James Robinson, 'Wars and state-making reconsidered: The rise of the developmental state', *Annales: Histoire, Sciences Sociales* 71, no. 1 (2016), 5–36.

Pocock, John G.A., *Barbarism and Religion*, 5 vols. (Cambridge: Cambridge University Press, 1999–2011).

Pocock, John G.A., *The Discovery of Islands: Essays in British History* (Cambridge: Cambridge University Press, 2005).

Pocock, John G.A., *Barbarism and Religion. Vol. I: The Enlightenment of Edward Gibbon, 1734–1764* (Cambridge: Cambridge University Press, 1990).

Postma, Johannes, *The Dutch in the Atlantic Slave Trade 1600–1815* (Cambridge: Cambridge University Press, 1992).

Postma, Johannes, 'The dimension of the Dutch slave trade from Western Africa', *Journal of African History* 13, no. 2 (1972), 237–48.

Prakash, Om, *Precious Metals and Commerce: Dutch East India Company in the Indian Ocean Trade* (Aldershot: Variorum, 1994).

Prévélakis, Georges, 'Les diasporas comme négation de l'idéologie graphique', in L. Anteby-Yemini, W. Berthomière and G. Sheffer (eds.), *Les diasporas. 2000 ans d'histoire* (Rennes: Presses universitaires de Rennes, 2005).

Price, Richard, 'Créolisation, creolization and créolité', *Small Axe* 21, no. 1 (2017), 211–19.

Prior, Charles, 'Beyond settler colonialism: State sovereignty in early America', *Journal of Early American History* 9, no. 2–3 (2019), 1–25.

Reid, John G. and Thomas Peace, 'Colonies of settlement and settler colonialism in Northeastern North America, 1450–1850', in Edward Cavanagh and Lorenzo Veracini (eds.), *The Routledge Handbook of the History of Settler Colonialism* (London: Routledge, 2016), 356–426.

Reynolds, Henry, *The Other Side of the Frontier: Aboriginal Resistance to the European Invasion of Australia* (Sydney: University of New South Wales Press, 1981).

Richter, Daniel K., 'His own, their own: Settler colonialism, Native peoples, and imperial balances of power in Eastern North America, 1660–1715', in Ignacio Gallup-Diaz (ed.), *The World of Colonial America: An Atlantic Handbook* (New York: Routledge, 2017), 209–33.

Riello, Giorgio, *Cotton: The Fabric That Made the Modern World* (Cambridge: Cambridge University Press, 2013).

Ritchie, Robert C., 'London merchants, the New York market, and the recall of Sir Edmund Andros', *New York History* 57, no. 1 (1976), 7–19.

Ritvo, Harriet, 'Animal planet', *Environmental History* 9, no. 2 (2004), 204–20.

Rodger, Nicholas A.M., *The Wooden World: An Anatomy of the Georgian Navy* (London: Collins, 1986).

Rommelse, Gijs, 'The role of mercantilism in Anglo-Dutch political relations, 1650–74', *Economic History Review* 63, no. 3 (2010), 591–611.

Roper, L.H., *Advancing Empire: English Interests and Overseas Expansion, 1613–1688* (New York: Cambridge University Press, 2017).

Roper, L.H., 'The fall of New Netherland and seventeenth-century Anglo-American imperial formation, 1654–1676', *New England Quarterly* 87, no. 4 (2014), 666–708.

Roper, L.H., *The English Empire in America, 1602–1658* (London: Pickering & Chatto, 2009).

Roper, L.H. and Bertrand Van Ruymbeke (eds.), *Constructing Early Modern Empires: Proprietary Ventures in the Atlantic World, 1500–1750* (Leiden: Brill, 2007).

Rosenberg, C.M., *Losing America, Conquering India* (Jefferson: McFarland & Co Publishers, 2017).

Ross, Robert, *A Concise History of South Africa* (Cambridge: Cambridge University Press, 1999).

Ross, Robert, *Status and Respectability in the Cape Colony, 1750–1870: A tragedy of Manners* (Cambridge: Cambridge University Press, 1999).

Ross, Robert, 'The first imperial masters of colonial South Africa', *South African Historical Journal* 25, no. 1 (1991), 177–83.

Ross, Robert, 'The Cape of Good Hope and the world economy', in Richard Elphick and Hermann Giliomee (eds.), *The Shaping of South African Society* (Middletown: Wesleyan University Press, 1989), 243–80.

Ross, Robert, 'The first two centuries of colonial agriculture in the Cape Colony: A historiographical review', *Social Dynamics* 9, no. 1 (1983), 30–49.

Rossum, Matthias van, 'Running together or running apart? Diversity, desertion and resistance in the Dutch East India Company empire, 1650–1800', in Marcus Rediker, Titas Chakraborty and Matthias van Rossum (eds.), *A Global History of Runaways: Workers, Mobility, and Capitalism 1600–1850* (Berkeley: University of California Press, 2019), 135–55.

Rossum, Matthias van, *Kleurrijke tragiek: de geschiedenis van slavernij in Azië onder de VOC* (Hilversum: Uitgeverij Verloren, 2015).

Rossum, Matthias van, *Werkers van de wereld: globalisering, arbeid en interculturele ontmoetingen tussen Aziatische en Europese zeelieden in dienst van de VOC, 1600–1800* (Hilversum: Verloren, 2014).

Rothschild, Emma, 'Late Atlantic history', in Nicholas Canny and Philip D. Morgan (eds.), *The Oxford Handbook of Atlantic History* (Oxford: Oxford University Press, 2011), 634–48.

Rothstein, Natalie, 'The calico campaign of 1719–1721', *East London Papers* 7 (1964), 3–21.

Roulet, Eric, *La Compagnie des îles de l'Amérique 1635–1651* (Rennes: Presses Universitaires de Rennes, 2017).

Roulet, Eric (ed.), *Les premières compagnies dans l'Atlantique, 1600–1650*, 2 vols. (Aachen: Shaker Verlag, 2017).

Rudé, George F., *Europe in the Eighteenth Century: Aristocracy and the Bourgeois Challenge* (Cambridge, MA: Harvard University Press, 1972).

Rueda Hernanz, Germán and Consuelo Soldevilla Oria, *Españoles Emigrantes en América (Siglos XVI–XX)* (Madrid: Arco, 2000).

Rupert, Linda M., *Creolization and Contraband: Curaçao in the Early Modern Atlantic World* (Athens: University of Georgia Press, 2012).

Rutherford, Stephanie and Sharon Wilcox, 'Introduction: A meeting place', in Sharon Wilcox and Stephanie Rutherford (eds.), *Historical Animal Geographies* (New York: Routledge, 2018), 3–10.

Sabanadze, Natalie, *Globalization and Nationalism: The Cases of Georgia and the Basque Country* (Budapest: Central European University Press, 2010).

Sahle, Esther, *Quakers in the British Atlantic, c. 1660–1800* (Martlesham: Boydell & Brewer, 2021).

Saler, Bethel, *The Settlers' Empire: Colonialism and State Formation in America's Old Northwest* (Philadelphia: University of Pennsylvania Press, 2015).

Salinero, Grégoire, 'Aux Indes! Motivations et conditions des migrations entre l'Espagne et les Indes, XVIe–XVIIe siècles', in C. Moatti, W. Kaiser and Ch. Pébarthe (eds.), *Le Monde de l'Itinérance en Méditerranée de l'Antiquité à l'Époque Moderne* (Pessac: Ausonius Éditions, 2009), 405–26.

Salinero, Grégoire, 'Sous le régime des licences. L'identification des migrants vers les Indes espagnoles, XVIe–XVIIe siècles', in C. Moatti and W. Kaiser (eds.), *Gens de passage en Méditerranée de l'Antiquité à l'Époque Moderne. Procédures de Contrôle et d'Identification* (Paris: Maisonneuve et Larose, 2007), 345–67.

Schiltkamp, Jacob A., 'Legislation, government, jurisprudence, and law in the Dutch West Indian colonies: The Order of Government of 1629',

Pro Memorie: Bijdragen Tot de Rechtsgeschiedenis Der Nederlanden 5, no. 4 (2003), 320–34.

Schiltkamp, Jacob A. and J. Th. de Smidt, *West Indisch plakaatboek. Plakaten, ordonnantiën en andere wetten uitgevaardigd in Suriname, 1667–1816* (Amsterdam: Emmering, 1973).

Schmidt, Benjamin, *Innocence Abroad: The Dutch Imagination and the New World, 1570–1670* (Cambridge: Cambridge University Press, 2001).

Schnakenbourg, Eric and François Ternat (eds.), *Une Diplomatie des Lointains. La France face à la Mondialisation des Rivalités Internationales, XVIIe–XVIIIe siècles* (Rennes: Presses Universitaires de Rennes, 2020).

Schoeman, K., *Cape Lives of the Eighteenth Century* (Pretoria: Protea Book House, 2011).

Schutte, G., 'Company and colonists at the Cape, 1652–1795', in Richard Elphick and Hermann Giliomee (eds.), *The Shaping of South African Society* (Middletown: Wesleyan University Press, 1989).

Serra Santana, E., 'Mito y realidad de la emigración femenina española al Nuevo Mundo en el siglo XVI', in Claire Pailler (ed.), *Femmes des Amériques* (Toulouse: Université de Toulouse-le-Mirail, 1986), 31–42.

Seth, Suman, 'Materialism, slavery, and the History of Jamaica', *Isis* 105, no. 4 (2014), 764–72.

Shäfer, Ernesto, 'La Casa de la Contratación de Indias durante los siglos XVI y XVII', *Archivo Hispalense* 5, no. 13–14 (1945), 149–62.

Shaw Romney, Susannah, 'Settler colonial prehistories in seventeenth-century North America', *WMQ* 76, no. 3 (2019), 375–82.

Shepherd, Verene A., *Livestock, Sugar and Slavery: Contested Terrain in Colonial Jamaica* (Kingston: Ian Randle Publishers, 2009).

Sheridan, Richard B., *Sugar and Slavery: The Economic History of the British West Indies, 1623–1775* (Barbados: Canoe Press, 2000).

Sicroff, Albert, *Les Controverses sur les Statuts de Pureté de Sang en Espagne, du XVe au XVIIe siècles* (Paris: Didier, 1960).

Slack, Paul, *The Invention of Improvement: Information & Material Progress in Seventeenth-Century England* (Oxford: Oxford University Press, 2015).

Sleeper-Smith, Susan (ed.), 'The Middle Ground revisited', *WMQ* 63, no. 1 (2006), 3–96.

Smith, Andrew B., 'The French period at the Cape, 1781–1783: A report on excavations at Conway Redoubt, Constantia Nek', *Military History Journal* 5, no. 3 (1981), 107–13.

Smith, Edmond, *Merchants: The Community That Shaped England's Trade and Empire* (London: Yale University Press, 2021).

Smith, Edmond, 'The social networks of investment in early modern England', *Historical Journal* 64, no. 4 (2021), 912–39.

Smithers, Gregory D. and Brooke N. Newman (eds.), *Native Diasporas, Indigenous Identities and Settler Colonialism in the Americas* (Lincoln: University of Nebraska Press, 2014).

Smolenski, John and Thomas J. Humfrey (eds.), *New World Orders: Violence, Sanction and Authority in the Colonial Americas* (Philadelphia: University of Pennsylvania Press, 2005).

Soll, Jacob, 'For a new economic history of early modern empire: Anglo-French imperial co-development beyond mercantilism and laissez-faire', *WMQ* 77, no. 4 (2020), 525–50.

Spear, Jennifer M., 'Beyond the Native/settler divide in early California', *WMQ* 76, no. 3 (2019), 427–34.

Spiegel, Marjorie, *The Dreaded Comparison: Human and Animal Slavery*, rev. ed. (New York: Mirror Books, 1996).

Steensgaard, Niels, 'Companies as a specific institution', in Leonard Blussé and Femme Gaastra (eds.), *Companies and Trade: On Companies during the Ancien Régime* (The Hague: Nijhoff, 1981), 245–64.

Steiger, Heinhard, 'Was haben die untertanen vom frieden?', in H. Duchhardt and M. Espenhorst (eds.), *Utrecht-Rastatt-Baden 1712–1714. Ein Europäisches Friedenswerk am Ende des Zeitalters Ludwig XIV* (Göttingen: Vandenhoeck & Ruprecht, 2013), 141–66.

Stern, Philip, *The Company-State: Corporate Sovereignty and the Early Modern Foundations of the British Empire in India* (New York: Oxford University Press, 2012).

Stern, Philip, 'British Asia and British Atlantic: Comparisons and connections', *WMQ* 63, no. 4 (2006), 693–712.

Stipriaan, Alex van, 'Watramama/Mami Wata: Three centuries of a water spirit in West Africa, Suriname and Europe', *Matatu* 27, no. 1 (2003), 321–37.

Studnicki-Gizbert, Daviken, *A Nation upon the Ocean Sea* (Oxford: Oxford University Press, 2007).

Sturman, Rachel, 'Indian indentured labor and the history of international rights regimes', *American Historical Review* 119, no. 5 (2014), 1439–65.

Sutton, Elizabeth, 'Bittersweet: Sugar, slavery, and science in Dutch Suriname', *Midwestern Arcadia: Essays in Honor of Alison Kettering* (2015), 143–53, doi:10.18277/makf.2015.13.

Swan, Robert J., 'First Africans into New Netherland, 1625 or 1626?', *de Halve Maen* 66 (1993), 75–82.

Tardieu, Jean-Pierre, *L'Inquisition de Lima et les Hérétiques Étrangers (XVIe–XVIIe Siècles)* (Paris: L'Harmattan, 1995).
Tarrade, Jean, *Le commerce colonial à la fin de l'Ancien Régime. L'évolution du régime de « l'Exclusif » de 1763 à 1789* (Paris: Presses Universitaires de France, 1972).
Tilly, Charles, *Coercion, Capital, and European States, AD 990–1992* (Cambridge: Cambridge University Press, 1990).
Toit, André du and Giliomee, Hermann, *Afrikaner Political Thought: Analysis and Documents. Volume One: 1780–1850* (Berkeley: University of California Press, 1983).
Van der Cruysse, Dirk (ed.), *Mercenaires français de la VOC. La route des Indes hollandaises au XVIIe siècle. Le récit de Jean Guidon de Chambelle (1644–1651) et autres documents* (Paris: éditions Chandeigne, 2003).
Van der Cruysse, Dirk, *Louis XIV et le Siam* (Paris: Fayard, 1991).
Vandersommers, Dan, 'The "animal turn" in history', *Perspectives on History* (November 2016), www.historians.org/publications-and-directories/perspectives-on-history/november-2016/the-animal-turn-in-history.
Van Ruymbeke, Bertrand, *L'Amérique avant les États-Unis. Une histoire de l'Amérique anglaise 1497–1776* (Paris: Flammarion, 2013).
Veevers, David, '"Inhabitants of the universe": Global families, kinship networks, and the formation of the early modern colonial state in Asia', *Journal of Global History* 10, no. 1 (2015), 99–121.
Veevers, David, '"The Company as Their Lords and the Deputy as Great Rajah": Imperial expansion and the English East India Company on the west coast of Sumatra, 1685–1730', *Journal of Imperial and Commonwealth History* 41, no. 5 (2013), 687–709.
Veracini, Lorenzo, 'Historylessness: Australia as a settler colonial collective', in Pramod K. Nayat (ed.), *Postcolonial Studies: An Anthology* (Hoboken: Wiley–Blackwell, 2016), 161–74.
Veracini, Lorenzo, '"Settler colonialism": Career of a concept', *Journal of Imperial and Commonwealth History* 41, no. 2 (2013), 313–33.
Veracini, Lorenzo and Gabriel Piterberg, 'Wakefield, Marx and the world turned inside out', *Journal of Global History* 10, no. 3 (2015), 457–78.
Vries, Jan de, 'The Dutch Atlantic economies', in Peter A. Coclanis (ed.), *The Atlantic Economy during the Seventeenth and Eighteenth Centuries: Organization, Operation, Practice and Personnel* (Columbia: University of South Carolina Press, 2005), 1–29.
Vries, Jan de and Ad van der Woude, *The First Modern Economy: Success, Failure and Perseverance of the Dutch Economy 1500–1815* (Cambridge: Cambridge University Press, 1997).
Ward, Russel, *The Australian Legend*, 2nd ed. (Melbourne: Oxford University Press, 1966).

White, Richard, *The Middle Ground: Indians, Empires, and Republics in the Great Lakes Region, 1650–1815* (Cambridge: Cambridge University Press, 1993).
Wijnholt, Meindert Rutgert, *Strafrecht in Suriname* (Deventer: Kluwer, 1965).
Wild, Antony, *The East India Company: Trade and Conquest from 1600* (London: Harper Collins, 1999).
Williams, Greg H., *The French Assault on American Shipping, 1793–1813: A History and Comprehensive Record of Merchant Marine Losses* (Jefferson: McFarland & Company, Inc., 2009).
Witgen, Michael, 'A nation of settlers: The early American Republic and the colonization of the Northwest Territory', *WMQ* 76, no. 3 (2019), 391–8.
Wolfe, Patrick, *Traces of History: Elementary Structures of Race* (London: Verso, 2016).
Wolfe, Patrick, 'Settler colonialism and the elimination of the Native', *Journal of Genocide Research* 8, no. 4 (2006), 387–409.
Worden, Nigel and Gerald Groenewald, *Trials of Slavery: Selected Documents Concerning Slaves from the Criminal Records of the Council of Justice at the Cape of Good Hope, 1705–1794* (Cape Town: Van Riebeeck Society, 2005).
Working, Lauren, 'Tobacco and the social life of conquest in London, 1580–1625', *Historical Journal* 65, no. 1 (2022), 30–48.
Yun Casalilla, Bartolomé, *Iberian World Empires and the Globalization of Europe 1415–1668* (New York: Palgrave Macmillan, 2018).
Yun Casalilla, Bartolomé and Patrick K. O'Brien, *The Rise of Fiscal States: A Global History, 1500–1914* (Cambridge: Cambridge University Press, 2017).
Zwart, Pim de, *Globalization and the Colonial Origins of the Great Divergence* (Leiden: Brill, 2016).

Index

abolition of enslavement
 in British Empire 70
Aboriginal nations *see* Australia
Ambon
 and Anglo-Dutch
  relations 52, 76
Andrews, Thomas
 and English imperial vision 75
Anglo-Boer Wars 194
Angola
 and traffic in enslaved Africans
  72, 120–1
Aruba 121
Australia
 and settler colonialism
  153, 157, 162
Ayscue, Sir George
 and subjugation of Barbados
  and Virginia 77
Azore Islands 51, 213

Banda Islands
 and Anglo-Dutch relations
  52, 74, 78
 enslavement in 131
Barbados
 colonisation of 70
 and English overseas initiatives 73
 and equine trade 204–5,
  207, 216
 and Restoration empire 80
 subjugation of by English
  Commonwealth 76–7
 and traffic in enslaved Africans
  76, 117, 121
Barbary
 and equine trade 201,
  207–8, 211
Batavia
 colonisation of 74
 enslavement in 12, 130–2, 135,
  137–9, 141–2
Batavian Republic 189
Belknap, Jeremy 225
 and colonisation 166–72
Bell, Philip 73
Bengal
 British takeover of 52–4
Berbice
 enslavement in 130, 135,
  140, 142
 and traffic in enslaved Africans
  136, 140
Berkeley, Sir John 80
Berkeley, Sir William, Governor of
  Virginia 118, 160
Beverley, Robert 164
Bodin, Jean 24
Bombay 79–80
Bonaire 121

Index

Braganza, Catherine of, Queen of England and Portuguese princess 79
Brazil 4, 46, 70
   Dutch capture of 113–15
   Dutch colonisation of 122
Bredero, Gerbrand, Dutch playwright
   and traffic in enslaved Africans 111
Breedon, Thomas 81

Canada 31, 217
   and equine trade 205
   as imperial example 28
Canary Islands 27, 51
Cape Colony
   abolition of slavery in 189, 193
   British rule of 193
   enslavement in 12, 131, 133–4, 137–8
   government of by VOC 180–4
   indentured servitude in 193
Cape Fear
   failure of English colony at 80
Cape Verde Islands 27
   and equine trade 210
Carolina proprietorship 79
Cartagena 98
Carteret, Sir George 80
Cartier, Jacques 31
Casa de contratación
   regulation of migration by 93–7
Ceylon
   and defence of India 190
   enslavement in 130–1, 133, 135
   see also Colombo
Chamberlain, Joseph, Colonial Secretary 194
Chamberlayne, John (*Magnæ Britanniæ Notitia*, 1737) 212
Champlain, Samuel de 31

Charles II, King of England 79, 81
Charpentier, François 32
Chennai *see* Madras
Chile 93
cochineal
   and French colonisation 56
cocoa
   and French colonisation 56
   importance of to French economy 50
Coen, Jan Pietersz 74
coffee
   and French colonisation 56–7
   production of and equine trade 216
   production of and traffic in enslaved Africans 227
Colbert, Jean-Baptiste
   imperial policy of 6, 32–3, 48
Colombia
   and traffic in enslaved Africans 116
Colombo
   enslavement in 131
Commission on Trade and Plantations (English) 81
Commonwealth (of England) 26, 76
Compagnie des Cents Associés (Compagnie de la Nouvelle France) 31
Compagnie des Habitants 31
Compagnie perpétuelle des Indes 32
Connecticut
   and equine trade 203, 210–11, 213–17
   establishment of 73
   expansionist desires of 80
conquistadores 25, 27–8
cotton 34
   and French colonisation 56
   importance of to French economy 37, 50

Courteen, Sir William
  Caribbean operations of 69–70
  imperial plan of 74–9
Crispe, Sir Nicholas
  and traffic in enslaved
    Africans 72
Cromwell, Oliver 77–8
  see also Jamaica
Cuba
  and equine trade 206
Curaçao
  Dutch colonisation of 122
  enslavement in 130, 133, 135, 140, 142
  and equine trade 204–5
  and traffic in enslaved Africans 114, 116–17, 132–3

Defoe, Daniel
  views on merchants 6
Demerara
  enslavement in 130
  and traffic in enslaved
    Africans 140
Dulany Sr, Daniel 163–4, 170
Dumas, Pierre-Benoît 55
Dupleix, Jean-François, Governor-General of French Asia 53
Dutch East India Company (VOC) 129
  as imperial vehicle 112
  relations of with English 74
  see also Cape Colony, Coen, Jan Pietersz
Dutch Republic
  administrative character of 109
  imperial government of 129
  relations with England of 80, 121
  relations with France of 31–3, 81
  relations with Habsburg monarchy of 72, 110, 115, 122
  and traffic in enslaved
    Africans 122

Dutch West India Company 129
  imperial activities of 112–14
  as imperial vehicle 108
  and traffic in enslaved Africans 110, 114–18
  see also Stuyvesant, Petrus

Elfrith, Daniel 73
English Civil Wars 26, 82
English East India Company
  as imperial vehicle 38, 74, 78, 87
  monopoly position of 35–8
  Sumatran operations of 82
Essequibo
  enslavement in 130, 135
  and equine trade 212
  European colonisation of 70
  and traffic in enslaved
    Africans 140

Forbonnais, François Véron Duverger de 51
Fourth Anglo-Dutch War 184, 186
Free Port Act (1766) 202
French East India Company (CIO) 6, 9
  formation of 32
  see also Dumas, Pierre-Benoît, Dupleix, Jean-François, Raynal, Guillaume-Thomas François
French West Indies
  and equine trade 203
  trade between and New England 50

Georgia 219
  and equine trade 203
Georgia Trustees 82
ginger
  importance of to French economy 37, 50
Glorious Revolution 82

Gold Coast 72, 74, 76, 80, 113
  see also Guinea
Gournay, Vincent de 49, 51
Grillo, Domingo, trafficker in enslaved Africans 116–17
Grotius, Hugo 29–30
  and traffic in enslaved Africans and empire 111
Guadeloupe
  and equine trade 206
  and traffic in enslaved Africans 58
Guiana 70
  enslavement in 131, 133
  and traffic in enslaved Africans 133
  see also Berbice, Demerara, Essequibo, West Indies
Guinea 71–2, 76, 78–9, 120
  English trade with 71, 75
  and European trade with Asia 74

Hakluyt, Richard 26
Havana 98
Heyn, Piet
  capture of Spanish treasure fleet by 113
hides
  and equine trade 216
Histoire des deux Indes see
  Raynal, Guillaume-Thomas François
Hobbes, Thomas 24, 29–30
Holy Roman Empire 26
Huber, Ulric, Dutch jurist
  and traffic in enslaved Africans 111
Huguenots
  and Cape Colony 182–4
Hume, David 30, 33

Iberia
  and equine trade 201, 207
Ile de France (Mauritius) 185

India
  and British empire 24
  European importation of fabrics from 9, 33–4, 37
  importance of Cape Colony to defence of 190
  indentured servitude in 74
  see also Bengal, Bombay, Madras
indigo
  and French colonisation 56
Ireland 36, 161

Jafar, Mir, Nawab of Bengal 53
Jahangir, Mughal Emperor 74
Jamaica 57
  English conquest of 77–8
  and equine trade 201, 206, 216
  and traffic in enslaved Africans 117, 120
  see also Long, Edward
James II
  and Restoration empire 79
Java
  and Anglo-Dutch relations 52, 74
  enslavement in 131
  see also Batavia
Jessop, William 73
Johan Maurits van Nassau-Siegen *see* Brazil

Khoikhoi nation 188, 191–3
  see also Cape Colony

Lomellino, Ambrosio, trafficker in enslaved Africans 116–17
Long, Edward, Jamaican historian 166–71
Louis XIV, King of France 6, 32–3, 81, 224
Louis XV, King of France 49

Louisiana 160, 217
  as imperial example 28
Lyon 15, 223–6, 229

Madagascar 48
Madeira Islands 27, 51
Madras 74
Maine
  and equine trade 207
Māori nation *see* New Zealand
Marlowe, Christopher 26
maroon society
  formation of in Cape
    Colony 134
Marseille 34, 225
Martin, Samuel 203
Martinique
  and equine trade 203–4
  and traffic in enslaved
    Africans 58
Maryland
  colonisation of 164
  colonist views of empire
    in 170
  and equine trade 217
  Native–colonist relations
    in 163
  see also Dulany Sr, Daniel
Massachusetts
  and equine trade 206, 212, 214
  expansion of 73
  and relations with neighbours 81
  and settler colonialism 164
Massachusetts Bay Company 73
Massachusetts Historical
  Society 168
Maverick, Samuel 81, 207
mercantilism 3, 77, 108
  and equine trade 202
Mexico
  and traffic in enslaved
    Africans 116
Milner, Alfred, High Commissioner
  for South Africa 194

molasses
  production of and equine trade
    204–5, 216
Monts, Pierre Gua, Sieur de 31
Moyer, Samuel
  and English imperial vision 75
Mumbai *see* Bombay

Nadir Shah
  sack of Delhi by 55
Natchez War (1729) 160
nationalism 23–5, 35, 39,
    110, 168
Native Americans
  as Calvinist converts 112
  colonial desire to eliminate 160
  colonist views of 163
  enslavement of 82
  responses of to colonisation 155
  and settler colonialism 155–8
  see also Raynal, Guillaume-
    Thomas François, United
    States of America
Navigation Acts 77, 228
New England
  migration to 73
  and Providence Island
    colonisation 73
  and smuggling 50
New Hampshire
  and equine trade 207
  see also Belknap, Jeremy
New Haven
  founding of 73
New Netherland
  conflicts with New England 80
  Dutch colonisation of 122
  English capture of 80, 121
  and traffic in enslaved
    Africans 119
New Plymouth 73
New Spain 91
  ecclesiastical concerns in 94–5
  migration to 98–100

New York
  capture of by Dutch 81
  as imperial case 109
New Zealand
  and settler colonialism 160–2
Noell, Martin 81

Ohio Company of Virginia 82
Orange Free State 193–4
Ovando, Nicolas de, Governor of Hispaniola 93

Parliament (of England) 26, 36–8, 60, 80
Pennoyer, William
  and English imperial vision 75
  and traffic in enslaved Africans 76
Pennsylvania
  and equine trade 217
  and traffic in enslaved Africans 228
Peru, Viceroyalty of 92, 100
Philip II, King of Spain 97, 99–100, 111
Philip IV/III, King of Spain and Portgual 72
Philippine Islands 93
Philipse, Frederick 121–2
Physiocrats see Raynal, Guillaume-Thomas François
piracy 12
  attitudes of colonial governments towards 109, 117
  concerns of English East India Company regarding 76
  conducted by Dutch against English and Spanish 116–18
  and traffic in enslaved Africans 109, 114, 118
Portugal
  and equine trade 201, 211
  imperial character of 27, 29
  relations with Dutch 72, 111–12
  and traffic in enslaved Africans 114
Povey, Thomas 81
Providence Island
  English colonisation of 72–3
  and English imperial vision 78
Providence Island Company 72–3
Puerto Rico
  and equine trade 206
  and traffic in enslaved Africans 116
Pufendorf, Samuel von 29–30

Quakers 160
Quesnay, François 50

Raleigh, Sir Walter 26
Ramsay, David 165
Raynal, Guillaume-Thomas François
  and American colonisation 56–9
  and European interests in Asia 51–6
  intellectual influence of 223–7
  views of on trading companies 47–51
Rhode Island
  and equine trade 205, 207–8, 210–11, 216
  founding of 73
  relations with neighbours 80
Rhodes, Cecil 82, 194
Rich, Robert, second Earl of Warwick
  anti-Spanish activities of 69, 74
  colonising activities of 69
  and Guiana 70
  and piracy 71
  and Providence Island colonisation 73
  and Providence Island Company 72
  rebellion of against Charles I 75

Richelieu, Armand-Jean du Plessis,
    Cardinal
  imperial policy of 31
roucou
  and French colonisation 56
Royal African Company 80
Royal Company of Adventurers
    Trading into Africa 79
rum
  production of and equine trade
    204–6, 216
  production of and traffic in
    enslaved Africans 136

Saint Pierre, Abbé de 33, 38
Saint-Domingue
  and equine trade 206
Santo Domingo
  and English imperial vision 78
  and traffic in enslaved Africans
    58, 116
Second Anglo-Dutch War 117
Seven Years' War 24, 32, 49,
    155, 160
Shah Jehan, Mughal Emperor 74
Shakespeare, William 26
Slagtersnek Rebellion *see*
    Cape Colony
Smith, Adam 50, 168
Smith, Captain John 59, 163
Somerset v Steuart (1772) 170
South Africa
  and settler colonialism 162
South Carolina
  and enslavement of Native
    Americans 82
  and equine trade 200
  as imperial example 28
Spanish monarchy
  imperial character of 27, 29
  see also Dutch Republic, Philip
    II, Philip IV/III
Spenser, Edmund 26

Sri Lanka *see* Ceylon
St Christopher's
  colonisation of 70
St Eustatius
  and equine trade 194–200,
    203, 206
St Helena 185
  and English imperial vision 78
Stuyvesant, Petrus, Director-
    General of New Netherland
    114, 117–18
sugar
  and French colonisation 56
  importance of to French
    economy 37, 50
  production of in Brazil 113
  production of as colonisation
    model 70
  production of and equine trade
    200–7, 212, 216–17
  production of and traffic in
    enslaved Africans 76, 113,
    136, 227
Sumatra 52, 82
Suriname 132
  Dutch capture of 80
  Dutch colonisation of 122
  enslavement in 12, 130–1, 133,
    135–7, 139–42
  and equine trade 204–7
  founding of English
    colony at 80
  and traffic in enslaved
    Africans 133

Tangier 80
Third Anglo-Dutch War 81
Thompson, Maurice
  and Anglo-Dutch relations 76
  and English imperial
    vision 75, 79
  as leader of English East India
    Company 78

and Providence Island
  colonisation 73
and Providence Island
  Company 72
and rebellion against
  Charles I 75
and traffic in enslaved
  Africans 72, 76
and 'Western Design' 77–8
see also Courteen, Sir William,
  English East India Company,
  Madagascar, Providence
  Island Company
tobacco
  importance of to French
    economy 37, 50
  production of and English
    colonisation model 70
  production of and traffic in
    enslaved Africans 136
  and progress of English
    colonisation 70
  smuggling of by Dutch 76
Tortola
  and equine trade 216
traffic in enslaved Africans
  abolition of 228
  by English 71–3
  by French 58–9
trafficking in enslaved
  Africans
  by Dutch 114–17
Transvaal 193–4
Treaty of Paris (1763) 46
Treaty of Tordesillas 114
Treaty of Utrecht (1713)
  and international
    relations 30, 33
Tucker, Josiah 50
Turgot, Anne Robert 50
Turner, Frederick Jackson
  'frontier thesis' of 157–8,
    165–6

United States of America
  226, 228–9
  and indentured servitude 70
  and settler colonialism
    67, 154–60
  see also Turner, Frederick
    Jackson
Usselincx, Willem 112

Valderrama, Jeronimo 99
Vassall, Samuel
  and Providence Island
    colonisation 73
  and traffic in enslaved
    Africans 72
Venezuela 100
  and equine trade 206
  salt pans at 70, 114
  and traffic in enslaved
    Africans 116
Vera Cruz 98
Vermont
  and equine trade 200
Verrazzano, Giovanni da 31
Virginia
  destruction of tobacco fleet by
    Dutch 81
  and equine trade 217
  and indentured servitude 70
  and Native–colonist
    relations 59
  subjugation of by English
    Commonwealth 76–7
  and traffic in enslaved Africans
    72, 115, 118
Virginia Company 69, 163
  dissolution of 5, 69
  and indentured servitude 70
Voortrekkers 193

War of the League of Augsburg 48
War of the Spanish
  Succession 33, 49

Washington, George
  and equine trade 209–10, 213
West Indies
  and equine trade 200–2, 205–10, 212–13, 216–17
  and French colonisation 56–9
  and settler colonialism 154, 162
  Spanish migration to 91
  and traffic in enslaved Africans 56, 60, 116, 121
William V of Orange 186
Willoughby of Parham, Francis, Lord 79–80
Wilson, Rowland
  and English imperial vision 75

Winslow, Edward
  and participation in 'Western Design' 78
Winthrop, John Jr 80
Winthrop, John Sr 164
Wood, John
  and English imperial vision 75
  and traffic in enslaved Africans 72, 76

Xhosa nation 191–2, 194
  see also Cape Colony

Zulu nation 194
  see also Cape Colony

EU authorised representative for GPSR:
Easy Access System Europe, Mustamäe tee 50,
10621 Tallinn, Estonia
gpsr.requests@easproject.com

www.ingramcontent.com/pod-product-compliance
Lightning Source LLC
Chambersburg PA
CBHW052058300426
44117CB00013B/2179